Profound Spiritual
From a Living Tra

Jaguar Wisdom presents, for the first time, an accessible introduction to the spiritual teachings and practices of the contemporary Mayan people. A vast system of correspondences and folklore, the Sacred Calendar is the back-bone of an indigenous magical tradition that has flourished throughout Mexico and Guatemala. Now *Jaguar Wisdom* reveals the basics of divination, ritual magic, and herbalism as practiced by modern Mayan Daykeepers.

Practical and fascinating, *Jaguar Wisdom* provides you with a clear and accessible introduction to the essential spiritual beliefs and practices of the ancient and modern Mayan people. Find out your day-sign using the simple yet beautiful system of Mayan astrology based upon the Sacred Calendar. Discover a simple yet accurate form of divination that provides real advice to help you through the challenges of continued spiritual evolution.

About the Author

Kenneth Johnson holds a degree in Comparative Religions with an emphasis on the study of mythology. He is the author of *North Star Road* (Llewellyn, 1996), co-author of *The Silver Wheel* (Llewellyn, 1996) and *The Grail Castle* (Llewellyn, 1995) with Marguerite Elsbeth, and *Mythic Astrology* (with Ariel Guttman, Llewellyn, 1993). Born in southern California, he has lived in Los Angeles, Amsterdam, London, and New Mexico, and currently resides on California's central coast.

To Write to the Author

If you wish to contact the author or would like more information about this book, please write to the author in care of Llewellyn Worldwide and we will forward your request. Both the author and the publisher appreciate hearing from you and learning of your enjoyment of this book and how it has helped you. Llewellyn Worldwide cannot guarantee that every letter written to the author can be answered, but all will be forwarded. Please write to:

Kenneth Johnson
c/o Llewellyn Worldwide
P.O. Box 64383, Dept. K372-7
St. Paul, MN 55164-0383, U.S.A.

Please enclose a self-addressed, stamped envelope for reply, or $1 to cover costs. If outside U.S.A., enclose international postal reply coupon.

Free Catalog from Llewellyn

For more than ninety years Llewellyn has brought its readers knowledge in the fields of metaphysics and human potential. Learn about the newest books in spiritual guidance, natural healing, astrology, occult philosophy and more. Enjoy book reviews, New Age articles, a calendar of events, plus current advertised products and services. To get your free copy of Llewellyn's *New Worlds of Mind and Spirit*, send your name and addres to:

Llewellyn's New Worlds of Mind and Spirit
P.O. Box 64383, Dept. K372-7
St. Paul, MN 55164-0383, U.S.A.

Contemporary Practices of Mayan Shamans

Jaguar Wisdom

MAYAN CALENDAR MAGIC

Kenneth Johnson

1997
Llewellyn Publications
St. Paul, Minnesota 55164-0383, U.S.A.

FIRST EDITION
First Printing, 1997

Cover art by Pat Gullett
Cover design by Tom Grewe
Interior illustrations by Marguerite Elsbeth (pages 12, 19 & 21) and
Lisa Novak (pages 10, 13-15, 19, 46, 49, 65-101)
Book editing, design, and layout by Astrid Sandell

Library of Congress Cataloging-in-Publications Data
Johnson, Kenneth, 1952–
Jaguar wisdom : Mayan calendar magic / Kenneth Johnson. — 1st ed.
p. cm.
"Contemporary practices of Mayan shamans."
Includes bibliographical references and index.
ISBN 1-56718-372-7 (pbk.)
1. Maya magic. 2. Maya calendar—Miscellanea. 3. Shamanism—Mexico. I. Title.
BF1622.M39J64 1997
133.4'3'089974152—dc21 97-5482
CIP

Printed in the United States of America

Llewellyn Publications
A Division of Llewellyn Worldwide, Ltd.
P.O. Box 64383, Dept. K372-7, St. Paul, MN 55164-0383

Other Books by Kenneth Johnson

North Star Road: Shamanism, Witchcraft & the Otherworld Journey, 1996

The Silver Wheel: Female Myths and Mysteries in the Celtic Tradition (with Marguerite Elsbeth), 1996

The Grail Castle: Male Myths and Mysteries in the Celtic Tradition (with Marguerite Elsbeth), 1995

Mythic Astrology: Archetypal Powers in the Horoscope (with Ariel Guttman), 1993

Forthcoming

Slavic Sorcery: A Personal Journey

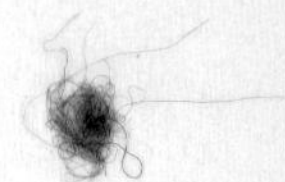

Table of Contents

1

The World of the Ancient Maya

The higher civilizations that took shape in Mexico and Central America have fascinated academics, occultists, and speculative mavericks of every variety. The Mayans and Aztecs built great and complex cities crowned by temple pyramids, yet never knew the use of the wheel except as a child's toy. All their architectural achievements were accomplished without the use of metal—their buildings were of stone, their swords of obsidian, and their metallurgy limited to the production of beautiful works of art. Despite the lack of what Westerners consider the essentials of "civilization," the Native peoples of North and South America were mathematical philosophers of a high order, as is evidenced by the system of cords and knots the Incas called the *quipu*, and by the great Long Count Calendar of the Classic Maya.

The influence of Mesoamerican civilization spread north over wide geographical regions. Its temple architecture inspired the Mound Builders of the American Southeast, whose mythology seems to have resembled that of Mexico and Central America. The presence of Mesoamerican religious ideas is noticeable among the Southwestern Anasazi and their present-day Pueblo descendants as well.

Few topics are capable of provoking as much argument as the origins of this civilization. Occultists and advocates of antediluvian continents believe that Mesoamerican culture, especially as exemplified by the Classic Maya, is of great antiquity and owes its beginnings to colonists from Atlantis (or perhaps the Pleiades). Archaeologists place the emergence of the Maya no earlier than the first few centuries before Christ and the birth of Mesoamerican civilization itself at about 1200 B.C.

According to the standard archaeological model, the cultivation of corn began perhaps as early as 6000 B.C. in Oaxaca, but the development of agriculture did not spark a "revolution" in Mexico as it did in the Old World. People continued living their traditional lives in small villages while the agricultural life-path spread slowly and without drama. Then, with surprising suddenness, a true civilization appeared, seemingly out of nowhere. Around 1200 B.C., large ceremonial centers began to be erected along the Gulf Coast in what is now the southern part of the state of Veracruz. Temples of earth and stone were raised in the jungle, and most of the themes which were to remain constant throughout the history of ancient Mexico made their first appearances in those ancient ceremonial precincts. The ritual handball game, so important to the Aztecs and the Maya, was first played in these early centers; the jaguar and the serpent, two animals which were of major religious significance to all the peoples of Mesoamerica, were worshipped here as well. Their images remain, carved in serpentine and jade.

We do not know what the inhabitants of those first cities called themselves. We have named them the Olmecs, a rather unfortunate term which means "the rubber people." Extracted in abundance from the tropical forests where the Olmecs lived, rubber was most notably used to make handballs. However, it was not the material keynote of Olmec civilization—that distinction belonged to jade. Whatever else they may have been, the Olmecs were dedicated traders in jade, sometimes traveling all the way to Belize on the Caribbean coast in search of the precious green stone. Jade was to the Olmecs what gold was to European conquistadors and alchemists: it was both materially valuable and spiritually empowered. A reverence for jade was part of the Olmec legacy to Mesoamerican civilization in general, and Aztec poets were still singing the stone's praises 2,500 years later on the eve of the Spanish Conquest.

Massive temples and urban-religious complexes, the serpent and the jaguar, the sacred handball game, and a love for jade: these essential elements of Mesoamerican civilization are all found among the Olmecs, who are widely believed to have been the "mother culture" of Mesoamerica. Their civilizing influence spread west to the highland plateaus of central Mexico. There, around the time of Christ, arose the great city of Teotihuacán, the "Abode of the Gods." Teotihuacán grew in power and strength; by A.D. 500 the city dominated central Mexico. During this same era the Classic Maya ruled the lands to the south.

Although it was believed until recently that Mayan civilization only began to flourish around A.D. 300, it is now clear that its roots are much earlier. In fact, Mayan civilization reached its first peak in ceremonial centers such as El Mirador as early as 300 B.C. For reasons we do not yet understand, these early cities were abandoned shortly before the time of Christ. Then, about a century later, a new constellation of urban-religious centers arose, marking the beginning of the Classic Period of the Maya, an epoch that lasted until about A.D. 900.

Today, we can read the story of the Classic Maya in their own words. Since 1841, when the American adventurer John Lloyd Stephens brought the Mayan ruins to the world's attention, it has been clear that the ancient Maya were a literate people. The walls of their great buildings are covered with hieroglyphics, as are the free-standing stone monuments, or stelae, which are scattered through the ruins. Ancient Mayan books written on folding sheets of bark paper, called codices, have come to light throughout the past few hundred years, but as long as the Mayan script could not be read, investigators could only deduce what their culture had been like through studying its visible remains—with the rest left to the imagination. Stephens was impressed by the sheer grandeur of the ruins and imagined the Maya as a great empire, the Egypt of the New World, its wars and conquests chronicled in works of monumental glory.

Other investigators were drawn to the mysterious side of the Maya. Even in the late nineteenth century, mystics and occultists camped in the jungles of Yucatán to contemplate the ruins in splendid isolation. The best known of these travelers was the Frenchman Augustus Le Plongeon. In addition to being one of the first to indulge in mystical speculation about the Maya, he was an expert photographer and recorder of data. Le Plongeon believed—though entirely on intuitive grounds—that he could read the Mayan hieroglyphs. His theory proposed that they told a story of migration from Atlantis to Egypt and the New World.

In time, scholars began to decipher bits and pieces of the mysterious Mayan script. It became apparent that at least some of the hieroglyphics that covered the Mayan stelae and temples were comprised of dates—so many dates, in fact, that scholars began to conceive of the Maya as an empire of philosophers and priests, abstract thinkers who were more concerned with time and mathematics than with war and dynastic succession. Mayanist J. Eric S. Thompson in particular believed that the Maya were actually ruled by priestly mathematicians.

The great breakthrough in deciphering Mayan writing came from a most unexpected quarter—Soviet Russia. During the Second World War, a young Russian artilleryman named Yuri Knorosov took part in the fall of Berlin. When the National Library went up in flames, Knorosov rushed into the burning building, grabbed a single book, and rescued it from the conflagration. He later discovered that the volume that had come into his hands by seeming accident was none other than the published edition of the old bark-paper Mayan codices. Knorosov went on to study linguistics and mastered many languages, but remained fascinated by the people of the New World jungle whose books had literally fallen into his hands under such peculiar circumstances. In 1952, Knorosov was finally able to show that the Mayan hieroglyphics had a syllabic component as well as an ideographic one—if the sound values could be established, the script could be read in the Mayan language itself.[1]

Knorosov's brilliant surmise remained unknown to the world at large, for he wrote in Russian—a language that few American or Mexican archaeologists could read. One person who could read his work, however, was a young Russian refugee named Tatiana Proskouriakoff. Employed as a sketch artist, she accompanied the Carnegie Institute's archaeological expeditions to the Maya country. In 1960, Proskouriakoff recognized a pattern of dates at Piedras Negras in Guatemala as relating to the names and deeds of royal families.[2] Today she is credited with the first ground-breaking decipherment of a Classic Maya text.

It is now possible to read almost all of the Mayan hieroglyphs. The Maya are no longer "prehistoric;" they have entered the list of those historic cultures which left written records behind them. Thanks to the efforts of the many scholars who have played a role in the deciphering of the Mayan script, we can see that there were two unique factors that impelled the Mayan people on their spiritual and intellectual journey. One of these was the institution of sacred kingship; the other was the Long Count Calendar.

The rulers of the Mayan city-states were not just ordinary rulers; they were "sacred kings." Like the pharaohs of Egypt, they were believed to be earthly incarnations of the gods; and, again like the pharaohs, Mayan kings were priests, monarchs, and deities all rolled into one.

Divine or sacred kings ruled in many of the ancient hieratic civilizations of the Old World including Babylon, Japan, and China. In each of these civilizations there was a powerful class of priests or religious specialists who advised the king and directed his ritual activities. These advisors studied the stars and omens, harmonizing the precise interplay of real and sacred time which would result in growth and abundance for the king and his people. Most of what we now know suggests that, among the Maya, these religious or shamanic functions were vested in the royal families themselves rather than in a specific class of priests who orchestrated the activities of the kings. For example, the art that decorates ceramic funerary vessels had great spiritual significance and is replete with mythological themes. Artists' signatures have occasionally been identified on these vessels, and it is generally believed that these artists were of royal lineage. Furthermore, the word *dzib* (DZEEB) in Mayan designates both "painting" and "writing," which suggests that the same individuals were responsible for the religious art and hieroglyphic texts as well as the calendrical inscriptions of the Maya. They were simultaneously priests, painters, and literary men.[3]

When the Maya adopted the institution of sacred kingship, their world underwent a tremendous surge of growth. However, we do not know what the Maya called their sacred kings. Mayanists Linda Schele and David Freidel have suggested the term *ahauob* (ah-how-OBE), the plural of the Mayan word *ahau*, meaning "lord."[4] The advent of the ahauob among the Maya began around 200 B.C., coinciding with the erection of the first monumental buildings and temple pyramids. Each Mayan city or urban complex was the center of a small state, ruled by its own dynasty of ahauob. By way of analogy, we might imagine that the city-states of classical Greece were each ruled by a divine pharaoh. The ahau was first and foremost a ritual figure. As visible symbols of spiritual power, the Mayan sacred kings were responsible for renewing the vital spirit of their land and their people. The temple pyramids were the stages upon which they performed their rituals.

The other factor in the rise of the Maya was the development of the Long Count Calendar, a new way of reckoning cycles of time which allowed the Maya to probe the secrets of history in an ever more complex fashion (see Chapter 8). This concept of cosmic time as exemplified in the Long Count was based on a much older way of reckoning time, the Sacred Calendar, which was common to all the peoples of ancient Mesoamerica—Olmecs, Toltecs, Aztecs, and Maya. The Sacred

Calendar was so fundamental to the people of Mexico that it virtually defines Mesoamerican civilization. It is this great body of lore—as much a system of magic as it is a reckoning of time—which is commonly called the "Mayan" calendar. A large part of this book will be devoted to exploring how the Sacred Calendar is used.

The visible representative of this new religious concept—history perceived as a series of magical cycles which could be understood by cosmic mathematics—was the ahau, who was probably the titular head of the priestly establishment as well as the principal actor in rites of world-centering and world-renewing which were based on the Long Count. Scholars have suggested that the Long Count, as well as being a complex instrument for the contemplation of time and history, was also geared towards the worship of the ancestors (who, like the kings, were called ahauob) and the recording of royal lineages.[5]

Although the decipherment of Mayan hieroglyphics has added so much to our knowledge of the Classic Maya, it is still unclear why their civilization declined. But of one thing we may be certain: the ahauob lost their power. People ceased to believe in the divine kings. Had the Mayan elite become corrupt and unworthy of trust? Had they exhausted themselves in petty wars? Or did their elaborate civilization simply fall before the onslaught of more vigorous and warlike peoples from the north—people who, though ethnically Mayan, were strongly influenced by the changing cultures of central Mexico?

We do not know the full answer. Having reached the end of their days of glory, they seem to have walked away from it all and returned to a more traditional, tribal way of life. They returned to the jungle.

Such, at least, was the case in Guatemala and southern Mexico, though not in Yucatán. Around the same time that the great Mayan centers such as Tikal and Palenque were being abandoned, a new and aggressive people called the Itzá were making their way into the Yucatán peninsula. Scholars of an earlier day believed that the Itzá themselves must have been from central Mexico; hence older books on Mayan civilization speak of the "Toltec Period" or the "Toltec-Maya." It is now believed that the Itzá were Mayan, and that they were originally from the southern end of the Gulf Coast. Their links with central Mexico were indeed strong; they seem to have been traders of sorts, and to have come to Yucatán in great sea-going canoes. By 867 they had founded the city of Chichén Itzá, which dominated Mesoamerica for three hundred years. However, by 900, the art of hieroglyphic writing had disappeared at Chichén Itzá, and the Long Count Calendar had vanished from the Mayan world. The empire ruled by the lords of Yucatán was expansive, more like the empires of Teotihuacán or the Aztecs than the city-states of the earlier Classic Maya. Chichén Itzá itself was abandoned around 1200. It was succeeded by another confederacy in the Yucatán region, that of Mayapan, which lasted from 1250 to 1451. By the time Christopher Columbus encountered an ocean-going canoe full of Mayan merchants in the bay of Honduras in 1502, Mayan civilization was only a shadow of itself. The Spanish conquest of Yucatán began in 1526, and the last independent Mayan kingdom persisted until 1697.

The spiritual tradition of the Maya lives on to the present day. In some respects, Mayan spiritual beliefs have changed; a sometimes uneasy compromise has been reached with Catholic Christianity, but the old ways have continued with much of their primal vigor still intact, and a great many modern religious and magical practices have strong roots in the world view of the ancients. Let us examine the universe as it was conceived by the Classic Maya.

ENDNOTES

1. Michael D. Coe, *Breaking the Maya Code* (New York: Thames and Hudson, 1992), 145–66.
2. Tatiana Proskouriakoff, "Historical Implications of a Pattern of Dates at Piedras Negras, Guatemala." *American Antiquity* 25:454–475.
3. Coe, *Breaking the Maya Code*, 245–52.
4. Linda Schele and David Freidel, *A Forest of Kings: The Untold Story of the Ancient Maya* (New York: William Morrow and Co., 1990), 419, n. 1.
5. David Carrasco, *Religions of Mesoamerica: Cosmovision and Ceremonial Centers* (San Francisco: Harper and Row, 1990), 39.

2

The Mayan Universe

According to the Maya, the world has been created and destroyed a number of times. Each world the gods have brought into being has been created with the hope that humankind will worship the gods properly, and more often than not the gods have been disappointed. Their continuing attempts to create a perfect being, one who will honor the sacred, is the foundation of evolution. The Hopi Indians of Arizona, who were deeply influenced by the common spiritual heritage of Mesoamerica, say that humankind has been successively "emerging" through four different worlds. The Zuñi of New Mexico, with a similar mythology, say that man was created in the Underworld and looked first like a lizard or reptile, but has been evolving through different worlds ever since. The idea of mankind's spiritual evolution lies at the heart of the history of the cosmos as the Maya understood it.

The Creation of the World

The present world, the most recent in this succession of worlds, was created by a pair of gods—male and female—who were believed to be aspects of a single deity. The earliest known rendition of this creation story has been revealed to us only recently through the decipherment of Mayan hieroglyphics. It is inscribed on the walls of three different temples at Palenque and dates from the reign of Chan-Bahlum (Chawn-Ba-LOOM, 684–702), son of Pacal (Pa-KAHL) the Great.[1]

The new creation began on the day 4 Ahau, 8 Cumku, in the year we call 3114 B.C. First Father and First Mother were already present, for they had been born in the previous world and had done the work of world-making at the beginning of the new cycle, creating the world in which we now live. First Father shaped the universe and raised the great tree at the center of the world. As we shall see, this tree is everywhere, even within us; in celestial terms it is the Milky Way. First Father's celestial helpers laid the three sacred hearth-stones in the sky—stars that Westerners call the belt of Orion. In honor of that event, the Maya continue to place three stones in the hearth as the foundation of their homes. Meanwhile, First Mother gave birth to the three oldest gods: the God of the Four Directions, the Night Sun Jaguar, and the Serpent-Foot God.

The Cosmos of the Maya

The previous legend tells how our current world began. Further sources tell us of the nature of this universe created by First Mother and First Father as conceived by the Maya. It was divided into three parts: Heaven, Earth, and the Underworld. Heaven, the home of the gods, was comprised of thirteen layers shaped like a pyramid. Each of these thirteen layers of Heaven—or steps of the cosmic pyramid—was ruled by one of the gods.

As Heaven was a pyramid, so was the Underworld. The Underworld was regarded as an inverted pyramid of nine steps or layers. Hence the Mayan universe was comprised of two pyramids, an upper and a lower one (Figure 1). A dark land called Xibalba (Shee-bahl-BAH, "the awesome place"), it is ruled by the gods of death. Resembling skeletons and smoking large cigars, the nine lords of this Mayan Underworld are a colorful lot indeed. The bony figures

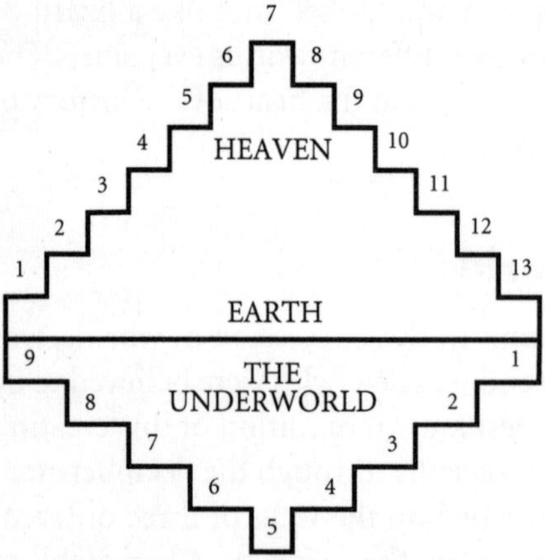

FIGURE 1 ***The Mayan Cosmos***

who preside over the Mexican Days of the Dead or ride the "death-carts" of the Penitente sect in New Mexico probably owe their symbolic attributes as much to these lords of Xibalba as they do to the Grim Reaper of European lore introduced by the Spanish.

Between Heaven and the Underworld lay the Earth and Sky, the world of men. The Earth was imagined as a flat expanse of land, resting on the back of a gigantic crocodile or caiman which floated on an enormous tropical pond full of water lilies, a concept known to all the peoples of Mesoamerica. In addition, the Maya recognized a great Celestial Serpent or Cosmic Dragon whose province was the sky. This Sky Serpent had two heads and two mouths; one opened upon Heaven, and the other upon the Underworld. The Underworld polarity of the Cosmic Serpent was similar, or perhaps identical, to the crocodile who carried the world on his back.

Therefore, just beneath the earth's crust a great reptilian creature was sleeping—a symbol of the generative power beneath the surface of things. From the body of the crocodile grew the World Tree, the great universal tree whose roots stretched down into the Underworld and whose branches stretched up into Heaven.

In 1773, Friar Ramon de Ordoñez y Aguilar became the first European to visit the ruins of Palenque. He was both mystified and inspired by a series of bas-relief sculptures in the buildings today known as the Temple of the Cross and the Temple of the Foliated Cross (two of the three temples that contain the Palenque creation story). The good father saw what he believed to be representations of the cross of Christ—hence the names of the temples (Figure 2). Pondering over how this symbol of the Christian religion could have reached the "benighted heathens" of Mexico well before the arrival of Columbus, Ordoñez and his contemporaries began to theorize about possible New World journeys by the lost tribes of Israel, the apostle Thomas, and others.

What the friar had seen in these temples were actually images of the Tree of Life, the central axis of the Mesoamerican universe. In equating the Tree of Life with the Christian cross, he was both nearer to and farther from the truth than he knew. For if his speculations about lost tribes and globe-trotting apostles proved to be fantasy, it is nevertheless true that the cross and the World Tree are the same symbol.

The Tree of Life is one of the few symbols that knows no cultural or ethnic boundaries. It is the tree that Siberian shamans climb when they visit the land of the spirits; it is the tree Yggdrasil that formed the central column of the Viking universe upon which Odin (another shaman) hung like a sacrifice in search of wisdom. It is the tree that stood in the center of the Garden of Eden, and had passed into Hebrew myth from older Babylonian stories. The cross of Christ is yet another World Tree; it was even said, in medieval legend, that his cross had been carved from a descendant of the Tree of Life which stood in the Garden of Eden. Sometimes the World Tree is perceived as a World Mountain, like Mount Meru in Vedic myth. The peoples of ancient Mexico honored both concepts of the center—tree and mountain. In any event, the Tree of Life represents the center of the universe, the axis around which everything else revolves. The pyramids of Teotihuacán and Chichén Itzá are images of this World Tree and World Mountain.

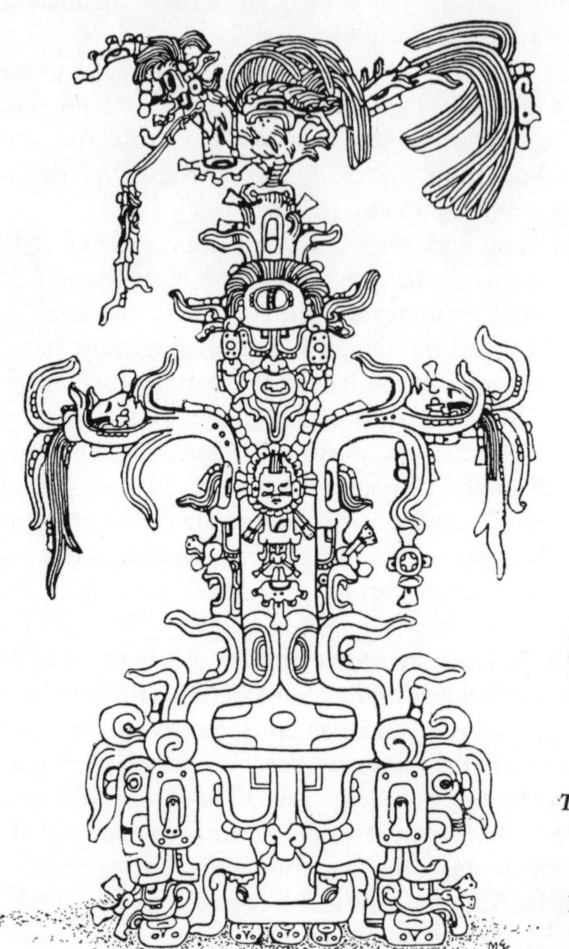

FIGURE 2
The Mayan Tree of Life

Temple of the Foliated Cross, Palenque

The Tree of Life was often represented in a T-shape, reminding Spanish priests of the cross. The T was symbolic not only of the tree, but of the vivifying energy contained within it. It rose from the back of the world-bearing crocodile and ascended into Heaven. The center of all things, it was the artery between the terrestrial and celestial worlds—the souls of the dead climbed it into the world of the gods. The Milky Way, visible symbol of the World Tree, was sometimes known as the Sac Be (SAHK BAY) or "White Road," and sometimes as the Xibalba Be (Shee-bahl-BAH BAY) or "Road to the Awesome Place." When the Milky Way lay upon the horizon in Maya Land, there was a black portion of sky above it which was called the Ek Ue (ECK WAY), the "Black Transformer" or "Black Dreamplace."[2] This was the dark hole into which souls vanished towards the Otherworld.

If the World Tree is the center, the world that First Father and First Mother made is a fourfold world, and its axes are the four cardinal directions: East, North, West, and South.

Many are familiar with the significance of the four directions in Native American thought, for they form the basis of the Medicine Wheel among the tribes of the Great Plains. The four directions are fundamental to most Native American spiritual traditions, not just those of Mesoamerica, and one finds variations in the colors and even the meanings attributed to these directions. Since this book is primarily concerned with the Maya, the scheme given below is gleaned from Mayan sources. Though there are differences between the Classic and contemporary concepts of the Four Directions, an underlying unity informs the entire symbolic system. What follows is based on both old and new concepts.

East

East is the direction of sunrise and of the spring. It is a symbol of beginnings, of the energy that gives birth to action and idea, just as the energy within the greening earth gives birth to the flowers of spring or the first rays of the rising sun give birth to a new day. East is the heavenly face of the Celestial Serpent, and red is the color associated the eastern direction. When a Mayan shaman works his path, he typically faces East; he is facing his future, in both the spiritual and material sense. Thus he attributes both his destiny and his physical children to the East.

West

West is the direction of sunset, the direction of autumn. In the West, all things come to an end; creatures die, just as the sun takes its nightly death when it dips below the western horizon, or as the leaves die and blow away in the fall. But what seems to be the end is, in fact, only one stage in an eternal process. Souls will be reborn in Heaven even as the earth will be reborn in spring. An action or idea which has its birth in the East may dip below the surface of the symbolic western horizon and experience an Underworld sojourn, but it will arise again reborn. Hence West is the direction of transformation, the Underworld face of the Celestial Serpent. Since the Mayan shaman typically faces East, the West is behind him. This is the place of the ancestors, of all who have come before him and who stand behind him to give him their support.

Both black and blue are colors associated with West. In Aztec poetry, "the red and the black" is a metaphor of wholeness, of completeness. It signifies the polar opposites of East and West, and hence the process of birth, transformation, and rebirth. On the cross of the four directions, the East-West polarity forms the horizontal arm, like a road. Among North American tribes this horizontal arm finds its equivalent in the Medicine Wheel as the "Good Red Road," the medicine path. This is the road that leads from birth to spiritual transformation, the Road of Life.

North

Another arm of the directional cross runs from North to South. In Classical times, North was equivalent to "above," the place of the sun at zenith. Like West, it was associated with the ancestral spirits who have departed this world. The road to the Underworld is the road to the north of the sky. Hence North has the meaning of wisdom, the wisdom we acquire from the ancestors. Its color is white.

When the Mayan shaman stands facing East, the North is on his left. As in other mystical systems around the world, the left is the feminine side. Hence, to the contemporary shaman, this direction represents women, relationships, and marriage.

SOUTH

In Classical times, the South was equivalent to "below." It was symbolic of the mysterious generative power that comes from beneath the soil and makes the plants sprout and grow. Its color is yellow, the color of the growing corn. South is symbolic of the generative power that gives life to all things. It is the direction of abundance. In the Sacred Calendar, each year is governed by one of the four directions. Years governed by the South are held to be the most favorable, especially in terms of agricultural cycles, for the growth of the soil. Facing East, the shaman has the South on his right side. Thus the South symbolizes male energy, the strength and abundance of one's family line.

CENTER

In the Mayan cosmology, there are in fact five directions rather than four, for the Center is itself a primary direction. The Yucatec Mayan word for Center is *yaxkin* (yawsh-KEEN), which has the word *yax* or "green" as its root, thus the color correspondence for the center is green. Center is also green because it is the spot where the Tree of Life grows. As we shall see, this is the direction wherein lies one's day-sign, the "face" we acquire from the spirit world.

Sacred Geomancy

The World Tree as the center of a cosmos from which four sacred directions emanate had powerful resonances in every aspect of Mesoamerican civilization, but nowhere more so than in city planning. Each of the great Mesoamerican cultures based itself in a monumental city or capital. These capital cities were designed according to a concept we call geomancy—a sacred form of architecture wherein buildings, even whole cities, are constructed as models of the cosmos.

Native American chronicles that survived the conquest of Aztec Mexico affirm that the mythical founders of Mesoamerican civilization, the Toltecs or "Makers," came from a place called Tula. At times, this Tula would seem to be a real, physical place "over the sea," but there is no agreement upon where this original Tula lay. The Aztecs, who provided the Spanish monk Bernardino de Sahagún with the information for his sixteenth-century encyclopedia of Aztec lore, placed it in the east. The Mayan chronicle entitled *The Annals of the Cakchiquels* places it in the west. At other times, there are said to be four Tulas, one for each of the sacred directions. Clearly, Tula remains as much a mythical as a geographical location.

Professor David Carrasco has argued that Tula is the "center place," itself the World Tree or World Mountain around which the four directions revolve.[3] He goes on to theorize that successive cultures erected their capital cities as geomantic models of the original Tula. The great sacred city was always Tula, the original center place re-created again and again. This, according to Carrasco, is why so many different locations in Mexico—Teotihuacán, Xochicalco, Cholula, and Tula Hidalgo—are all identified with Tula. The wandering Mayan sea traders who founded Chichén Itzá regarded their own capital as a similar geomantic world center, a Tula, as did each dynasty of kings that ruled the city-states of the Classic Maya.

Herein lies the explanation for the remarkable astronomical and geomantic alignments that characterize these Mesoamerican centers—they were not merely cities, they were mandalas or cosmograms. They were worldly manifestations of the archetypal Tula, mental maps constructed according to the dictates of an intricate geomancy. The great temple of Feathered Serpent at Chichén Itzá, for example, is a true World Mountain. It has four stairways, one running up each of its four sides to symbolize the four directions of time. The axes of the northeast and southwest corners of the pyramid are oriented towards the summer solstice sunrise and the winter solstice sunset.

Many tourists and New Age travelers continue to gather in Chichén Itzá on the spring equinox to watch an amazing spectacle which was planned by the Maya. The balustrades along the four stairways descend to earth in the shape of feathered serpents. The main doorway of the temple that crowns the pyramid opens to the north, the road to the center of the sky. On the equinoxes, shafts of sunlight ripple down the backs of the two great serpents lining the northern staircase. Here is a truly wonderful example of Mayan sacred geomancy—the Cosmic Serpent who forms the central energetic pole of the World Mountain and World Tree becomes illuminated, charged with power, pointing the way to the ancestral well of souls that lies to the north.

The central plaza of Chichén Itzá, like the great plazas of other Mayan cities, symbolizes the ocean of creation from which all things have arisen. In the center of this plaza is a simple platform with four stairways oriented to the solstitial directions and symbolizing once again the four directions that the gods established at the beginning of the world. The "northern path" through Chichén Itzá leads from the World Mountain, down the backs of the feathered serpents to the cosmic sea, through the original center place where the gods established the four directions, and on to the so-called Great Sacrificial Well, which surely represented the entrance to the Underworld, the cave of souls.

The Inner Tree

Just as the World Tree or World Mountain is a universal symbol that transcends cultural boundaries, so is the idea that the central tree or mountain is actually within the human body. There is a precise correspondence between the architecture of Heaven, the macrocosm, and the constitution of man, the microcosm. As there is a central tree or axis that forms the pivotal point of the world or the universe, likewise there must be a central axis that forms the pivotal point for man as a spiritual entity. According to Hindu thought, the spinal column is the human analog of Mount Meru. According to Kabbalistic Judaism, the Tree of Life is found not only in the mythical Garden of Eden, but within the human body, where it, too, corresponds to the spinal column.

Just as the vital energy from within the earth travels up the World Mountain or Tree of Life and the life-giving power of the gods flows down it, there is an equivalent that flows in the spinal column giving life to the inner or spiritual man. Hindus call it the kundalini; Kabbalists know it as the Shekinah. To the Classic Maya it was *itz* (EETZ), the "dew of heaven," while to modern-day Mayan Calendar shamans, it is *coyopa* (koy-oh-PAH), "the lightning in the blood."

Though no authentic teachings regarding the esoteric nature of the human body remain from the period of the Classic Maya, Aztec sources tell us that, in fact, the people of Mesoamerica had highly developed teachings about the nature of spiritual energy in the human body.[4] The vital force which traveled up and down the World Tree—and, by extension, up and down the spine—was called *malinalli* (mah-lee-NAH-lee) in the Nahuatl language, equivalent to the Mayan itz. According to the Aztecs it consisted of two streams; one flowed downwards from Heaven, and the other flowed upwards from the Underworld. Together, the two streams combined in a double helix, like the

DNA spiral. The flow of malinalli concentrated itself in three specific centers within the human body. These centers form an obvious analogy to the Hindu doctrine of the chakras, the "subtle centers" or, more literally, "wheels" of psycho-spiritual energy within the body. In Hindu tradition, there are seven such centers, whereas the fragmentary sources surviving from Aztec times mention only three. There may well have been others, the knowledge of which has not been preserved.[5] A diagram preserved in one of the old Aztec books (now known as the *Codex Borgia*) links the day-signs of the Sacred Calendar with various parts of the human body and suggests an awareness of the crown, heart, navel, and root chakras. Thus, like the World Tree, the entire Calendar is within us as well as outside of us—it is part of our essence as well as a measure of time (Figure 3).

The first of the three known centers has its locus in the crown of the head; the energy associated with it is called *tonalli* (toh-NAH-lee) in Nahuatl. The word signifies a warmth that originates in the sun and radiates through each human individual as a link with the solar force. Tonalli is placed in the mother's womb through the agency of the Creator; as the spark of light that links each of us to the gods, it is the locus of our higher individuality, our personal essence. Tonalli is closely related to the Hindu concept of the *atman*, and is equivalent to the lotus or crown chakra of Hindu tradition.

The second esoteric center is in the heart; the vital force that animates this center is called *teyolia* (tay-OH-lee-ah) in Nahuatl and is the source of emotion, memory, and knowledge. Teyolia is the "divine fire" that shapes our patterns of thought and habit. The teyolia may be transformed into a "divine heart" even in this lifetime. In Aztec tradition those who played the roles of the gods at religious festivals and those who dedicated their lives to the composition of spiritual poetry were believed to be especially filled with teyolia. Teyolia is a substance found everywhere, not only in the heart chakra. It is present in mountains and lakes, and in temples and pyramids as well.

The third center lies in the liver; its associated force is called *ihiyotl* (ee-HEE-yotle). This ihiyotl is like a "luminous gas," a subtle energy that is the source of our emotions: hatred, desire, courage, and love. To examine one's own motivations and thus seek the truth of one's being was a process that the Aztecs called "discovering one's liver." It is the energy called ihiyotl that projects itself to others, creating tentacles of charm and attraction.

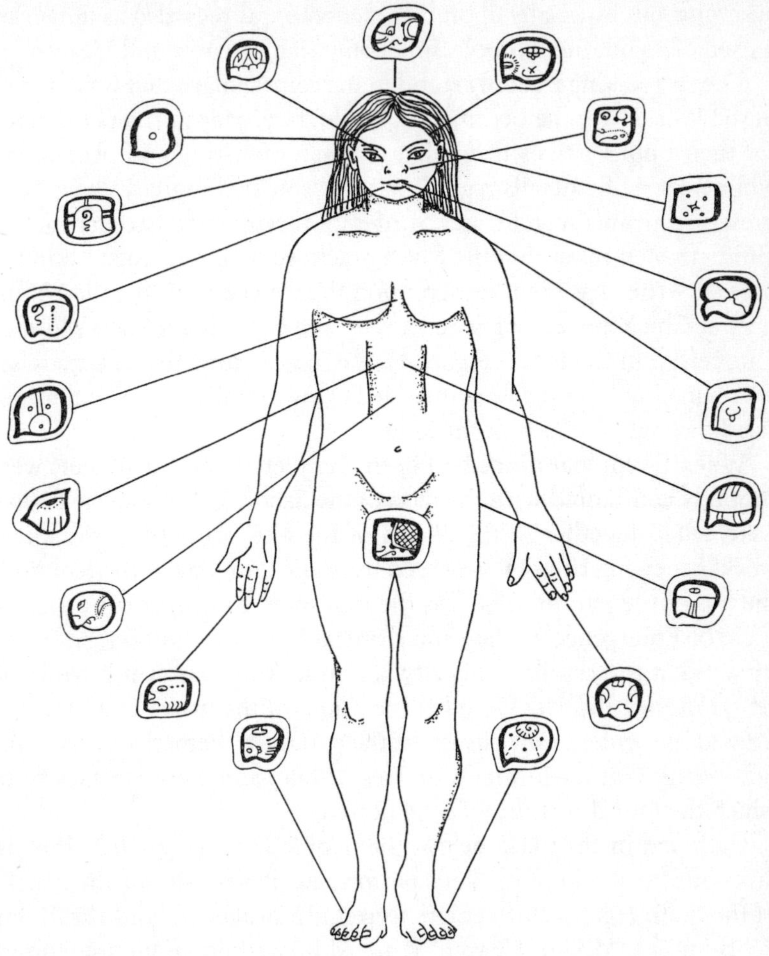

FIGURE 3 ***The Calendar and the Human Body***

A World in Balance

This, then, was the inner and outer world that First Father and First Mother made, on a day in 3114 B.C., which was also a day in mythological time—a time beyond time. However, this world is still in a state of emergence. It is constantly developing, and hence unstable. Therefore it must be maintained. It is only through the prayers of human beings, through their devotion to the gods, that the world's equilibrium is made possible. To worship the gods was impingent upon everyone, but especially upon the ruler who was regarded as the incarnation of a god, the symbolic link between his people and Heaven.

The sacred king not only stood in the central place that was the axis of the World Tree: he became the World Tree. Mayan rulers prepared for their public rituals through a regimen of fasting and prayer, and while no specific details regarding these spiritual exercises have been preserved from ancient times, contemporary Mayan teachers such as Hunbatz Men insist that the Maya practiced a kind of yoga,[6] and the present writer has seen, carved upon the walls of the so-called Nunnery at Chichén Itzá, a bas relief scupture depicting a Mayan lord or king seated in full lotus (Figure 4). We may assume that the exercises preceding public ritual were intended to awaken the life-force that spiraled through the body of the king.

When the preparations had been completed and the planets were properly configured with the days of the Sacred Calendar, the people were called together in the "heart of the city" to witness the king's world-renewing rites. He emerged from the doorway of the temple at the top of the pyramid: he was the first man, coming forth from the Cave of Emergence at the center of the World Mountain. Atop the pyramid at the center of his city, a Mayan king was at the symbolic center of the universe. Placed at the center of the urban complex that formed the center of the city-state, the pyramids themselves were symbols of the World Mountain or Tree of Life, and were the axes from which the four directions of time flowed.

Gathered in the plaza below, the people watched as their human link with the world of the gods performed rites meant for the benefit of them all. His psychic centers were fully awakened, and the "body lightning" or "dew of Heaven" coursed up and down his spine in its sacred spiral motion. The king proceeded to invoke rulers long past, the spirits of the ancestors—an invocation that frequently took the form of a sacred "spirit dance." When the king mounted the pyramid, he was acting as the archetypal shaman who climbs the World Tree to visit the land of the gods.

Spilling blood was essential in bringing forth the spirits of the ancestors, just as it is essential in the Plains Indian Sun Dance, and for the same reason—to link one's spirit with the creative power of the universe. Mayan kings often used stingray spines to slit the penis and spill the blood into a bowl or onto specially prepared bark paper. At other times they pierced their tongues. This was the preferred blood-letting practice for Mayan women, and a relief at Yaxchilan (Yawsh-chee-LAHN)

FIGURE 4 ***Mayan Lord in Meditation***
"The Nunnery," Chichén Itzá

shows a certain Lady Xoc (SHOKE) passing a thorny vine through her tongue—which surely must have been as painful as any Sun Dance. Meanwhile copal incense burned in a nearby censer, producing huge billows of dark smoke.

The spilling of blood and the arduous ritual it entailed, together with the preparatory meditations or vision quests that awakened the inner centers, combined to induce a visionary state in the ritual performer. Emerging from the billows of copal smoke, the serpent that formed the Underworld polarity of the Cosmic Dragon or Celestial Serpent appeared to the Mayan lord or lady performing the ritual. From the jaws of the serpent, as if from the mouth of the Underworld, a human face would come forth—the spirit of an ancestor returning to provide guidance and vision to his people. Representations of these visions remain, including a dramatic carved record of a ritual performed by Lady Xoc in A.D. 709. It depicts Yat-Balam (YAHT-Ba-LAHM), founder of the Yaxchilan Dynasty (c. A.D. 320), emerging from the mouth of the Vision Serpent amid clouds of copal smoke.[7]

Thus, through spiritual contact with those ancestors who had become one with the heart of the world, the universe was renewed and maintained.

ENDNOTES

1. Schele and Freidel, *Forest of Kings*, 244–56.
2. David Freidel, Linda Schele, and Joy Parker, *Maya Cosmos: Three Thousand Years on the Shaman's Path* (New York: William Morrow and Co., 1993), 64–107.
3. David Carrasco, *Quetzalcoatl and the Irony of Empire: Myths and Prophecies in the Aztec Tradition* (Chicago and London: University of Chicago Press, 1982).
4. Carrasco, *Religions of Mesoamerica*, 65–70.
5. The Hopi Indians of Arizona recognize five such centers, corresponding to the crown, third eye, throat, heart, and navel chakras of Hindu and Buddhist tradition. See Frank Waters, *Book of the Hopi* (Harmondsworth: Penguin, 1978), 9–10.
6. Hunbatz Men, *Secrets of Mayan Science/Religion*, translated by Diana Gubiseh Ayala and James Jennings Dunlap II (Santa Fe: Bear and Co., 1990), 109–45.
7. Schele and Freidel, *Forest of Kings*, 265–8.

3

The World of the Four Directions

The great Mayan cities were abandoned; the Long Count was kept no more. The people were conquered by the Spanish and converted (however unwillingly) to Christianity. The old ways were never entirely forgotten, however, and it is a common saying among anthropologists that the conquest of the Maya is still incomplete. Not only have the Maya risen in rebellion a number of times, but they have maintained their old "pagan" beliefs to an astonishing degree. Nowhere is the conquest of the Maya more incomplete than in the spiritual realm.

Many traditionalist Maya still honor the ancient shrines and heed the teachings of the village shamans. The Quiché Maya of the Guatemalan highlands, however, have a reputation for being the most deeply traditional, largely because they keep the most complex surviving form of the old Sacred Calendar. Their shamans, in fact, are called Daykeepers, signifying those who understands and interprets the Calendar. Let us take a brief look at the Native spiritual practices of the contemporary Maya.

The Making of a Daykeeper

Not everyone can become a Calendar shaman or Daykeeper. In some conservative Quiché communities, like Momostenango, only those who are born on special days of the Sacred Calendar are believed to be naturally endowed with coyopa, the "lightning in the blood" which is the modern term for what the Classic Maya called itz and the Aztecs malinalli. Without the body lightning—a natural surplus of kundalini power—it is difficult to succeed in becoming a Daykeeper. Nevertheless, even those who have not been born with a great deal of natural coyopa inherent in their day-signs may still manage to acquire a powerful quantum of "body lightning" through intensive training and spiritual practice

Whether born or made, the potential Daykeeper—like shamans everywhere—must come into the profession by way of a vision, an illness, or often both. According to Dennis and Barbara Tedlock, two American anthropologists initiated as Daykeepers in Momostenango, such "illnesses" usually involve severe cramps in the joints or muscles, severe stomach cramps, a tendency to simply fall down without warning or reason, as well as more "psychological" afflictions such as habitually losing one's money to thieves or drinking too much.[1]

The shamanic illness is generally the first sign that an individual is destined to take the ancient or traditional way. Some writers have called this traditional path *costumbre*, which encompasses the entire body of Native ways and lore. However, Martin Prechtel, an American who was initiated as a Daykeeper and shaman in Guatemala, insists that, to the true Mayan esotericist, costumbre is simply folklore, and that the old Mayan religion itself is more properly called "Walking the Path of the Sun" or "Walking the Path of the Days." Flordemayo, a *curandera* or healer who has also studied with Guatemalan Daykeepers, calls it *Caminando La Bara*, which is Spanish for "walking the teachings" or "walking the knowledge."

If a person is born on an appropriate day or acquires the requisite amount of coyopa, suffers from one of the shamanic illnesses, and has powerful or unusual dreams that indicate a special destiny, then this individual may be trained as a Daykeeper. The aspirant is apprenticed to an older Calendar shaman to learn the lore of the Sacred Calendar.

Essentially, the Sacred Calendar plays three important roles in the lives of the modern Maya:

- It is a system of "astrology,"
- it is a technique of divination, and
- most importantly, it is a ritual cycle according to which the spiritual life may be lived.

We will explore all these dimensions of the Sacred Calendar in the course of this book.

At the beginning of apprenticeship, a novice shaman collects a personal bag of divining seeds from the sacred ceiba tree, along with crystals that sometimes represent the spirits of divination and the Sacred Calendar, but which may sometimes be used as "seeing stones" or divinatory tools in their own right. On special days determined by the Calendar, the novice is permitted to practice techniques of divination. He or she is also instructed in the traditional prayers and the lore of sacred days upon which one visits the shrines or climbs the sacred mountains. Progress is monitored by the teacher through dreamwork—the novice's dreams are discussed with the teacher, who prescribes a path of training accordingly. Finally, all those who have been trained during the past 260-day period are initiated on a special day. In Momostenango this day is 8 Monkey, and in Chichicastenango it is 8 Deer. Martin Prechtel was initiated into a tradition that recognized 8 Eagle as its principal ceremonial day. ("We're bird people," he proclaims.)

After becoming a Calendar shaman, one may specialize in a number of different spiritual arts. A singer, for example, is usually male and concerns himself with the chants, prayers, and rituals of the Calendar. A marriage spokesman (also male) must memorize long passages of oratory connnected with betrothal and marriage ceremonies. Midwives (always female) are also considered shamans after a fashion.

Two shamanic practitioners, because of their importance, deserve our special attention.

The Healer

A traditional Mayan healer is sometimes called a bone-setter, and operates through Native techniques of massage therapy combined with herbalism. In ancient times, Mayan herbalism was a highly developed art; however, it declined steadily from the Conquest period until the present day. The last of the great Mayan herbalists, Don Eligio Panti of Belize, saved much of what is left of this knowledge by transmitting it to his American disciple, Rosita Arvigo.[2]

The following list includes just a few of the herbs in Don Eligio's vast pharmacopoeia:

ALLSPICE (*pimienta gorda*) leaves and berries aid fever relief, indigestion, stomachache, and colic. A crushed berry placed over the gum of an aching tooth will quickly ease the pain.

AMARANTH (*calalu*) leaves are high in iron and calcium; the seeds are rich in protein. Served warm with a touch of milk and honey, this South American "pot herb" is a great energy booster.

CHAMOMILE (*manzanilla*) is used by Mayan healers as a mild tea for insomnia, nerves, colic, and indigestion.

CILANTRO is a flavorful garden vegetable used to season soups, salads, and sauces. Boil the seeds and serve the liquid as a tea when you can't sleep or your stomach is upset.

COPAL TREE (*pom bark*), boiled into a tea, may aid indigestion.

CORN (*im che*) is a medicinal food sacred to the Maya. Cornsilk is boiled and served as tea for kidney and bladder problems.

LEMON GRASS (*zacote limon*), a refreshing rain forest herb, can be used to reduce fever.

LINDEN FLOWERS (*flor de tilo*) make a mild, calming tea.

MEXICAN WORMSEED (*epasote*) can take away a hangover when you drink tea made from its root.

ROSEMARY (*romero*) will help to cleanse the stomach of mucus.

RUE (*sink in*) is a popular Mayan remedy with a variety of uses. Hysteria, stomachache, menstrual cramps, delayed menses, labor, and childbirth all improve when you drink water into which the fresh plant has been squeezed.

The Spiritualist

A spiritualist may be either male or female, and is considered not only the most powerful of all Calendar shamans, but also the most feared. These individuals, who conduct séances at midnight and speak with the spirits of the dead or with the spirits resident in caves, often cross the thin boundary between shamanism and "witchcraft." Like the Mayan kings of old, they unite themselves with the ancestors and spirits who dwell in mountains and caves. Though the spiritualists are greatly feared, they are also greatly respected. The senior Calendar shaman or Mother-Father in a given region is often a spiritualist.[3]

The spiritualist's ability to walk a metaphysical tightrope between healing and sorcery illustrates an important point about contemporary Mayan life. Many Mayan people fear sorcery and spend a great deal of time protecting themselves from the attacks of malevolent shamans. The most important ingredients in their protective magic are:

COPAL resin, gathered from the sacred copal tree, the worldly correspondence of the great World Tree and a spirit in its own right, is capable of overcoming evil. Copal incense is burned to protect against evil forces, black magic, and such spiritual diseases as envy, fright, and grief. It is also used to summon the ancestors.

RUE is universally recognized as the herb of grace. This strong spiritual medicine is best known for its ability to ward off evil spirits. Rue can be mixed with skunk root (*zorillo*) and powdered white stone (see below, *piedra de Esquipulas*) to banish jealousy or a bad case of nerves.

HOLY WATER, collected from the nearest Catholic church, can be sprinkled about the house or grounds, or used to anoint and bless a spiritually troubled person.

PIEDRA DE ESQUIPULAS, a calcium-based stone, is found at a sacred mountain in Guatemala. It is named for the "black" or Native statue of Christ at the shrine of Esquipulas. The stone is ground to a fine powder and added to a tea also containing skunk root, rue, and holy water. Drink it three times a day to break enchantments and avert the envy of others. This may be a bit hard to come by if you live north of the border, though there is another healing Christ of Esquipulas at the village of Chimayo in northern New Mexico. The sanctuary there contains a pit of "healing earth." Gather a bit of it and mix it in water, as with the piedra de Esquipulas.

BASIL, called *ca cal tun* (kah kahl TOON) in Yucatán, is a familiar wild and cultivated spice used in a variety of ethnic recipes; in the rain forest it is also used to break enchantments and ward off evil spirits. Burn it for seven Fridays to clear an unpleasant atmosphere in the home.

ROSEMARY burned with copal resin makes an incense to ward off evil spirits and envy. For protection, a mixture of copal and rosemary can be burned for nine Fridays.

SKUNK ROOT is an herb used by Mayan shamans to increase their powers. Boil the root or bark and drink it as a tea.

Say this prayer when using any of the above remedies:

May all harmful evil depart from this place. In the name of the Creator. So be it.

There are many more techniques of spiritual protection which form part of the Mayan magical tradition. Amulets are especially popular. To make one, place a sprig of rue, a chip of copal incense and a tiny segment of Esquipulas stone (or Chimayo dirt) on a bit of balsam bark. Fold a square of black silk or cotton around the items to create a small, neat bundle. Sew up the edges with black thread. Wear the pouch around your neck or keep it on or about your body at all times.

Living at the Center of the World

The Maya continue to live in a fourfold world. In many highland communities, four local mountains are accounted sacred and are said to represent the energies of the four directions. The Yucatec Maya still recognize four spiritual guardians for the sacred directions, though now those guardians have taken on different names—St. Dominic rules in the East and St. James the Younger in the West, while Gabriel the Archangel guards the northern direction and Mary Magdalene (a fitting patroness of fertility) is in the South.[4]

The four directions give the shaman the principal magical correspondences—colors, seasons and metaphysical concepts—though the true complexity of Mayan magic is only revealed through a study of the Sacred Calendar. In order to understand how the Mayan shaman perceives the spiritual universe, make use of this very simple exercise.

Meditation: The Four Directions

1. Stand facing the East.
2. Take a deep breath and close your eyes. Imagine that you stand in the center of all things, the very navel of the universe. You are the World Tree. Your roots stretch down to the Underworld, and your mind touches the heavens. Above your head shines the North Star. You are the Milky Way, the great cosmic highway.
3. Now imagine that a spiral of energy is rising up out of the earth, traveling up the back of your legs, then up your spine, the trunk of your own inner World Tree. This energy is solid, stablizing, and abundant. In fact, all possible abundance and good fortune comes to you as a result of this earthy power.
4. Now imagine another spiral of energy, flooding down from the heavens above, entering your body through the crown of your

head and traveling down your spinal column into the abundant earth. This force embodies spiritual power; it is symbolic of your inspiration, your connection with the divine. This is the energy the Classic Maya called itz, the "dew of heaven."

5. Visualize these two energetic forces as spirals of white light, one moving from the sky into the earth, the other from the earth into the sky. Together they form a double spiral traveling up and down your spine, like the double helix of a DNA molecule.

6. Now stretch your arms out from your sides, so that you stand as a cross in the center of all things. Remember, to the Maya the Christian cross is but a symbol of the cross of the four directions, the World Tree, and of the fourfold universe itself. You are that universe.

   At your right hand, to the South, are gathered all the male powers of the universe. Since the Maya trace their ancestors through the father's side, these "male powers" include all the living members of your family. In Mayan magic we learn to honor all our relations, so for the moment you must forget about any psychological "issues" you may have with these people. Love them anyway. Also at your right hand are all the psychological attributes we generally associate with maleness, including your sense of authority, assertiveness, power, and command.

   Now concentrate on your left hand. Here, in the North, are gathered all the female powers of the universe. Some traditional shamans say that the marriage ceremony itself is symbolically "to your left." So, whether you are male or female, see all your intimate relations, as well as the actual women who come into your life, on your left hand. Once again, forget about any issues you have with these people, and simply love them.

   In back of you, to the West, stand all your ancestors, whether from your own family or the world at large. Here lies the collective spiritual power of all those who went before you. When your own time comes to die, you will become part of this great collective human unconscious that resides in the "pool of souls." We will explore the pool of souls later, but for now simply acknowledge the power of the ancestors behind you.

   In front of you, to the East, lies the future. Do you have children of your own? They are in the East, for they are part of your future. This is where your spiritual path lies, for on the spiritual path we always walk forward, never back. Because magical or ritual practice is part of the spiritual path, and because divination with the Sacred Calendar helps us to understand the future, some Mayan shamans say that divination is "in the East."

7. Breathe and reflect quietly on this, your own World Tree, until it becomes part of you.

Making an Altar

Many Mayan communities have their own "world center," which is usually a pagan shrine somewhere in or near the village. Like the ancient temples, it serves as a power spot representing the axis of the world, the sacred tree or mountain. Such a shrine usually consists of a natural stone altar in a rural setting—fragments of broken pottery, balls of burnt copal incense, and mounds of candle wax abound. Many traditional Mayans, especially shamans or other practitioners of the "old ways," also work from private altars in their homes. By making such an altar, you create the center of the universe, the pivot of the four directions, in your own living space.

An altar may be a simple thing—in fact, the simpler the better. In Mayan villages, where money is a rare thing, an old bench or card table may serve for an altar, even among the most powerful shamans. Begin by finding an appropriate piece of furniture.

Very few Maya would place an altar dead center in the middle of a room—after all, families are large and space is limited. The best place for an altar is against a wall or in a corner.

Now you may begin to decorate your altar. Among the Maya, this is a highly individual and improvisational affair. An altar may be a model of the world axis, but it is also an artistic expression of you.

Here are some things one might find on a traditional Mayan altar:

A CROSS—To enter a Mayan home and view the family altar with its prominent cross may give a visitor the impression of conventional Catholicism. Mayan crosses are more properly symbolic of the World Tree and the four directions; their meaning goes back much further than Christian hegemony in the New World. A Mayan altar cross, for example, may be garbed in a *huipil* or traditional Mayan dress, as well as in beads, charms, and so on. If crosses bother you in general, you don't need one, but if you can appreciate the ancient symbolism and the artistic possibilities, try draping a cross with your favorite magical objects, or even "dressing" it in doll's clothes.

CANDLES—Candles represent forgiveness or pardon. They correspond to the day-sign Vulture in the old calendar; the vulture, who eats carrion, is a symbol for "karmic clean-out." Similarly, the candle is also a purifying agent, burning up our "sins."

IDOLS—Mayan people, at least until recently, used to find ancient statuettes or other objects in the ruins and bring them home. This practice, of course, has become more rare as local authorities become increasingly severe about "pot-hunting" in archaeological sites. In any event, it is very unlikely that you live in a zone where such antiques would be available (and it would be wildly illegal to take them, anyway). If you like the idea of placing statues with a Mayan "look" to them on your altar, you will have to make do with store-bought reproductions. Also note that some Catholic saints appear to have taken on the meaning of old gods, and what looks like a saintly icon may in fact be a reminder of the ancient ways. Simon Peter, for example, is the contemporary equivalent of the old pagan Earth Father, whom we shall meet shortly.

FOOD, FLOWERS, AND PHOTOS—Mayan people may reverence their ancestors by placing their pictures on the altar—Grandma's photo honors Grandma's spirit and helps keep her valued or much-loved energy in the home. By the same token, food may sometimes be left on an altar "for the dead." This practice, of course, is part of the popular Mexican holiday called the Day of the Dead, celebrated on November 1. To place family photos, objects that remind you of loved ones, or the occasional burrito on an altar creates a very colorful space, and altars throughout backwoods Mexico are colorful—bright woven tablecloths or sarapes, vibrant flowers, bottles of alcohol, wedding cake figures, even Christmas tree lights are all popular. Use your imagination. "Spiritual" doesn't have to mean drab or colorless.

INCENSE—Among the Maya, incense typically means copal. You can burn it on anything, whether it be an old plate, a fancy incense burner, or just a rock. Copal is readily available in most American health food stores.

DIVINATION BAG—A Calendar shaman usually keeps his bag of divining seeds on or near the altar. This is a special topic, which we shall cover in Chapter 7.

CRYSTALS AND OTHER STONES—This too is a special topic. With some stones, you may establish an especially powerful relationship. Such a stone—one that fills you with a feeling of power and the sacredness of life—may in fact be a "seeing stone" or "stone of light," known in Yucatec Maya as a *sastun* (sahs-TOON).

Finding Your Stone of Light

A sastun can be anything—for the great contemporary shaman and healer Don Eligio Panti, it was a simple child's marble, while for his principal student, Rosita Arvigo, it is a "New Age type" crystal.

If you possess a stone or crystal so special to you that you suspect it may be your seeing stone or sastun, you can use this ritual, as taught by Don Eligio, to "test" it.[5] Even if your stone doesn't turn out to be a true sastun, the first half of the ritual will "power up" or charge any crystal or stone. Another way to charge a stone is to keep it overnight in a glass of brandy after praying over it, as is done in Yucatán.

According to Don Eligio, the following ritual should be performed on a Friday.

1. Hold your crystal in one hand. Dip the fingers of your other hand into a glass of some kind of liquor—Don Eligio used rum, while in Yucatán they often use brandy, which is my own preference. After dipping your fingers, make the sign of the cross on both sides of your stone.
2. Speak the following words:

   Sastun, sastun, I ask that you tell me all I want to know. Teach me to understand signs. Visit me in all my dreams. Give me the answers I seek. I have faith that this sastun will answer all my prayers. God the Father, God the Son, and God the Holy Spirit.

   (As will become clear in a few pages, one could also say "In the name of God, in the name of the Earth Father, and in the name of the Ancestors.") Repeat the dipping and the prayer nine times.

3. Go to sleep with your stone or crystal nearby—in your hand, under your pillow, or wherever it feels right. If your stone is actually a sastun, the spirits will come to you in a dream and instruct you in its proper use.

   If you want to enhance the possibility of a powerful, significant dream experience, you can do what some Mayan shamans do when they are "seeking a dream." Drink a glass of warm water mixed with a tablespoon of lemon juice in order to clean out your system. Do this about an hour after dinner in order to give yourself time to digest first, as well as giving yourself time to make a few trips to the bathroom before retiring.

4. If the spirits come to you in a dream to confirm your stone as a sastun, they will give you very specific instructions as to how your stone should be used. Every person and every stone is unique; hence every set of magical instructions will be different from any other. Follow instructions to the letter.

5. If you do have a dream, and if the stone in your possession is in fact your sastun, continue to honor it by signing the cross with alcohol and saying the prayer nine times every Friday night.

Though some shamans use a seeing stone in combination with Calendar divination, this is an extremely advanced technique. If you discover your seeing stone, you will probably wish to set it aside, keeping it separate from the rest of your divining equipment (see Chapter 7).

The Earth Father

The Quiché recognize their own trinity, which is quite different than the trinity of the Catholic Church. The Quiché terms are Tiox, Mundo, and Nantat.[6] The word Tiox (tee-OSHE) is a Quiché translation of the Spanish word *Dios*, meaning God: Tiox includes the Christian God and all his saints, the entire Catholic pantheon.

Mundo, of course, is the Spanish word for earth, and includes not only the earth itself, but specifically caves and mountains, for caves and mountains were regarded as gateways to the Underworld in pre-Columbian times. Santo Mundo or Saint World, the second person of the Native Mayan trinity, is an ambivalent character.

Like the old Underworld gods, this Earth Father is treacherous and somewhat untrustworthy. Yet the Maya realize that it is Santo Mundo—trickster though he may be—who is responsible for all worldly prosperity. After all, he lives below the earth, and anyone can see that this is the place where the green plants, especially the life-giving corn, have their origin. All our natural food—and hence all our natural abundance—arises from the earth. The Earth Father may be a tempestuous and unpredictable force; some might even call him evil, for he is believed to be responsible for all our madness and craziness. Yet it is he who gives us all the good things of this world.

In the village of Santiago Atitlan, a Guatemalan town that is well known for its adherence to costumbre and the traditional ways, the Earth Father goes by the name of Maximon. (His role as Earth Father, however, is a highly ambivalent one. Martin Prechtel, who knows him well, says: "He isn't really a he.")

The name itself is revealing—it is a combination of *Maam*, the old Mayan word for the Earth Lord or (sometimes) the spirit of the year, and *Simon*, from St. Simon Peter. Let it be noted, however, that in many traditional Central American communities St. Simon is a "patron saint" of sorcery and black magic rather than a peaceful fisherman. He plays much the same role as does St. Cipriano, who, in South America, has numerous grimoires and books of spells dedicated to his name. Let it be noted, also, that even the highly significant name of Maximon is just a veil for deeper truths—Martin Prechtel also says: "Maximon is not his real name."

Maximon represents nature in the raw, the destructive power of nature which manifests in earthquakes, floods, and storms. He is a wanderer who travels on foot, and may strike a man with madness or snakebite. He is worshipped at the mouths of caves, which of course is where the Underworld gods have always been worshipped. He may be the spiritual descendant of the old Mayan god called Pauhatun (Pow-ah-TOON), an Underworld god who presided over what we might call "the psychedelic enema"—Mayan ahauob often took enemas of the juice of psilocybin mushrooms in preparation for their rituals. In any event, most contemporary Mayan people fear Maximon, and only the people of Santiago Atitlan pay him such special reverence.

Maximon is an idol, almost life-sized, whose *cofradia* or tutelary society keeps him stored in the rafters of their "dawn house" for most of the year. He sports a black coat and hat, a black beard, and a big cigar. Sometimes he is depicted with a bottle of booze as well. Just before Lent, the young men of Santiago Atitlan go into the mountains to gather various flowers and fruits for Maximon. They go without their wives, but they are encouraged to go wild with sexual activity when they return. After all, Maximon is the patron saint of worldly abundance, and is believed to be a powerful sexual force who will lend vigor and potency to the young men. The flowers and fruits they gather are stored next to Maximon in the dawn house.

When the people celebrate his power during Lent, Maximon will come down from the rafters, the mountain offerings will be presented to him, and the people will dance and sing. Maximon will be taken to the church, borne on the shoulders of his "horse," a specially chosen cofradia member. A pole symbolizing the World Tree will be raised in a side chapel. Maximon will be raised up on the pole; in other words, he will hang from the World Tree as do all good shamans during their initiation—including Christ.

As for Christ himself, the more staunch Catholic members of the village have made him the star of a ceremony very similar to Maximon's. On Good Friday, an effigy of Christ is carried to the church, and hanged on yet another World Tree which is raised in a small pit of earth called "the center of the world." This Christ, like Maximon, is a nature spirit, for within his cloak one can see fruit and small animals. In time, he is taken down and placed in a glass-covered casket covered with flowers and decorated with Christmas tree lights. Christ and Maximon exit the church at the same time, and engage in a kind of ritual confrontation—during which, according to the devotees of Maximon, Christ will be "impregnated" by Maximon. Thus, the New Year may begin, for all seasonal forces may be resolved to the dualism of Light (Christ, yang) and Darkness (Maximon, yin).

For the most part, this dynamic tension between Christ Lord of Heaven and Maximon the Underworld Father is a balanced cosmic dance. However, outright conflict sometimes develops. In 1950, a Catholic priest, convinced that Maximon was actually Judas, the slayer of Christ (which is in fact only one of his many attributes), stole the Maximon idol from the dawn house. Somehow it ended up in the Musée de l'Homme in Paris, where it was enshrined for many years. Then, in 1978, Martin Prechtel, along with the poet Nathaniel Tarn, negotiated the return of Maximon to Santiago Atitlan. The French ambassador rented a launch and sailed across Lake Atitlan accompanied by a female diplomat who carried the mask in a suitcase chained to her wrist. Thus Maximon returned home.

Sadly enough, the conflict has continued. Martin was driven out of Guatemala by government death squads who strafed his house. The growing strength of both Catholics and Evangelicals in the Guatemalan highlands presents an ongoing danger to the devotees of Maximon.

But, for the moment, Maximon continues to survive.

The Pool of Souls

The "third person" of the Mayan trinity is Nantat (nahn-TAHT), which signifies the Ancestors and corresponds to the ahauob of times past who were ritually invoked by the Classic Mayan kings. The Ancestors are everywhere; their spirits permeate our lives. The Maya ask permission of the Ancestors before undertaking any operation—such as building a house—which might influence the family structure, for the Ancestors remain guardians of the family. The Ancestors may also return to us, taking on new life, for the Maya (or some of them) have a concept of reincarnation.

Most Mayan peoples believe that there are in fact two souls. Conceptions about these two souls differ widely; the summary here is based on information from the Quiché Maya of Momostenango.

Every human being has a "life-soul," one that is linked with the body and that, should it depart from the body, would cause the person's death within a short time. This life-soul is also called the *uxlab* (oosh-LAHB) or "breath soul," as well as the *anima*, a Spanish or Latin word for soul. This soul arrives at birth and is lodged in the heart.

There is another component of this life-soul, which may sometimes be regarded as a separate entity altogether. This is the coyopa or "body lightning," which we have already discussed. Because not everyone is born with coyopa (though it may be acquired through ritual), to possess this powerful energy is to be marked for a shaman's destiny.

The second soul is the "free soul." This soul differs from the life-soul for several reasons. The life-soul, for example, is tied to the body, while the free soul may literally roam free without harming its possessor. One suspects that the free soul corresponds to the "astral body" or "astral soul" of other occult traditions around the world.

Still, there are differences. The free soul is sometimes called the *nagual*, which is actually a term borrowed from Nahuatl. The traditional definition of a nagual is a guardian spirit or animal totem which presides over an individual's destiny. One may discover this guardian spirit through a dream, or, among some Native peoples, by noting the first animal to cross the newborn's path. A nagual may also be a force of nature—for instance, a thunderbolt—rather than an animal. The link between a person and his nagual or totem is indissoluble and lifelong. In Mayan thinking, one's nagual is linked with the day one is born. To be born on the day Eagle, for example, indicates that the eagle is your nagual. There are other terms for this link between the free soul and the day-sign of one's birth: either one may be described as your "face" or "destiny."

It is this free soul that, after an individual's death, travels on and may in time reincarnate. Mayan souls are sometimes said to journey to the "pool of souls," from whence they may reach back to us and communicate with us through caves—doorways to the Underworld. In Quiché territory, for example, a cave near Utatlan is especially reverenced as the great entryway to the Underworld. In essence, any cave may serve, and shamans who wish to communicate with the spirits of the Ancestors will often journey to the nearest cave to perform rituals.

The sanctity of caves is taken very seriously. In the late 1960s, an archaeologist named Dennis Puleston got the notion that he would excavate the caves of Belize, hoping to find ritual objects from the Classic Period. The traditional Maya in the area refused to help him; the only workers he could obtain were those who were strongly influenced by Western society and had ceased to believe in the ways of their fathers. Puleston didn't get far with his excavations, however. He was struck by lightning and killed while standing on the top of the great pyramid of Chichén Itzá during a thunderstorm. His archaeological colleague, Barbara MacLeod, proved to be wiser—she returned to Belize and hired local shamans to help her make atonement at the mouths of the very caves she had once planned to excavate.

Deep below the surface of the earth, then, lies the pool of souls, where the naguals of the departed wait. If honored properly, they may communicate with us through dream, vision, or through the voice of a shaman, much as the ahauob of the Classic Period spoke through the priest kings who performed their rituals atop the pyramids—which, like caves, were gateways to the world beyond.

In time, a shaman may help a departed soul to return. Many Daykeepers practice a ritual called "planting," wherein the soul of an ancestor is magically "planted" in the body of a pregnant woman, and thus enabled to return to earth once more.

And so the cycle of life goes on.

Celebrating the Days of the Dead

Throughout Mexico (and, increasingly, throughout southern California and the American Southwest), the Days of the Dead are celebrated on Halloween and on the days immediately following. The "official" Day of the Dead is November 1. Altars are erected in homes and dedicated to departed members of one's family. Colorfully decorated, these altars contain religious icons and objects as well as photographs of the deceased. Food is cooked and placed upon the altar to feed the dead. After the deceased have taken their invisible portion, the family will eat the actual meal. Candies made in the shape of skeletons are particular favorites among the children.

During the Days of the Dead, Mexican families visit the graves of deceased relatives in their local cemeteries. They decorate the graves, so that the cemeteries become colorful, magical places. Picnics are held, and in this way, too, families symbolically feast with their ancestors. The people say that the spirits of the dead will walk abroad at night during these days, and search for their previous homes. Paths of marigolds, the flowers of the dead, are often strewn in front of houses. It is believed that a path of these flowers will assist the spirits of the deceased in finding their way home.

To maintain a close and friendly connection with the Ancestors is a way of assuring that the whole community—both living and dead—will maintain its spiritual health, and that a continuity with tradition and with the past will be preserved in the present. Most of us may not live in small villages that constitute worlds unto themselves, but we all live in some kind of community, and we all have a duty to help our community maintain its spiritual health—even, or perhaps especially, if we have come to perceive that community as global in nature. After all, healing the tribe is the proper business of shamans. One of the most important ways that we can do this is to honor the Ancestors.

The traditional time for this practice is Halloween or All Souls' Day, but it may be done at any time.

A Traditional Celebration

1. First, you will need photographs or other mementos of your dead. In Mexico, the altars for the Days of the Dead are decorated with framed photographs, portraits, and personal objects owned by one's departed parents, grandparents, siblings, and so

on. These mementos are set forth upon your altar as images and reminders of those who have passed beyond.

The notion of honoring deceased relatives may be troubling for some, especially if you've gone through therapy encouraging you to find the source of your own negative habit patterns in parental programming. Why pay homage to a mother who was abusively cold, or a father who was a chronic alcoholic? Why should you honor a grandmother who shattered the family structure for generations to come by running off with a carnival barker long ago? Aren't these the very people from whom you are attempting to liberate yourself?

But the Feast for the Dead is a much more ancient tradition than any current brand of therapy, and it may force you to see things in a different light. To honor the dead is an act of love which requires that we forgive our own past and all the people in it. What you honor in your father is not his alcoholism—it is his immortal soul, a soul in which you share simply by virtue of being human. What you honor in your cold or abusive mother is not her fierce rigidity, but the fierce fire of spirit that once burned within her and which burns within all living. Following a shamanic path means that you must learn to nurture a loving concern for the Ancestors, for all the departed souls of your total human community, which goes beyond mere emotional attachment or aversion. This can only be defined, as the Buddhists define it, in terms of compassion.

2. Now you must feed the dead. What shall you feed them? Anything you like! In Mexico, it would not be unusual to cook up Grandpa's favorite enchilada recipe and place it on the altar next to his picture.
3. When you leave food and drink on the altar, try to hold good thoughts for those to whom the food is dedicated. Contemplate, reflect, imagine. What was good about that person, or those people? What was beautiful, a part of their essential immortality of spirit? Sit and meditate on these things. When your heart is filled with love for your particular ancestors, you may send forth that love all over the world, to all our ancestors, and to the living as well.

4. Leave the food on the altar for as long as is practicable (considering the nature of the food, its perishability, the temperature of the room, etc.). Take it off the altar and eat it while it is still fresh and nourishing. If you can, share it with like-minded relatives who honor the same dead, or with friends who have their own ancestors to salute. Eat in silence, and in reverence for the souls and spirits of those who came before you. Cherish them with each bite, drink deep of their spirit with each sip.

Mayan magic and spirituality is an immensely complex topic; only the merest outlines of this extraordinary system can be given here. There is, however, one subject that must be understood in depth in order to gain any degree of real knowledge about the Mayan Tradition. This is the Sacred Calendar.

ENDNOTES

1. Barbara Tedlock, *Time and the Highland Maya* (Albuqerque: University of New Mexico, 1982), 54–8.
2. Rosita Arvigo, with Nadine Epstein and Marilyn Yaquinto, *Sastun: My Apprenticeship with a Maya Healer* (San Francisco: Harper and Row, 1994).
3. Tedlock, *Time and the Highland Maya*, 71–4.
4. Irene Nicholson, *Mexican and Central American Mythology* (London: Paul Hamlyn, 1967), 22.
5. Arvigo, Epstein and Yaquinto, *Sastun*, 117–21.
6. Tedlock, *Time and the Highland Maya*, 41–2.

4

The Sacred Calendar

The Sacred Calendar is about time.

We all know what time is—or think we do. It is a succession of dawns and sunsets, days and nights and seasons. We may divide it into hours and minutes or years and centuries, but we can never step outside of it—except perhaps in moments of special awareness which constitute the peak experiences of life. Time is one of the essential words. Life itself is subject to the regimen of time—not just human and animal life, but the life of planets and galaxies as well. Time is the one inescapable fact of existence.

Be that as it may, our personal quantum of biological energy will wind down, in time, and time will overcome us in the end. We as a species have always been inclined to regard time as a kind of taskmaster, a relentless clock that holds us always in its grasp, ticking away the minutes toward our eventual extinction. Time is the linear reality that gives shape and pattern to our lives, defining our mortality.

According to many traditional societies, there are two dimensions of time: ordinary time and sacred time. What has just been described is ordinary time.

If ordinary time represents a process to which all of us are subject and before which all of us are ultimately powerless, then sacred time represents cosmic order. It is the foundation of rhythm and motion. It is the glue that binds the universe together. Without the sense of cosmic order implied by this sacred dimension of time, nothing could happen. There would be no loom upon which to weave the tapestry of life. In many ancient mythologies, the gods do their work of universal creation in a world where time does not yet exist. Time itself is the summit of creation, for it is only when time exists that the new-made world is ready for humankind. The creation of time replaces original chaos with cosmic order. Marduk, king of the gods of ancient Babylon, slays the primordial serpent Tiamat, symbolic of chaos, and when he is done he "sets the stars in their courses" and thus establishes the calendar. Similarly, the Viking god Odin and his brothers slay the great frost-giant Ymir, fashioning the world from his carcass and, finally, attending to the calendar by putting the heavens in order.

Sacred time exists contemporaneously with ordinary time. It is fashioned of the same elements—seasonal and celestial—which comprise ordinary time. It is simply our altered or ritualized perception of time that allows us to enter its sacred dimension.

When the shaman draws his magic circle, or when a priest approaches the altar to celebrate the mass, he enters ritual space. This is a sacred place where the ordinary laws of reality do not apply. This is where magic happens. The center of the shaman's circle, the altar with its bread and wine—here lies the center of the universe.

We enter ritual space in our daily lives whenever we pray or meditate, whenever we create—in short, whenever we pay homage to the presence of the divine in our lives. For that moment, we are at the center of the universe. Whenever we enter ritual space, we enter ritual time as well. Ordinary time may be going on all around us, but we are no longer a part of it. Our perception of time has changed. It is no longer a mere progression of hours and minutes, but a living, vital, spiritual presence. This is what the sacred dimension of time is all about.

According to Chinese tradition, the primeval sage Fu Hsi "looked upward and contemplated the images in the heavens; he looked downward and contemplated the patterns on earth."[1] From this original act of contemplation arose three different ways of measuring sacred space and time: astrology, geomancy, and the *I Ching*. Both ordinary and sacred time are generally measured by the patterns of heaven and earth, for it is these patterns, these constantly recurring cycles, that integrate us with the cosmic order underlying all things. Honoring these recurring changes is yet another way for us to enter the sacred dimension of time.

Thus humanity has devised rituals to mark the four major changes of the solar and seasonal year—the equinoxes, when day and night are of equal length, and the solstices, when the sun appears to stand still and then "turn back" to the north or south. Priests and magicians of all cultures have charted the progress of planets and fixed the positions of the stars, for the orderly cycles of the heavens are among the most potent symbols of the cosmic order—remember, Marduk and Odin created time by "setting the stars in their courses." The yogi honors the rising of the sun each day, and so pays homage to the sun as a symbol of the Self; thus he enters into ritual time—which, paradoxically, is timeless, even as the Self is eternal.

The Mesoamerican spiritual tradition exemplified its vision of the universe in mandalas or cosmograms, diagrams of the infinite. The double pyramid construction of the Mayan universe was one such diagram; the geomantic city was another. But these cosmograms are essentially static; they are not in motion. The Maya believed that the universe, both human and cosmic, was constantly evolving through different worlds or "suns," different epochs of cosmic time. They believed that every moment in time was in a state of flux, a shifting tapestry of energies that manifested in earthquakes and volcanoes, in the wars of gods and men and the changes of the human heart and spirit. Hence the theme of transformation is central to all Mesoamerican mythology. In one story, a deformed and rejected god is transformed into the glorious sun of the new world epoch. In another, the god-king Quetzalcoatl is transformed into the planet Venus. The world is constantly evolving.

However, an evolving world is a world in turmoil, and therefore it needs to be centered, equilibrated, and maintained so that it shall not become *koyanisqaatsi*, a Hopi term meaning "world out of balance." Human beings must constantly struggle for the sense of universal order and harmony even as they struggle towards their own evolution.

To pluck order out of chaos we must understand the nature of both polarities, the very rhythm of emergence. How, then, shall we measure the ebb and flow of energy in time, the vast transformations and metamorphoses that make up life on earth? How shall we find the sense of cosmic order in this shifting, restless world of volcanic passions, both human and terrestrial? How shall we sense both the order and the chaos entwined in one vast scheme?

For this, the people of ancient Mesoamerica needed a cosmogram or mandala that was fluid rather than static—a cosmogram that moved in time, capable of embodying the flux and reflux of life.

This was the Sacred Calendar.

The Structure of the Calendar

When we talk about the Sacred Calendar, we are really talking about two calendars—one that measures ordinary time, and one that measures sacred time. These two calendars interpenetrate in such a way as to integrate and synthesize the secular and sacred dimensions of reality. In this book we shall be primarily concerned with the measure of ritual time, sometimes referred to as the Ritual Almanac or Divinatory Almanac. To lay the groundwork for discussion, we shall consider briefly the nature of both calendars and the manner in which they combine to weave the patterns of human life and history.

Let us first consider the solar calendar, the yardstick of secular time. The Maya recognized the solar year of 365 days, just as we do. However, they divided it differently. Whereas we use a calendar of twelve months, each of approximately thirty days, the Maya divided the year into eighteen months, each one of twenty days, followed by five extra days at the end of the year. In Figure 5, the names of the months in Yucatec Maya are given with the hieroglyphic symbol used by the Classic Maya to denote each month.

FIGURE 5 ***The Mayan Solar Months***

This solar calendar is called the *haab* (HAHB) in Mayan, and it has several peculiarities that are worthy of our notice. For instance, there is the matter of the twenty days within each month. The days are not numbered from one through twenty. Instead, the first day of each month is called the "seating" of that month (i.e., the seating of Pop, the seating of Uo, and so on). This terminology derives from the fact that each month was a kind of deity or spiritual entity unto itself, and, like a chieftain or lord, took its "seat" upon its throne. The first day of each month—the seating day—is numbered 0, then the days proceed from 1 through 19. At the end of 360 days come five final days, called the *uayeb* (wye-EB). These five days were traditionally considered unlucky, especially by the Aztecs who fasted, prayed, and quenched all fires throughout the uayeb period.

Note that the haab equals 365 days, whereas the true solar year is a little longer than that. This is why our Gregorian Calendar includes an extra day every four years—to bring the 365-day calendar back into harmony with the actual cycle of the sun. The Mayans were aware of the true duration of the year, but for reasons of ritual timing they made no attempt to reconcile the haab with the solar cycle; the haab kept moving ahead of the solar year. In 1553, the first day of the solar year, 0 Pop, occurred July 26 (according to the most recent revision of the Gregorian Calendar), whereas the Calendar shamans of Guatemala now celebrate the arrival of 0 Pop near the end of February.[2]

This, then, is the haab, the solar calendar and measure of secular time. Let us now consider the yardstick of ritual time. We do not know what the ancient Maya called this ritual or sacred aspect of the Calendar. Some scholars use the word *tzolkin* (tzohl-KEEN, from *tzol*=count and *kin*=day, hence "count of days"), but this is purely a term of convenience and may not have been used by the Maya. The tzolkin is a unique method of reckoning time. It consists of twenty named days combined with thirteen numbers. Each day-name is repeated thirteen times during the Calendar cycle, for a total of 260 days (13 x 20=260). The twenty days, with their glyphs, directional correspondences, Mayan names, and their most commonly accepted meanings among contemporary Daykeepers, are given in Figure 6 on the following page.

Because the tzolkin is comprised of twenty days but only thirteen numbers, the cycle of days and numbers will soon set up an interlocking rhythm of its own design. Beginning with 1 Crocodile, the days will proceed in order until 13 Corn. Then will come 1 Jaguar, 2 Eagle,

Glyph	Direction	Mayan Name	Meanings
	East	Imix (ee-MEESH)	The Crocodile
	North	Ik (EEK)	The Wind
	West	Akbal (ack-BAHL)	The Night
	South	Kan (KAHN)	The Lizard
	East	Chicchan (chick-CHAHN)	The Serpent
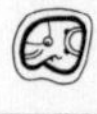	North	Cimi (kee-MEE)	Death
	West	Manik (man-EEK)	The Deer
	South	Lamat (lah-MAHT)	The Rabbit
	East	Muluc (moo-LOOK)	Water
	North	Oc (OKE)	The Dog
	West	Chuen (choo-EN)	The Monkey
	South	Eb (EB)	The Road
	East	Ben (BEN)	The Corn
	North	Ix (EESH)	The Jaguar
	West	Men (MEN)	The Eagle
	South	Cib (KEEB)	The Vulture
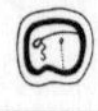	East	Caban (kah-BAHN)	Incense
	North	Etznab (etz-NAB)	Flint
	West	Cauac (kow-OCK)	The Storm
	South	Ahau (ah-HOW)	The Ancestors

FIGURE 6 ***The Twenty Day-Signs of the Sacred Calendar***

3 Vulture, and so on until 13 Death, which is followed by 1 Deer. At last, the final day 13 Ancestors will be reached, after which the whole cycle begins again with 1 Crocodile, repeating eternally.

We begin our count with the day 1 Crocodile. The complex interpenetrating cycles of the Sacred Calendar and the twenty-year cycles called *katuns* (kah-TOONS) made 1 Crocodile a logical place to begin the counting of days, and hence 1 Crocodile was sometimes called the "beginning." However, this is an arbitrary point of origin. The rhythm of the Sacred Calendar is circular; many contemporary Calendar shamans insist that it has neither beginning nor end. Nevertheless, we will follow tradition and use 1 Crocodile as a convenient "beginning."

The 260 days of the Sacred Calendar can be arranged in diagram form (Figure 7). The diagram resembles a sort of calendar board, and there is evidence that calendar boards of one kind or another were used for divinatory purposes in ancient times. Also, let us note a particular mathematical property of the Sacred Calendar.[3] The numbers 1 through 13, like any series of odd numbers, form binary pairs that mirror each other:

1 2 3 4 5 6 7 8 9 10 11 12 13

The mirroring pairs formed by this series are 1 and 13, 2 and 12, 3 and 11, and so on. Each of these pairs, when added together, equals 14. This, of course, is 2 x 7, and 7 is the number in the center, the number that has no mirror. This is not simply a mathematical curiosity; it has a practical application. The binary pairs may be arranged diagrammatically to form a symbol we shall call the Pyramid of Time (Figure 8). This Pyramid of Time is identical to the upper portion of the diagram we have already called the Pyramid of Heaven (see Chapter 2), and it gives us an important clue as to the inner meaning of the Sacred Calendar. The Sacred Calendar is a pyramid, hence another World Tree or World Mountain.

The Mayan Calendar is a symphony of cycles within cycles. The 260-day tzolkin is interwoven with the solar year, and with larger cycles of time called katuns, which span about twenty years each. The tzolkin may be divided into four "seasons" of sixty-five days each, and most importantly, into twenty periods of thirteen days. Our pyramid of days reveals the inner meaning of these thirteen-day cycles.

CROCODILE	1	8	2	9	3	10	4	11	5	12	6	13	7
WIND	2	9	3	10	4	11	5	12	6	3	7	1	8
NIGHT	3	10	4	11	5	12	6	13	7	1	8	2	9
LIZARD	4	11	5	12	6	13	7	1	8	2	9	3	10
SERPENT	5	12	6	13	7	1	8	2	9	3	10	4	11
DEATH	6	13	7	1	8	2	9	3	10	4	11	5	12
DEER	7	1	8	2	9	3	10	4	11	5	12	6	13
RABBIT	8	2	9	3	10	4	11	5	12	6	13	7	1
WATER	9	3	10	4	11	5	12	6	13	7	1	8	2
DOG	10	4	11	5	12	6	13	7	1	8	2	9	3
MONKEY	11	5	12	6	13	7	1	8	2	9	3	10	4
ROAD	12	6	13	7	1	8	2	9	3	10	4	11	5
CORN	13	7	1	8	2	9	3	10	4	11	5	12	6
JAGUAR	1	8	2	9	3	10	4	11	5	12	6	13	7
EAGLE	2	9	3	10	4	11	5	12	6	13	7	1	8
VULTURE	3	10	4	11	5	12	6	13	7	1	8	2	9
INCENSE	4	11	5	12	6	13	7	1	8	2	9	3	10
FLINT	5	12	6	13	7	1	8	2	9	3	10	4	11
STORM	6	13	7	1	8	2	9	3	10	4	11	5	12
ANCESTORS	7	1	8	2	9	3	10	4	11	5	12	6	13

FIGURE 7 *The Calendar Board*

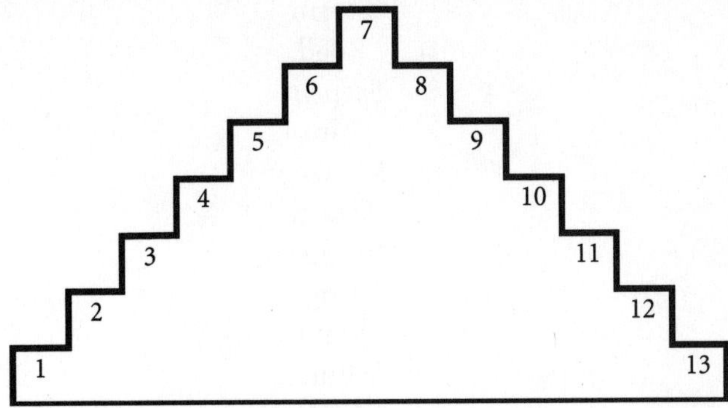

FIGURE 8 ***The Pyramid of Time***

The Wave of Time

The thirteen-day periods can be a bit confusing when it comes to names. We don't know what word the Classic Maya used to refer to a cycle of thirteen days. Many writers have followed the lead of the Spanish chronicler Sahagún, who refers to such a period as a "week." The term is misleading, inasmuch as the period in question is actually closer to two of our weeks. I have used the term "fortnight" throughout this book to refer to the thirteen-day cycles embedded within the Sacred Calendar. Though from the ethnographic standpoint there is no good reason to use the term, it is commonly used in the English-speaking world to denote a period of two weeks.

The fortnightly periods are essential to an understanding of the Calendar. The number cycle runs from 1 through 13, then returns to the number 1 again. Each time the number 1 recurs, it will do so on a different day-sign. So we get twenty fortnights, each one "ruled" by whichever day-sign begins that particular fortnightly period.

The order of fortnights differs from the order of days. For instance, we may begin with 1 Crocodile, but this initial fortnightly period will come to a close with 13 Corn, as can be seen in Figure 7. The next cycle begins with 1 Jaguar, the next with 1 Deer, and so on. The order of the fortnights is as follows:

Crocodile
Jaguar
Deer
Ancestors
Corn
Death

Storm
Road
Serpent
Flint
Monkey
Lizard
Incense
Dog
Night
Vulture
Water
Wind
Eagle
Rabbit

Though the order of the fortnights may be different than the order of days, one thing has not changed: the sequence of the four directions. The four directions of time continue in their appointed rounds, whether in the cycle of days or of fortnights. Take a look at the first four periods: Crocodile is attributed to the East, Jaguar to the North, Deer to the West, Ancestors to the South, and then we return to the East again with Corn.

The fortnights are the essential component of what we may call "living the Calendar." They set the clock for the major rituals of Mayan life. The Daykeepers of Guatemala say that low numbers are "weak" and lack strength, while the middle numbers—6, 7, 8, and 9—represent the days of balanced energy and power. The final days, 10 through 13, are "too strong," so powerful as to be potentially dangerous. Therefore, all major rituals are performed on the days of balanced power at the center of each fortnight. A cycle of ritual activity for any given fortnight typically begins at sunset of day 7 (or sometimes on day 6), continues through day 8, and reaches a conclusion on day 9.[4] The hieroglyphic dates on monuments from the Classic Period show that 5, 6, 7, 8, and especially 9 appear more often than other numbers.[5] From this, we may assume that the Classic Maya, like their modern descendants, also performed their important rituals on these days.

If we return to our Pyramid of Time diagram, we can see a definite pattern emerging. The energy inherent in a particular fortnightly cycle is still tentative or weak in the beginning, not yet fully established in its own nature. As it climbs the pyramid, it begins to grow in power. It reaches the peak of the pyramid on day 7. Since the Maya count their days from sunrise to sunrise, the exact middle of any given cycle must occur at sunset of the seventh day. This is the top of the pyramid—and precisely when many Daykeepers begin the round of ritual appropriate for each given fortnight. As the current cycle begins its course down the pyramid, it will grow in power, just like a wave that has reached its crest and then begins to crash downward. This descent of power is still in a balanced condition on the eighth and ninth days; after that, the energy inherent in the current cycle of time becomes more and more intense—too intense to be safely dealt with on ritual terms. The Aztecs thought of these days as "holy" rather than "dangerous." Were the Aztecs, a warrior people, attracted to precisely those moments of power that were too intense for others to handle? One is reminded of Barbara Tedlock's statement that everything in Zuñi spirituality can be classified as either "the beautiful" or "the dangerous," and that sometimes the two polarities overlap—the beautiful may become dangerous and vice versa.[6]

If, for the moment, we leave behind the somewhat static or architectonic image of the pyramid, we may return to the metaphor of the wave as a concept that is closer both to the world of nature and the world of post-Einsteinian physics. Each fortnightly cycle may be regarded as a particular quantum of energy, an energy that travels in a wave-like motion. Precisely like a wave, it begins as an underground surge, symbolized by the sun's emergence from the Underworld on the first day of the cycle. This wave of energy grows in power until it crests. Then it begins to descend, discharging its quantum of energy in a thundering crash to the shore. As the energy inherent in the wave trickles away into the sand on the night of the thirteenth day, a new cycle has already begun farther out at sea. The power of the day-sign that will begin the new fortnight is already present. At sunset on the thirteenth day, the Daykeepers welcome the spirit of the coming day, the one who will begin the next fortnightly cycle. They think of the next day as a "guest" who is already entering the sacred space limned by their communal and family altars.

Each fortnight has its own meaning and particular character. This character is not necessarily formed by the first day or 1 day of the cycle. Rather, it is dependent on the middle days (7, 8, and 9), the days of balanced power.

The Year Lords

Now let us look at the way in which the haab and the tzolkin combine. Each day has a position in both the secular and sacred calendars—a specific resonance in terms of both ordinary and sacred time. Consider the date March 2, 1977. This was the Mayan New Year's day, 0 Pop. In terms of the Sacred Calendar, it was also the day 4 Wind. Because of the disparity between the number of days in these cycles, the Sacred Calendar completed an entire cycle and returned to the day 4 Wind on November 17, 1977, while the solar calendar had only reached the day 0 Kankin.

How long will it take before 4 Wind and 0 Pop once again fall on the same day? How long a time must pass before the solar and sacred calendars once again coincide? The answer is 18,980 days—just a few days short of fifty-two years. On February 28, 2029, it will once again be 4 Wind 0 Pop.

This cycle of fifty-two years is called the Calendar Round. It was recognized as a significant cycle by the Maya, and attained paramount importance among the Aztecs, who referred to it as a "bundle of years." The Aztec New Year was celebrated with a ritual called the New Fire Ceremony, in which all the hearthfires extinguished during the five unlucky days of the uayeb were once again rekindled. By combining the Calendar Round with the cycle of the planet Venus, the Aztecs selected a special day every fifty-two years when the New Fire Ceremony became a ritual of cosmic significance symbolizing the renewal of the entire world.

The cycle of fifty-two years was also meaningful to each individual. Let us say that you were born on September 10, 1963, which would be 9 Ancestors 8 Mol. The day 9 Ancestors would come around again every 260 days. The day 8 Mol would recur every 365 days. But the combination 9 Ancestors 8 Mol would only recur after 18,980 days—in this example, on September 2, 2015.

This fifty-two year Calendar Round "birthday" probably symbolized a second birth among the peoples of Mesoamerica. This, presumably, was the date that marked one's passage into full maturity; this was when one became an "elder."

Due to the way in which the two calendars interpenetrate, the New Year's day of 0 Pop can only coincide with one of four tzolkin day-names. These four New Year's days were called Year Bearers by most Mesoamerican cultures, and different Native cultures used different sets of Year Bearers. For instance: the Aztecs used Corn, Flint, Night, and Rabbit as their Year Bearers, while the Yucatec Maya, during early Spanish Colonial times, used Water, Jaguar, Storm, and Lizard. The great Mayan city of Tikal, as well as Teotihuacán, celebrated New Year's on Wind, Deer, Road, and Incense. The Quiché Maya of today use the same Year Bearers; we shall do the same. There is some evidence, however, that the earliest set of Year Bearers—used during Olmec times—was Crocodile, Death, Monkey, and Vulture.[7]

Although this may all seem a bit arbitrary and confusing, there is a kind of logic to it. As shown in Figure 6 (page 46), each day-sign of the tzolkin is associated with one of the four cardinal directions.[8] No matter which four days were designated as Year Bearers, there was always

Direction	I	II	III	IV	V
East	Crocodile	Incense	Corn	Water	Serpent
North	Death	Wind	Flint	Jaguar	Dog
West	Monkey	Deer	Night	Storm	Eagle
South	Vulture	Road	Rabbit	Lizard	Ancestors

FIGURE 9 ***The Year Bearers***

one day for each direction, as seen in Figure 9 above. Any given year had certain characteristics according to the directional attribute of the day that served as Year Bearer. Years governed by the East and South were considered more favorable than those governed by the North or West.

The years succeeded each other in an orderly fashion. As we have seen, 0 Pop fell on the day 4 Wind in 1977. Thus the year received the name 4 Wind. In 1978, 0 Pop fell on 5 Deer, in 1979 upon 6 Road, and in 1980 upon 7 Incense—the number of the year increasing by one each time. By 1986, 13 Deer had been reached, so that 1987 received the name 1 Road. How long will it take until our initial year 4 Wind comes around again? The answer, of course, is fifty-two years (4 day-signs x 13 numbers=52). The year 2019 will be 4 Wind. This progression of the Year Bearers played a major role in what we might call "political astrology"—the prediction of future events through studying the cycles of time. The Year Bearers were also important in the prediction of climatic and agricultural cycles, forming a kind of "farmer's almanac" for the Maya.

The Meaning of the Calendar

What, then, does the Sacred Calendar symbolize? Why thirteen numbers and twenty day-signs? What sort of cycle is this that chronicles the sacred dimension of time?

One clue, of course, lies in the fact that there are thirteen divisions of Heaven in the Mayan cosmos. Therefore, we may say that the number 13, far from being "unlucky" as it is in Western folklore, was to the Maya a symbol of Heaven itself.

Martin Prechtel, however, has a more "grass-roots" interpretation. "The thirteen numbers correspond to the thirteen joints in the human body," he says. These are: the two ankle joints, the two knees, the two hips, the hands, the elbows, the shoulder joints, and, finally, the neck or thirteenth joint.

The twenty day-signs may also be related to the human metaphor, the microcosm as macrocosm. The number 20 was regarded in ancient times as the number of humankind, because it is the number of all the digits—fingers and toes—on the human body. Thus, the equation 13 x 20 unites Heaven with humankind.

Esoteric writers have theorized that the Sacred Calendar may include even more complex cycles, and that it may, in fact, be a cosmogram that embodies the orbital periods of various planets. Mars takes 780 days to circle the sun, and 260 x 3=780. The synodical period of Venus is 584 days, and 58.4 revolutions of the Sacred Calendar will equal 26 synodical Venus years.[9]

Anthropologists working among the contemporary Maya have asked their informants what the Calendar symbolizes. The answer given by Mayan Calendar shamans is remarkably consistent: It is the term of pregnancy, the cycle of human gestation. This, they say, is the foundation of the Calendar.[10]

Scientifically, we know that the actual period of pregnancy is somewhat longer than 260 days. The 260-day interval is a fair rule of thumb for the period which elapses between the time a woman first misses her menses to the time when she gives birth; hence the tzolkin is symbolic of the gestation period. It is primarily an earthly, human cycle rather than an astronomical one—though as we shall see, the cycle of the sun's zenith passage also played a role in its formation.

Though it is the cycle of human gestation that, after so many centuries, the Maya still cite as the basis of the tzolkin, the gestation cycle itself is yet another metaphor. All the world's great myths are essentially concerned with the journey of human consciousness—the archetypal hero's journey. The Mayan Calendar is no different. Consciousness, like life, must journey from conception to full birth. If we take Crocodile as the "beginning" of the tzolkin, we may say that the Calendar begins its cycle in the primordial swamp of the unconscious with the day-sign Crocodile, and culminates with the union of human and divine consciousness in the sign Ancestors, symbolizing the spirit of the enlightened collective mind and often represented by a flower. However, if we rely on a more contemporary teaching, we may note that the day-sign Eb in Yucatec Mayan signifies "the road"—what other Native Americans have called the Road of Life. In Yucatec Maya, the word *eb* also means "stairway"—perhaps in reference to the stairways that led to the top of Mayan temples by which the ancient kings mounted to the world of the gods. The Calendar, as a symbol of the growth of human consciousness, leads us up the Pyramid of Time. It is the Road of Life, and its roots lie in the eternal journey we all must make, the journey from conception to birth.

The Origins of the Calendar

The gestation cycle of humanity, a metaphor for the Road of Life, may explain the meaning of the Calendar, but it doesn't tell us how or where it came to be.

Zelia Nuttall pointed out that 260 days is one of the intervals between zenith transits of the sun at 15 degrees of north latitude.[11] When we see the sun shining above us at noon, it appears to be at the zenith, the point directly overhead. This, however, is a purely visual perception. In fact, the sun only transits over the true astronomical zenith at variable intervals that are determined by latitude. At 15 degrees north latitude, a geographic region comprising a large portion of present-day Guatemala and Honduras, the sun transits the zenith forty days after the spring equinox—approximately April 30. After 105 days, it transits the zenith again, this time around August 12 or 13, about forty days before the autumn equinox. Then there is an interval of 260 days until the next zenith passage, which again falls somewhere near April 30. Just as significant is the fact that the interval between the spring and summer zenith passages is 105 days. Half of 105 is 52 ½, providing one of our most important tzolkin numbers, 52.[12]

We know that the sun's zenith passage was important to the astronomers of ancient Mexico, for it is marked by architectural alignments at Monte Alban in Oaxaca.[13] Also, it can hardly be coincidence that the "creation date," August 13, 3114 B.C., falls on a zenith transit.

The Maya of today link the tzolkin with the period of pregnancy, but 260 days is an imprecise approximation of that period. Other numbers could have been chosen—some more accurate—to approximate the gestation period. Why, then, was it fixed at 260 days? Perhaps because 260 days correlated to the solar zenith cycle.

This surmise, however, only makes sense if the Sacred Calendar originated at 15 degrees north latitude, since that is the only place in Mesoamerica where the sun's zenith transit equals exactly 260 days. It was for this reason that Nuttall's suggestion was categorically rejected by J. Eric S. Thompson. The latitude in question was strongly suggestive of the Mayan city of Copan (now in Honduras), known to be one of the intellectual centers of Mayan civilization. Thompson, however, saw no reason to believe that Copan was an especially early site; certainly it did not seem to be early enough to serve as a potential point of origin for the Sacred Calendar.[14]

Recent excavations, however, prove that Copan has a very long history indeed, with evidence that the valley was inhabited as early as 1100 B.C. By 900 B.C. the people of the valley had already developed a society governed by powerful chieftains or kings, for the early tombs of Copan were constructed for rich and powerful individuals. Copan lay on the Olmec trading route to Belize, a source of precious jade. The city may well have reached such an early peak of sophistication because of this favored location.[15] In addition, monuments have been discovered at Copan which mark the sunset on the days that fall midway between the vernal equinox and subsequent zenith passage, as well as between the second zenith passage and the autumn equinox shortly thereafter. The first sunset marker, equivalent to a date in early April, would have been important as an indicator of the beginning of the rainy season.[16]

At present, the Sacred Calendar maintains most of its ancient glory only in the highlands of Guatemala—a region which also lies at 15 degrees of latitude. Scholars dismiss the notion of a highland origin for the Sacred Calendar. They say that Classic Mayan civilization never reached a particularly high development there, nor an especially early one, and that it is simply the isolation of the mountains themselves that accounts for the survival of the tzolkin there. Martin disagrees: "I think the Calendar originated in the highlands. It didn't start somewhere else and then just end up there. It was always there, right from the very beginning, and that's why it's still there. It doesn't just mark the zenith passage, either—that's much too simple. And the human gestation cycle? That's one of the most basic levels, a mere gingerbread story. The Sacred Calendar embodies all kinds of different astronomical cycles, including the Venus cycle."

Mayan civilization itself is clearly much older than we once believed. The largest Mayan city known to us at present is El Mirador. This gigantic ceremonial complex dates back to 300 B.C., and was virtually abandoned by 50 B.C.—a date that is several centuries earlier than the beginning of the so-called Classic Period. Controversial dates from Belize indicate that village farmers may have developed a culture that was identifiably Mayan as early as 2000 B.C.[17]

We call the Olmecs the "mother culture" of Mesoamerica for one reason: we have found no evidence of earlier civilizations there. But this does not mean that such civilizations did not exist. The Olmecs themselves were unknown to us before the 1930s. The early Mayan center of El Mirador was only discovered in 1981, when bush pilots flying over a remote part of the Mexico-Guatemala border spotted its pyramids peeking above the jungle canopy.

Living the Calendar

The Sacred Calendar is used in three basic ways—as a system of personal astrology, a tool of divination, and as the key to a ritual cycle.

To live in ritual time is to honor the wave of time as it flows past your doorstep. This, in essence, is what all Mayan shamans do. This is why such individuals are referred to as Daykeepers. In order to work with the Sacred Calendar as a system of magic, one must learn to keep the days.

Turn to the tables in the appendix of this book beginning on page 181, and study its use. Become familiar with its structure. Then ascertain the answer to this question: What day is it today?

Use this date as your starting point for living the Calendar. Just start keeping the days. At first, this may not be quite as easy as it sounds. The rhythm of the Sacred Calendar can be a difficult one for Western (or non-Indian) minds to access, but in time you will get the hang of it. Don't be embarrassed if you must continually refer to the Calendar

Board and the Mayan Calendar Tables in order to figure out what day it is. Just keep trying. After a while, you will begin to sense the rhythm of the wave of time.

Living the Calendar can be either a very private or a very public affair. In some parts of Guatemala, the major Calendar ceremonies are conducted in the center of town, with the entire village participating. You, however, will more likely celebrate the days in private.

How does one celebrate the days? How does one live the Calendar?

When you celebrate a Calendar day, it is proper to begin at dawn—or as early in the morning as is possible, given your personal schedule. Light the candles on your altar as well as copal incense. Copal and candles are standard among Mayan Daykeepers: copal symbolizes the ancient ways of costumbre, the ways of the Ancestors. To light copal is to honor tradition and your own ancestral stream. Candles represent purification, your own desire to keep working towards inner growth.

After your altar has come alive with copal and candles, you may pray or meditate. A traditional Daykeeper typically relies more on prayer as opposed to what we would term "meditation." He calls upon the spirit of the day, addressing it as an entity. "Lord 3 Rabbit," he might call out, "here I am!" Following this, he intones or chants a long, fervent, and poetic prayer of his own invention. The art of prayer-making, incidentally, is characteristically Mayan. As we noted in the last chapter, there are some shamans, called "singers," who specialize in chants, prayers, and ritual formulas. I urge you to try creating your own prayers—there is nothing quite so helpful in entering into the spirit of Mayan daykeeping.

But what to pray about? This, of course, depends on the nature of the day itself. Each day-sign of the Sacred Calendar has its particular traditional lore, as we will learn in Chapter 5. On favorable or "lucky" days, give thanks for the specific blessings that fall under the power of that day. On difficult days, pray for release or relief from the troubles and imbalances characteristic of that day's energy. Pray not only for yourself, but for your family and friends as well. Better still, pray for the whole world.

If the idea of speaking extended, poetic prayers makes you uncomfortable, you can always sit in silent meditation, turning your mind towards thanksgiving on the favorable days, and towards purification or the healing of difficulties on the unfavorable days.

How many days should you celebrate in this fashion? It is, of course, theoretically possible to light your candles and incense and pray every day. In traditional Mayan society, however, it is more customary to observe:

1. The "1" day or beginning of each fortnightly cycle, and
2. The 6, 7, 8, and 9 or "middle days" of each cycle.

In a busy world, where most people work from nine to five, even this can be difficult. If all else fails, at least try to keep the six most important days for giving thanks—days that are publicly celebrated with great fanfare in many traditional Mayan communities:

8 Deer—the celebration of the ancestors

8 Jaguar—the celebration of the Earth (Santo Mundo)

8 Road—the celebration of one's own personal life

8 Rabbit—the celebration of the fields (i.e., abundance)

8 Corn—the invocation of your "destiny animal"

8 Monkey—the celebration of the Sacred Calendar

Some of these ideas, such as the celebration of Santo Mundo or the invocation of your "destiny animal," may seem a bit strange. These concepts will become much more clear, however, after you familiarize yourself with the symbolism and significance of the days themselves.

Read on, then, and let us explore the meanings of the twenty day-signs of the Sacred Calendar.

ENDNOTES

1. Richard Wilhelm, trans. *The I Ching or Book of Changes*, English trans. by Cary F. Baynes (Princeton: Princeton-Bollingen, 1970), 328.

2. Tables for conversion of Mayan dates into Gregorian dates and a discussion of the correlation between them, are found at the back of this book, beginning on page 179.

3. The "mathematical magic" of the Sacred Calendar has been discussed by two of the more esoteric writers on the subject: Tony Shearer, *Beneath the Moon and Under the Sun* (Santa Fe: Sun Books, 1987); and Jose Arguelles, *The Mayan Factor: Path Beyond Technology* (Santa Fe: Bear and Co., 1987).

4. Tedlock, *Time and the Highland Maya*, 107–8, and Ruth Bunzel, *Chichicastenango* (Seattle: University of Washington Press, 1959), 283–5.
5. Thompson, *Maya Hieroglyphic Writing*, 93.
6. Barbara Tedlock, *The Beautiful and the Dangerous* (New York: Viking Penguin, 1992).
7. Munro S. Edmonson, *The Book of the Year: Middle American Calendrical Systems* (Salt Lake City: University of Utah Press, 1988), 8–10.
8. The fifth set of Year Bearers, beginning with Serpent, is included purely for the sake of completeness. Though it is possible to use these days as Year Bearers, we have no that evidence any Mesoamerican civilization did so.
9. Shearer, *Beneath the Moon and Under the Sun*, 80.
10. Tedlock, *Time and the Highland Maya*, 93.
11. Zelia Nuttall, "Nouvelles lumiéres sur les civilisations americaines et le système du calendrier," in *Proceedings of the 22nd International Congress of Americanists*, Rome, 1926, Vol. 1 (1928):119–48.
12. Anthony F. Aveni, "Concepts of Positional Astronomy in Ancient Mesoamerican Architecture," in *Native American Astronomy*, ed. Anthony F. Aveni (Austin: University of Texas Press, 1977), 9-14.
13. Anthony F. Aveni, "Astronomy in Ancient Mesoamerica," in Dr. E.C. Krupp, ed., *In Search of Ancient Astronomies* (New York: McGraw-Hill, 1979), 185–90.
14. Thompson, *Maya Hieroglyphic Writing*, 98.
15. Schele and Freidel, *A Forest of Kings*, 306–8.
16. Aveni, "Concepts of Positional Astronomy."
17. Schele and Freidel, *Forest of Kings*, 421, n. 22.

5

The Book of Days

The interpretation of the day-signs given in this book is rather different from some of the more recent esoteric material on the Calendar, and requires some explanation. For the most part, I have focused on some of the more basic meanings of the day-signs as explained by contemporary Quiché Daykeepers in Momostenango and Chichicastenango. However, the esoteric meanings of the day-signs are never revealed to non-initiates; each master Daykeeper may have his own personal, slightly different interpretation of the signs. I have also used quotations from the so-called "prophetic books" or *Chilam Balam* manuscripts of colonial Yucatán (written after the Spanish Conquest but preserving a great deal of material from more ancient times). In addition, I have drawn upon day-sign lore surviving from the Aztec version of the Calendar, and even upon parallel concepts among North American Indians. For the most part, I have focused on myths and stories, whether Maya or Aztec, preferring an intuitive and poetic rather than a scholarly approach. There are, to be sure, some comments drawn from modern academic research, although even these are included without footnotes, in hopes that you may allow the lore of the day-signs to speak through the heart rather than through the mind alone.

Readers who have studied Jose Arguelles' "Dreamspell" version of the Mayan Calendar, or Bruce Scofeld's writings on the Aztec version of the Sacred Calendar may wonder at some of the English-language names I have chosen to designate the day-signs. For example, I have used "Crocodile" to signify Imix, which is in accordance with Scofeld but seemingly very far from Arguelles' "Dragon." However, Scofeld uses "Flower" for Ahau, while I use "Ancestors." This requires some explanation: In general, I have chosen English names that embody the most common meanings for the day-signs throughout the indigenous Mesoamerican world.

You may ask, why bother using English names at all if it's so convoluted and variable? Why not just use the familiar Yucatec names—which, after all, are printed in this book along with the English translations? The reason is that it is better for the average reader to use only the English names when working with the Sacred Calendar.

Among the indigenous peoples who still keep the Calendar, a given day may have a variety of names. For example, in Quiché Maya, the "first" four days are Imox, Ik', Ak'abal, and C'at—meaning Alligator, Wind, Night, and Lizard respectively, while in the more familiar Yucatec it's Imix, Ik, Akbal, and Kan—which have pretty much the same meanings. Among the Mixe people of Oaxaca, the four days in question are Hukpii, Xa'a, How, and Huu'n—which mean Root, Wind, Palm, and Hard!

It's all the same, but it's all different.

Martin Prechtel explains that: "The days are not simply units of time; they are gods. They were regarded as gods in ancient times, and they are regarded as gods today. Even those of us who are initiates must never speak their names in a non-sacred context; and those who are not initiated had best not speak their names at all.

"The gods are capricious, inimical to humankind. They may lodge themselves in a tree or a stone or anywhere they please. They are hungry and demand to be fed. If we don't call on them properly, with the proper ceremony and the proper respect, they may cause an untold amount of damage—danger, sickness, and even death."

The Mayan language is regarded by traditionalists as a sacred vehicle, the language in which the gods must be called, addressed, and propitiated. The reader who is merely curious about such matters should always use the English—non-sacred—names for the Gods of Time.

The Crocodile

IMIX

Imix is the name of all secret or hidden things.

—Chichicastenango

The Crocodile is the primal spirit that sleeps beneath the surface of the earth, the embodiment of birth and generation, the life-giving power that flows up from the Underworld. The Classic Maya knew this power not only as a crocodile or caiman, but as the primordial Earth Monster who symbolizes the holiness of the world.

The Earth Monster, or primordial crocodile, floats in the ocean beneath the World Tree, bearing the earth upon his back. This cosmo-conception was widespread throughout pre-Columbian America. In more northerly regions, such as the Great Lakes, the primal reptile or world-bearer was a turtle. This is the origin of the aboriginal name for our North American continent—Turtle Island. The idea of a crocodile floating in a hot tropical swamp, on stagnant water thick with water lilies, might well be reminiscent of the "primordial soup" from which, according to the current scientific world view, all life began.

The Mayan glyph for Imix, or Crocodile, represents a water lily, often found on tropical ponds where caimans and crocodiles live. The water lily is itself a symbol of the earth's abundance because of its very high food value. The Earth Monster is often shown with corn and water lilies sprouting from his head. In this sense, this day-sign has a strong link with abundance and growth.

The day of the Crocodile also has strong roots with the Underworld—its power reaches down as well as up. The famous sarcophagus of Pacal the Great of Palenque depicts the king being swallowed by the Earth Monster—beginning his journey to the Land of the Dead. The Tree of Life grows from his stomach (or liver), ascending to Heaven as the king plunges below. This, as we have seen, is the psychic center associated with that power the Aztecs called ihiyotl—which, according to the map of the Sacred Calendar inside the human body (Chapter 2, Figure 3), also constitutes the physical correspondence of this day-sign, linking it with the Tree of Life growing from the body of the primordial crocodile. This day-sign is both the Sacred Tree and its primal source.

Crocodile is the fundamental ground of being, the unity from which individuated consciousness emerges. The psychologist C. G. Jung called this primal unity the collective unconscious, the group mind common to us all. Symbolized in many different spiritual traditions as water or as a dragon, it is aptly represented in Mayan thought as a saurian beast afloat on a cosmic ocean. The power of the collective mind is a deeply ambivalent thing; all our great dreams, visions, and spiritual experiences emerge from its depths, but so do all our nightmares. The Maya say the dark power made manifest in insanity and possession is also one of the meanings of this day-sign. Indeed, the stormy visions of the mad flow forth from the collective mind just as surely as the exalted visions of artists and mystics.

Crocodile is the power of the earth itself, a tropical stew from which the sun coaxes abundant life. The collective unconscious is an equally deep and primeval foundation, like earth, mud, or water, from which all human consciousness emerges. Thus, Crocodile is an emblem of the great reservoir of abundance, both biological and psychological, which gives birth to all phenomena.

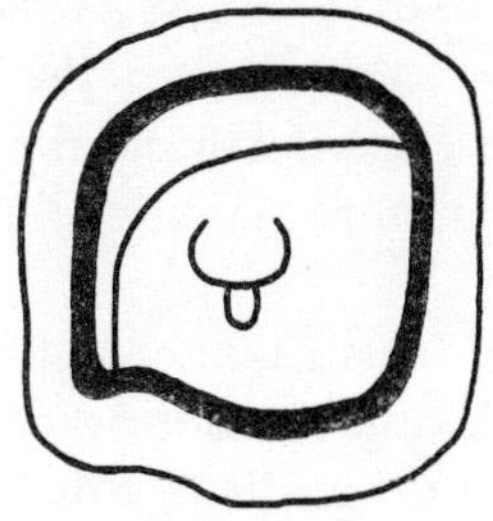

The Wind

Ik

The winds are your nagual...You have the spirit of a comet.

—The Book of Chilam Balam of Kaua

In general, Mayan people don't like the wind. They believe evil spirits dwell therein, blowing fiercely hither and thither, waiting for the opportunity to enter the human body and cause mental or physical illness. The Mayan healer Don Eligio Panti claimed that many of his patients had been made sick through magical rather than purely physical means, and that their sickness had been brought to them on the wind.

Similarly, people born on the day of the Wind are believed to be filled with anger and rage. These potentially dangerous qualities need to be controlled from the very day of one's birth. Yet anger, rage, or egotistical bluster are, on the esoteric level, simply lower or more unevolved manifestations of a power that, in its highest aspect, provides us with life itself.

On Mayan sculptures, a rather mysterious deity known to scholars as "God B" is often shown holding a T-cross, the symbol of the day-sign Wind or Ik. God B is believed to have been a god of rain and storms. The rain makes life on earth possible. It causes the growth of the crops, and it ought not to surprise us that the T-crosses held by God B are often depicted with corn sprouting from them.

The Aztecs placed this day under the rulership of Quetzalcoatl, the Feathered Serpent. Quetzalcoatl is best known as the bringer of civilization who taught a religion of higher consciousness to the people of ancient Mexico. The story of Quetzalcoatl's civilizing mission seems to have been based on the career of an actual person during the "historic Toltec" period (c. A.D. 908–1168), but Quetzalcoatl had already been worshipped as a deity for hundreds of years. The historic individual whose teachings are preserved under the name Quetzalcoatl may have been regarded as an avatar of the deity.

Quetzalcoatl, in addition to his role as the god of the morning star—the planet Venus—was also the god of the wind. As a wind god, he was called by the name Ehecatl, and it was this aspect of the Feathered Serpent who ruled over this day-sign. The wind brings the storm clouds that produce the life-giving rain, but more than that, the wind is symbolic of the breath of life itself.

The glyph for this day-sign is the T-cross. This T is known throughout Mesoamerica and the American Southwest. The doorways of the ancient cities of Chaco Canyon in New Mexico are frequently built in this T-cross shape. In some of the ancient codices or sacred books of the Aztecs and Mayas, the Tree of Life itself is shaped like a T, reminding us that trees play a role in the renewal of the world's oxygen—trees and the air are intimately linked.

Almost all of the world's spiritual traditions speak of the subtle or vital breath, the breath of life which is often the instrument of creation itself. In the Book of Genesis, the "Spirit of God moved upon the face of the waters" (1:2). The original Hebrew word for "spirit" is *ruach*—it is the vital breath of God that is active at the moment of creation. In Greek myth, Prometheus breathes his *pneuma* into the inanimate clay figure of the first man in order to bring him to life. In yogic philosophy, the vital breath or Sanskrit *prana* is the life-giving energy which, on the purely physical level, is made manifest in the breath. In the physical body, the day-sign Wind corresponds to the upper part of the diaphragm that fills with air during yogic breathing exercises. Because we breathe, we live.

Without the symbiosis of trees and wind, there would be no life on earth, nothing to breathe. What better symbol for the breath of life, then, than the T-cross with its dual meaning of "tree" and "breath"?

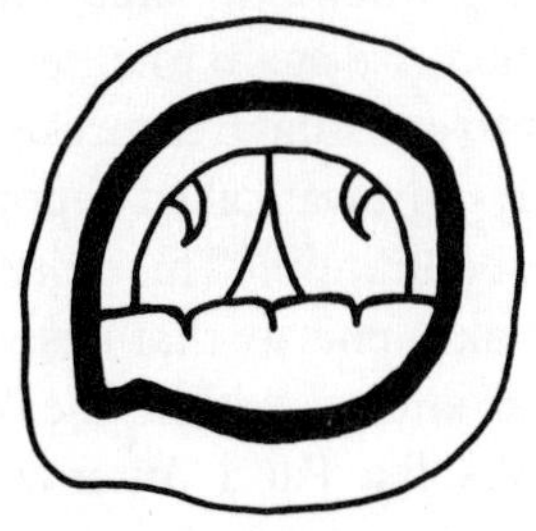

The Night

AKBAL

Nocturnal, dark.

—The Book of Chilam Balam of Kaua

No one knows exactly what the glyph for this day-sign was supposed to symbolize, though some Mayan scholars believe that it represents the Underworld. The Mayan word *akbal* means "darkness" or "night"; the Aztecs knew this day-sign as *calli* (cahl-yee) which means "house." The Underworld is the House of Darkness.

The great Mayan epic called the *Popol Vuh* (Po–POLE VOO) tells the story of twin brothers who travel to the Underworld to play a game of handball with the Lords of Darkness, forfeiting their lives if they lose. While waiting for the game to begin, they spend several nights in a succession of Underworld "houses" in which they must face and conquer terrible dangers. The twins meet each of these initiatory challenges. They win the handball game but, tricked by the Lords of Death, they are forced to sacrifice themselves anyway. Ritually slain, they return to life again. Thus, with this legend, the House of Darkness is the place where we face the perils of the soul, our personal netherworld where the ego dies only to be reborn in different form.

There is a mysterious lord who rules over this day-sign. His name is Pacal Votan (Pah-KAHL Vo-TAHN). When Friar Ramon de Ordoñez y Aguilar became the first European to gaze upon the ruins of Palenque in 1773, his Mayan guides told him the story of Pacal Votan, legendary founder of the city. This wise man had come from "the East," built Palenque, and then buried a treasure of sacred books and jade in a subterranean house on the Pacific coast of Chiapas. This underground "house of darkness" was inhabited by mysterious sentinels, including a woman who was guardian of the hieroglyphs, and jade. Jade was a precious and magical substance to all the ancient peoples of Mesoamerica, and hieroglyphic books symbolized wisdom.

The meaning of this myth is clear: wisdom is only to be found in the recesses of our personal "house of darkness," whence we must journey, face our fears, surrender our egos, and then rise again to a new birth when our trials have been transformed into spiritual treasures.

The Aztec deity associated with this day-sign was called Tepeyollotl (Tay-pay-yoh-LOHTL), the "Heart of the Mountain." This deity was a personification of the teyolia or heart chakra energy that lies within mountains. He was the psycho-spiritual energy within the World Mountain itself. He was a guardian of caves, like Pacal Votan with his underground sanctuary. Tepeyollotl, one of many manifestations of the Earth Father, was a Lord of Animals as well. Also called "Echo" or "lord of the drum," some modern Mayan tribes speak of a group of earth gods called the *tzultacah* (tzool-tah-KAH), the "mountain and valley gods." These spirits live in caves or beneath the earth where they cause earthquakes. The Maya descend into these caves to worship them. They are lords of animals and speak with the voice of thunder. This thunder, echoing through the mountains, is the echoing drum of Pacal Votan. Tepeyollotl rules volcanoes as well, a fitting symbol of the power of the unconscious erupting into the daylight world.

The day-sign Night represents that phase of human consciousness in which all of us must descend into the Underworld to experience spiritual death and rebirth. To the Maya, this inner darkness is the place where wisdom—symbolized by Pacal Votan's treasury of sacred books and jade—is to be found. Without this death-and-rebirth experience, there can be no growth in consciousness, no progress along the Road of Life. Thus this day-sign is preeminently a wisdom sign, aptly symbolized by the archetypal wise man, Pacal Votan.

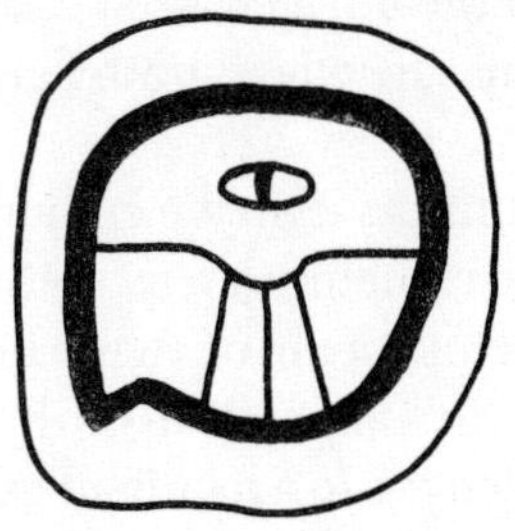

The Lizard

KAN

The precious singing birds are your birds.

—The Book of Chilam Balam of Kaua

I am the Lizard King. I can do anything.

—Jim Morrison (born on 4 Lizard)

In ancient times, the day-sign now called Lizard was a symbol of the growing corn. It represented fertility and the power of growth. The association between the lizard and the power of fertility runs strong and deep in Native American culture. The Pueblo peoples of the American Southwest, who have been deeply influenced by ancient Mexico, regard the lizard as a symbol of growth, sexuality, and the life-giving rain. Lizards, common themes in the rock art of Arizona, New Mexico, and Utah, are typically found in contexts suggesting fertility. The Aztec deity associated with this day-sign was Huehuecoyotl (Way-way-kye-OTLE), the "god of the dance." Over what manner of dance did this god preside? All over the Southwest, dances are held to celebrate the growth of the crops, especially the Corn Dance, performed in the summer. Today, the summer corn dances of the Southwest frequently employ parrot feathers as part of their sacred regalia, for parrot feathers are somtimes said to be symbolic of the South, and therefore of growth. In ancient times the Anasazi of Chaco Canyon used parrot feathers imported from Mexico in their ceremonies. In the ancient system of the day-signs, Lizard was also attributed to the direction South, symbolizing fertility, growth, and the summer season.

The name Huehuecoyotl means "Ancient Coyote," and herein lies another clue to the meaning of this day-sign. Coyote is a popular figure all over Native America. He is sometimes wise, but more often foolish, and the stories told about him are frequently obscene. Though he steps on his own tail, loses his own rectum, and is typically sent off howling at the end of the story, he is nevertheless reverenced as a wise creature, and sometimes as the creator of the universe itself. Coyote is the Trickster, that wild spirit of untamed nature who is both fiendishly clever and unabashedly sexual.

Both the abundance and sensuality of this day-sign are embodied in one of its other meanings, for the Quiché sometimes refer to this day as a "net." The *Popol Vuh* tells the story of a pair of twins born to Xmucane (Shmoo-kah-NAY) and Xpiyacoc (Shpee-yah-COKE), the primal creative pair. These twins are challenged to a handball game by the lords of the Underworld. The brothers fail, are sacrificed, and one of them ends up with his skull hanging in a calabash tree in the Underworld. Blood Woman, daughter of one of the lords of the dead, walks by the calabash tree and the skull spits in her hand. This makes her pregnant with another pair of hero twins who will brave the Underworld themselves and become the protagonists of the next divine handball game (see Night). Fearful of retribution from the lords of Xibalba, Blood Woman escapes to the upper world and seeks out Xmucane who refuses to believe that her son has impregnated Blood Woman unless she receives a sign. She sends Blood Woman to gather corn in a net from a garden her sons had planted. Blood Woman finds only a single clump of corn, but she pulls the cornsilk out of one of the ears and thus produces a net full of ears of ripe corn. Xmucane is amazed at the huge net full of corn, and goes back to the garden to find out what has transpired. There she sees the imprint of the net in the ground, which she takes as an omen that Blood Woman is, truly, to be the mother of her grandchildren.

This myth explains the connection between "net" and "ripe corn." The net is the container or vessel in which abundance, whether agricultural or human, is carried and nurtured. However, the vital growth force represented by the day-sign Lizard may all too easily express itself as pure unbridled sensuality. Thus the "net" also contains the copal incense which one must burn to atone for one's sensual indulgences. Both the positive and negative polarities of the day-sign Lizard may be carried in its symbolic net.

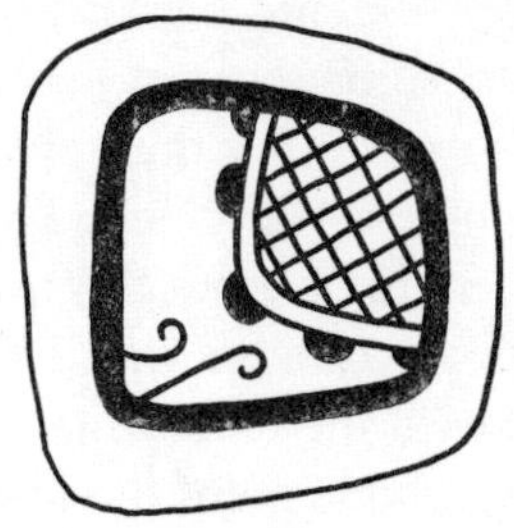

The Serpent

CHICCHAN

The rattlesnake is your nagual.... The fire is your spirit.

—The Book of Chilam Balam of Kaua

Among the native peoples of Mexico and the American Southwest, the serpent—like the lizard of the previous day-sign—is a bringer of rain, and, by extension, a symbol of fertility. The famous Snake Dance performed by the Hopis is essentially a rain dance, for the snakes who have been chosen for the ritual will later tell the rain-making kachinas how the Hopis honored them, inducing the kachinas to shower their blessings upon the Hopis in return.

Among the Maya there were four celestial serpents, the *chicchans*, who guarded the four quarters of the world. When they spoke to each other, thunder was heard, presaging rain. Though the sky was their primary domain, they had a residence on earth as well: lakes, streams, and the interior of mountains were sacred to the chicchans.

However, it is more accurate to speak of four aspects of a single deity than it is to speak of four deities. This four-in-one concept is a common theme among all the peoples of ancient Mesoamerica. The four chicchans are, in this sense, four aspects of the Sky Serpent who encircles the world—whose upper face looks toward Heaven and whose lower face forms the gateway to the Underworld. This Sky Serpent takes many forms; even the great civilizer Quetzalcoatl seems originally to have been an aspect of the Sky Serpent (as indicated by his name, Feathered Serpent).

Another aspect of the reptilian rain god was Chac (CHOCK), a long-nosed deity who appears frequently on the carved temple friezes of Yucatán. He was assisted in his rain-making activities by a group of helpers called chacs, in whom we may recognize another manifestation of the chicchans. Chac and his attendants were known to the Aztecs as Tlaloc (TLAH-loke), the rain god, and his tlaloques (tlah-LOH-kays).

Tlaloc ruled over one of the paradises to which the souls of the blessed might travel after death—Tlalocan—a land of mist, of rainbows and butterflies and lush green forests. Some scholars believe that Eototo, the chief of the Hopi kachinas, is none other than old Tlaloc himself, and that the kachinas are the tlaloques or chicchans. The symbolism of the Hopi Snake Dance would seem to bear out this notion.

In Anasazi petroglyphs, one frequently encounters the "lightning serpent," the image of a snake combined with the representation of a lightning bolt. This makes sense from a symbolic point of view, since rain and lightning are associated with one another. And if there is lightning in the sky, there is also lightning in the body. We have already remarked upon how the Mayan concept of the "body lightning" shares its serpent symbolism with the Hindu concept of the kundalini or serpent power. This power is stored in the root chakra at the base of the spine—which is this day-sign's correspondence in the human body. It is also worth noting that the image of lightning striking a sheet of water is, among the Maya, a metaphor for the body lightning.

The Aztecs linked the day-sign Serpent with the goddess Jade Skirt. Fittingly, she is the wife of Tlaloc the rain god. Jade Skirt is a goddess of love, beauty, and the life-giving water. As a goddess of both love and the life-force, her identification with the serpent power is strong. The day-sign of the Serpent is an emblem of that life-giving vital force that flows through the clouds and in the human body.

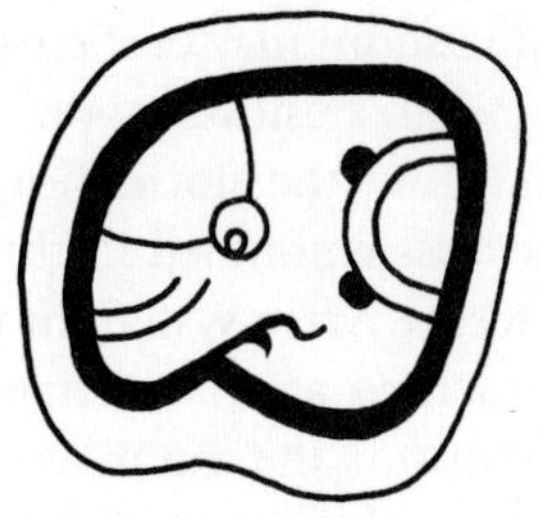

Death

CIMI

The day above all others for forgiveness...one's evil deeds will be forgiven.

—Chichicastenango

Marriage. The dead. Asking for good.

—Momostenango

In the *Popol Vuh*, the Lords of Death demanded the presence of the hero twins in the world below. The two most powerful chieftains of this Underworld realm—two animated skeletons with a penchant for cigars—were named 1 Death and 7 Death. The Hero Twins were subjected to numerous trials and initiatory experiences. They played handball with the Lords of Death, who tricked them into losing the game and forfeiting their lives. The twins sacrificed themselves by leaping into a fiery oven, but on the fifth day they rose again, emerging from the river of the Underworld as a pair of catfish.

This drama, in which the Lords of the Underworld play a treacherous but initiatory role, suggests that the day-sign Death is symbolic of transformation rather than physical death. If Night represents the place where transformation occurs, Death represents the transformative process itself. This is why Death is considered a very lucky day on which to be born.

Throughout ancient Mexico, a system of magical correspondences governed the meaning of each day-sign. One of the correspondences attributed to Death was the cardinal direction North. In ancient times, North was the direction that symbolized the Ancestors, but was only the direction of "death" in the sense that the Ancestors have departed the physical plane. Nevertheless, they continue to guide us with their wisdom, and seeking that wisdom was part of the essence of Mayan ritual practice. In the day-sign Death, we become one with those who went before us, and we partake of their wisdom. In the human body, Death is associated with the crown chakra, the sacred center through which solar enlightenment and ancestral wisdom may best enter into our own consciousness. Hence this day-sign bestows upon us the ancestral wisdom that guides us through all our transformations.

Another key to the transformative process embodied in this day-sign is the Moon God, who, according to the Aztec system of correspondences, ruled this sign. He is represented as an old man who carries a conch shell on his back. This conch is the moon as it rises over the ocean, illuminating the dark waters of the soul with its brilliant white light. Of course, the moon goes through a cycle of death and rebirth each month as it passes through its various phases. The Moon God is an elder, a wise old man, and the conch, because of its spiral shape, is a symbol of the eternal cycle of birth and death—yet another symbol of transformation. This wise old god sometimes wears butterfly wings, reminding us that the butterfly was a caterpillar until it wrapped itself in its transformative cocoon. It also reminds us that butterflies are said by the Maya to be the souls of the dead.

Both the Mayans and the Aztecs used an ideogram for this day-sign which depicted a skull, the image of the death god as well as the locus of the crown chakra to which this day-sign corresponds. Recently, archaeologists have discovered several skulls made of crystal that probably represent the death god. Exactly who made them is uncertain—they may be Aztec, Mixtec, or Mayan. Some psychics believe these skulls to have oracular properties and claim that they are powerful vehicles for the induction of prophetic trance states. This is reminiscent of practices that were common in ancient Europe, where the heads of slain heroes were likewise believed to speak with the voice of prophecy: for example, the head of Mimir in Norse myth, of Bran the Blessed in Celtic lore, and of Orpheus in Greek myth.

The day-sign Death, then, represents that process of transformation or inner death which leads to wisdom and the spirit of prophecy.

The Deer

Manik

The wild forester is your nagual. The cacao is your tree.

—The Book of Chilam Balam of Kaua

The day for giving thanks to the ancestors for all that one has from them...especially for ceremonies that come from ancient time.

—Chichicastenango

The day-sign of the Deer is one of extraordinary symbolic complexity. Though the meaning of its Yucatec name, Manik, is unknown, the hieroglyph for this day clearly represents a hand. In ancient codices, the gods of the sacred hunt are frequently shown with scorpions' tails, and these tails end in a human hand. The hand at the end of the scorpion's tail is the same hand we see in the glyph for this day-sign; it is the hand of the hunter.

In Mayan myth, the god of hunting was named Ek Zip (ECK ZEEP), or Black Zip—he survives in folklore to this very day as an old man with a long white beard who keeps all the world's animals in his magical corral, deep in the forest. Not only is Ek Zip the patron deity of hunters, he is also the protector of the deer, the hunted creature. When hunters approach, so the legend goes, Ek Zip whistles through closed hands to warn the deer of danger; one of his other names, in fact, is the Whistler.

This symbiosis between the hunter and the hunted is typical of Native American thinking. The hunter and his prey are not regarded as antagonists, engaged in a life-and-death struggle with one another. Rather, they are playing out their pre-ordained roles in the endless cycle of birth and death. They are part of the same cosmic dance. This is why Indian hunters all over the Americas say a prayer and ask divine permission before taking the life of any living creature. It is also why

Native hunters often disguised themselves in the skins of the animals they were stalking—so as to become one with the life-energy of that particular species. In Mayan iconography, Ek Zip frequently wears the antlers of the deer. He protects the hunter and the hunted.

He is called Black Zip because his face is always painted black, but Ek Zip is not the only black-faced god in the Mayan pantheon. According to the *Book of Chilam Balam of Kaua*, the cacao tree was one of the correspondences of this day-sign. This tree was the source of cacao or cocao beans, which were used all over pre-Columbian Mexico as currency or units of exchange. Hence, the cacao tree was especially sacred to Mayan merchants and traders as it was a symbol of their god Ek Chuah (ECK Choo-AH), who also had a black face (the Mayan word *ek* means black). The merchant class was the life-blood of ancient Mexico. Traders traveled the length and breadth of the land, from the jungles of Costa Rica to Chaco Canyon in present-day New Mexico. Not only did they bring goods to trade, they brought news, information, and the exchange of cultural values between very different peoples. Like the hunter and his prey, the traveling merchant was part of the sacred rhythm of life.

The Aztec ruler of this day was Tlaloc, god of the rain (see The Serpent). Tlaloc was among the most enduring and important gods of Mesoamerica. The principal deity of Teotihuacán, the City of the Gods, he was known to the Mayans as Chac, whose long-nosed effigy decorates the temples of Yucatán. The protector of the deer, Ek Zip was, like all other gods associated with the animal kingdom, an earth god. The earth gods dwell on the tops of mountains, where Tlaloc's rain clouds collect. Tlaloc ruled over Tlalocan, a very earthly sort of paradise filled with mists and lush forests, rainbows and butterflies. It was to Tlalocan that the souls of the blessed traveled after death.

The day-sign Deer is a symbol of the sacred rhythm of life, an earthly rhythm that includes the hunter and the hunted, the give and take of business or trade, the very craft of life itself.

The Rabbit

LAMAT

A day to give thanks for...harvest and planting.

—Chichicastenango

Though the meaning of the Yucatec Mayan word *lamat*, like that of Manik, is unknown, the significance of this day-sign is clear. It is a symbol of ripeness, abundance, and the growth of the corn.

There are other shades of meaning here, too, for the Rabbit's hieroglyph is the Mayan symbol for the planet Venus. To the Maya, Venus was not associated with the goddess of love, as it is in Western civilization. Instead, the Maya linked the cycle of Venus with powerful and dynamic events in the world of politics and ecology. The god Lahun-Chan (Lah-HOON CHAHN), with whom the Yucatec Maya associated the planet, was a deformed monster who wreaked havoc as he lurched drunkenly through the world of the gods.

This wild drunkenness was strongly associated with the day-sign Rabbit. The rabbit in question would seem to be "the rabbit in the moon." Whereas Westerners see a "man in the moon," both the Chinese and the Native peoples of Mesoamerica saw a rabbit. This mythic rabbit is a cheerful drunk, the companion of Mayahuel (My-ah-WELL), the goddess of drinking. It is in the story of Mayahuel, the Aztec deity who ruled this day-sign, that we can most clearly see its associations with alcohol and general indulgence, as well as with the spirit of growth and vitality, of "ripeness."

Mayahuel, it is said, was a virgin goddess under the protection of the celestial monster or Sky Serpent. Quetzalcoatl, in his cosmic form as the god of the wind (see The Wind), stole her from her guardian and fled with her to earth. He became one with her, and the two of them were transformed into a great tree with two branches: a male branch to represent Quetzalcoatl, and a female branch to represent Mayahuel. The Sky Serpent, angered, came with his celestial helpers and attacked the tree that held the spirit of his former ward. The female branch was torn to pieces: Mayahuel was dead. In sorrow, Quetzalcoatl returned to his customary form and buried the bones of the virgin goddess. From her grave sprouted the agave or maguey plant from which the liquor known as pulque is brewed.

The story of Mayahuel and Quetzalcoatl is an Aztec version of a myth common all over pre-Columbian America. The story of the goddess who dies, is buried, and returns in the form of growing things is fundamental to Native American mythology. It signifies that the earth is regarded as the physical body of the Divine Mother. In many versions of the myth it is corn, not agave, that grows from the body of the slain Earth Mother, as corn was the Native American "staff of life."

The story of this Aztec "corn mother" has an esoteric meaning as well. The tree into which Quetzalcoatl and Mayahuel are transformed is yet another symbol for the World Tree standing at the center of the universe. The World Tree is also within us as the spinal column, which carries the "body lightning" up and down in its spiral pattern. Other spiritual traditions concerning this life-force inform us that the "inner tree" has both a masculine or yang channel (Quetzalcoatl) and a feminine or yin channel (Mayahuel). In this Aztec myth we see a version of the "fall from grace"—the loss of that original male-female unity which, in spiritual traditions all over the world, is equated with the condition of paradise.

Paradise may be lost and regained within a human lifetime. Venus, the planet associated with this day-sign, also goes through a cycle of death and rebirth—it shines as the evening star, disappears, then returns again as the morning star. Though the god Quetzalcoatl appears here primarily as the god of the wind, in the best-known version of his story (see The Corn) Quetzalcoatl is a gifted but fallen spiritual leader who dies on a pyre of flames and is reborn as the planet Venus. Thus the story of Mayahuel's transformation symbolizes more than the loss of our original spiritual unity—it speaks of a continual process of death and rebirth, like the disappearance and return of Venus-Quetzalcoatl. The Divine Mother, who dies seasonally and passes beneath the earth, returns with the spring.

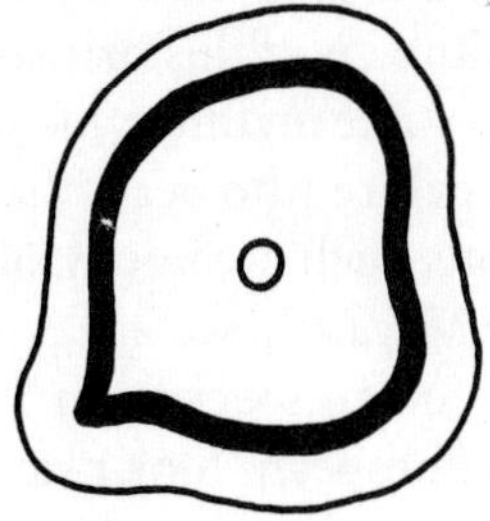

Water

Muluc

The shark is your nagual.

—The Book of Chilam Balam of Kaua

Payment.

—Momostenango

The most common name for this day-sign is Water, though the Mayan word *muluc* literally means "something that is gathered up" or "collected" in reference to the rain clouds that gather up or collect in the sky before a storm. This gathering together of the clouds is given artistic form by way of the "cloud terrace" motif (see Storm), which was common in both the American Southwest and ancient Mexico. Hopi and Pueblo art abounds with cloud terraces; the piling up of the clouds is visually represented by a geometric design that resembles a stepped pyramid. The image of impending rain, which will create new life, is symbolically linked to the pyramidal shape of the universe itself.

The Mayans taught that the power and energy of the rain was "collected" in water pots or vases, which were kept by the chacs, the helpers of the rain god (see Serpent). During a rain, the chacs pour forth the waters of abundance from their rain pots. Fierce storms occur when the rain pots, overburdened with water, burst open unexpectedly. A modern folktale from Guatemala tells the story of a runaway boy who takes refuge with a kindly old man who lives alone in the jungle. The old man leaves the boy on his own in the house, but insists that he must never open the jars in the back room. Of course, this is exactly what the boy does. The result is a tremendous tropical storm, quelled only when the old man returns to set things to right. He is, in reality, a chac, and the boy has opened his "collection" (muluc) of rain pots.

The Mayans chose a watery deity to rule over this sign: Xoc (SHOKE), the Great Fish, who is sometimes depicted as a shark, sometimes as a whale. Not a great deal is known of this primal water beast or its precise significance, but there is some mythic evidence that Xoc was yet another form of the primal creature who bears the world on its back. It may seem strange to encounter such oceanic symbolism here, for we do not ordinarily think of the Maya as a seafaring people. But the Mayans did live by the Caribbean coast, especially in Yucatán and Belize. Their first known contact with Europeans took place when Columbus encountered one of their gigantic trading canoes far out in that sea. The Itzá, who invaded Yucatán after the end of the Classic Period (c. A.D. 835) and founded the city of Chichén Itzá, were Caribbean traders who reached their new home by canoe. Also, when the Mayan ahauob spilled their blood in ritual, they used the spine of a stingray—another oceanic creature—for that purpose.

There is yet another symbolic attribute of Water, one that derives from the Mayan glyph for that day-sign. The ideogram for Water is the same as the symbol for jade, a stone that was blue-green, the color of the center of all things. We have already seen that jade was the most precious and sacred of stones; the buried kings of ancient Mexico were interred with treasures of jade. The emperors of China were also buried with jade all around them, for to the Chinese jade was a stone of life which was believed to preserve the body and spirit of the departed king. As jade was the most precious of stones to the people of Mesoamerica, so water—source of agricultural growth and hence the literal "water of life"—was the most sacred of natural forces. The rain both gave life and took it away, depending on whether it came as a gentle shower or a devastating flood. Hence jade and water correspond to each other symbolically as metaphors for the precious blue-green life force at the center of the four directions.

The Dog

Oc

The adorned one, of the easy life....

—The Book of Chilam Balam of Kaua

Although this day-sign is usually called the Dog and, in divination at least, represents sensual—especially sexual—energy pure and simple, there is also a deeper, more esoteric meaning to this symbol. Though one of the Classic Mayan hieroglyphs for this sign clearly depicts a dog, another glyph represents a human foot. As for the name of this sign in Yucatec Mayan, *oc* literally means a door or a gateway—which, as we shall see, sometimes signifies the gateway to the Otherworld, but which could also signify the gateway to a new year or Calendar cycle. The *Book of Chilam Balam of Chumayel* includes a myth about how time began. The foot (one of the glyphs for this day-sign) of a god paces across the universe, measuring out time. This foot is specifically linked with the day-sign Oc, which, in this myth, marks the beginning of the tzolkin.

One of the ancient hieroglyphs for this day-sign seems to represent the skeletal god who conducts us to the Underworld—which, of course, is but one more gateway or oc. Like everything else in Mesoamerican myth, this Underworld Guide has many faces. Among the Aztecs, he was called Xolotl (SHO-lotle), the "dark twin" of Feathered Serpent whose animal form is a dog. Among the tribal Lacandon Maya who live in the jungles of Chiapas, the dog is still the Underworld Guide. Until recently, Lacandon tribesmen fashioned statues of dogs from palm leaves to be placed at the four corners of each grave. It is also said that in ancient times, when an aristocrat or king died, his dog was sacrificed in order to join its master and conduct him across the river of the dead. Thus the dog represents a loyalty and faithfulness that survives even beyond death.

Xolotl, the "dark twin" of Feathered Serpent, represents the great civilization bringer's "shadow side," a psychological opposite that forms the converse image of his own dazzling persona. This shadowy twin was a skeletal figure who, hoisting the sun on his back, carries it into the Underworld at the end of every day. Here, in the "shadow" world, the dark twin carries the solar orb through the night, until it is time for the sun to be reborn once again.

The sun emerges from the Underworld at dawn and runs its course through the daylight world, the world of consciousness. Then it plunges. Like the sun, we too must one day die and journey into the Underworld, with only faith and loyalty (the dog) to guide us. In some stories it is the dog who brings fire to humankind and is often shown carrying a torch. This, perhaps, is also emblematic of the fire of faith that guides us through periods of darkness, for our journey through the Underworld occurs not only in death, but as an inner process. This inner transformative process is depicted several times in the Mayan Calendar—for instance, in the day-signs Night and Death. We have seen the motif of rebirth from the Underworld implicit in these same signs, as well as in the Rabbit, sign of the companion of Mayahuel, the goddess who dies and is reborn. The day-sign Oc is simultaneously our gateway into darkness, our feet passing through that gateway, and the dog of faith who guides us through the ensuing darkness. It is a complex symbol for that stage in the journey of consciousness when we must walk through the "dark night of the soul." There is a torch to guide us, and this torch is an emblem of the faith that sustains us in our darkest moments.

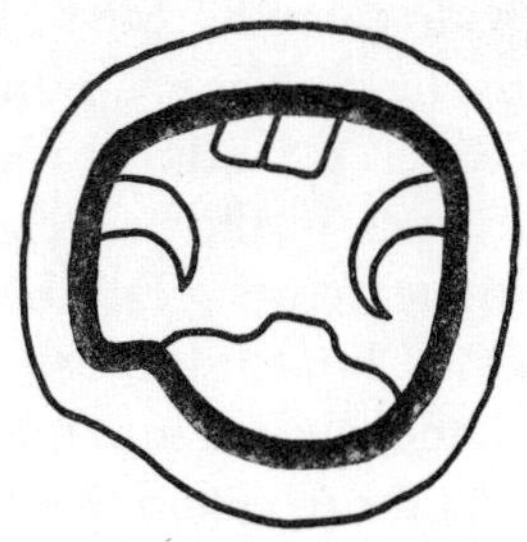

The Monkey

CHUEN

Masters of all the arts.

—The Book of Chilam Balam of Kaua

It is said, in the *Popol Vuh*, that First Mother and First Father gave birth to two sons, One Hunahpu (Hoo-nah-POO) and Seven Hunahpu. One Hunahpu in turn had two sons, One Batz and One Chouen (Chow-EN). The word *batz* means "monkey" and is the Quiché name for this day-sign. The word *chouen* is the same as Yucatec chuen; the literal meaning is "craftsman" or "artisan." Thus the twins One Monkey and One Craftsman are both manifestations of this day-sign.

One Batz and One Chouen were the primordial artificers and craftsmen. They were flute players, singers, writers, carvers, jewelers, and metalworkers. No wonder the Maya regard this day-sign as one of the most fortunate! All the fine arts are included in the meaning of the day of the Monkey. Creative excellence, as embodied in this day-sign, was one of the human qualities most deeply honored by the peoples of ancient Mexico. Artistic activity was, in and of itself, considered part of the spiritual path set forth by the original Toltecs, the mythic founders of Mesoamerican civilization.

There is an irreverent, rebellious, and sometimes even cruel quality to this day-sign as well. The *Popol Vuh* tells how Hunahpu and his brother journeyed to the Underworld to play handball with the Lords of Darkness. Though they played well, they were tricked and sacrificed by the dark lords. However, the spirit of One Hunahpu impregnated an Underworld girl called Blood Woman. She escaped to the upper world to bear her children, the hero twins Hunahpu and Xbalanque (Shba-lahn-KAY), but the hero twins were mistreated by their half-brothers, One Batz and One Chouen, who were jealous of them and who conspired with First Mother to make sure the younger brothers would receive no food at the family hearth. Instead, Hunahpu and Xbalanque were forced to hunt and provide game for First Mother, One Batz, and One Chouen. In the end, the hero twins got even. They coaxed One Batz and One Chouen into a tree, ostensibly to retrieve some birds killed by the hero twins but stuck in the branches. No sooner had the two artisans ascended than the tree magically began to grow into the sky, leaving One Batz and One Chouen stranded. Then, another magical transformation occurred: they turned into monkeys. They finally succeeded in getting down from the trees and to return to the home of their grandmother, but First Mother just laughed at their ridiculous appearance. They retreated back to the sanctuary of the forest, and remain monkeys to this very day. Despite the fact that they were humbled and turned into animals for their envy of their brothers and their excessive egotism, they were nevertheless "prayed to by the flautists and singers among the ancient people, and the writers and carvers prayed to them."

As well as being a tale of pride and its fall, the story of the artisan twins is also a symbolic representation of celestial phenomena. Because the orbital periods of planets are relatively constant, as are the days of the Sacred Calendar, it was only possible for a given planet to rise heliacally (i.e., with the sun) on particular tzolkin days. The planet Mars rose on Monkey days, and the two artisan twins are most likely connected with the red planet. The humiliating return of the new-made monkeys to the home of First Mother would then correspond to the retrograde period of Mars.

The funerary inscriptions on ancient Mayan ceramics make it clear that the Classic Mayan scribes were painters as well as literary artists and keepers of sacred lore. These members of the Mayan royal houses who specialized in knowledge recognized the Monkey God as their patron deity. Given such an intimate connection between sacred knowledge and creative artistry, we should not be surprised to learn that Monkey is still regarded as the day of the "masters of all the arts" as well as being one of the days dedicated to the Calendar keepers and their lore. Monkey is the day of the craftsman, the wisdom-keeper and the artist. It exemplifies both the spiritual and creative power as well as the over-reaching egotism of the artistic temperament.

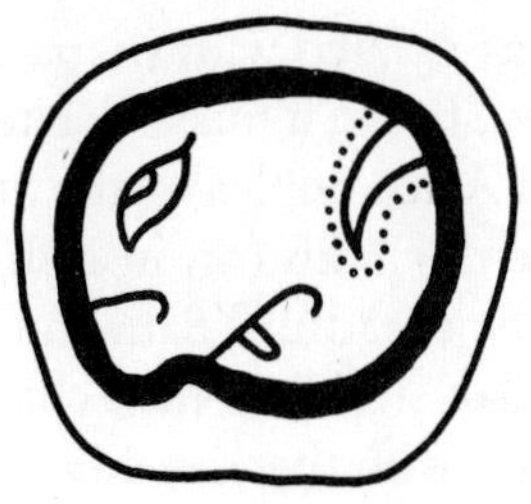

The Road

Eb

A good man, one whose riches are those of the community.... That which is of the community is your estate.

—The Book of Chilam Balam of Kaua

...That we be guided on our road, the good road, the straight road, the long road...

—Momostenango

The day-sign which, in Yucatec, is called Eb, or "stairway," is one of the most mysterious and misunderstood day-signs. Most interpreters of the Sacred Calendar have called it a negative, destructive influence, but in the *Book of Chilam Balam of Chumayel*, a creation story dated about 1562 tells us that on 2 Eb God "created the first ladder so that God could descend into the midst of the sky and the sea." Thus the idea of the day-sign Eb as a ladder or stairway is very old. In fact, the story describes the whole world as a kind of ladder.

The ladder of the *Chilam Balam of Chumayel* is clearly the pyramid of heaven and earth, which dominates Classic Mayan cosmology. To climb the ladder is to climb the pyramid. The modern Maya call this day-sign "the Road of Life." In many Native American philosophies, the Road of Life is the "Good Red Road" that leads from east to west and represents the spiritual path. To the Maya, walking the Road of Life means climbing the ladder or pyramid to the summit of creation, the thirteenth heaven.

Another clue to the esoteric meaning of this day-sign is provided by its Aztec name, Malinalli. Although this word may describe a kind of grass (hence the usual translation of this day-sign as Grass), it also refers to the vital energy that animates all life (see Chapter 2), the "dew of heaven" or "lightning in the blood." Hence this day-sign is a symbol of the vital energy and power that propels us along the Road of Life, as well as of the Road itself.

How, then, did this day-sign become associated with so many negative connotations? The answer, I believe, lies in a misunderstanding of an old "Book of Days" collected from Aztec nobles by the Spanish priest Bernardino de Sahagún. Here the day 1 Eb (or, in Nahuatl, 1 Malinalli) is called "a day of wild beasts, dreadful." Sahagún is not actually referring to the character of the day-sign Eb—he is characterizing the entire fortnightly cycle that begins with that day. Many scholars have not understood that the tone of a fortnight is not established by the first day of the cycle, but by the middle days. The middle days of Road's fortnightly cycle are 7 Flint and 8 Storm, which are rather ominous, but the days 7 and 8 Road crown fortnightly periods that are declared favorable by both Sahagún and the modern Daykeepers of Chichicastenango.

To further complicate matters, the old chronicles tell us that the woman known as Malinche or Doña Marina was born on the day 1 Eb (the name Malinche is probably a Spanish corruption of Ce Malinalli, which simply means 1 Eb in Nahuatl). This woman, born a princess but raised as a slave for the sexual pleasure of Aztec lords, was bestowed upon the conqueror Cortez as a gift. Her rage against her former masters, the Aztecs, led her to provide assistance to Cortez in toppling Montezuma's empire. She was his translator, lover, spy, and perhaps his principal strategist when it came to Native psychology. Hence some have called her "La Chingada," the great whore who betrayed her people to the Spaniards. Paradoxically, she also became the mother of the mestizo race by bearing Cortez's child, the first known union of Aztec and Spaniard. So she is the great mother of the Mexican people, as well as being the great whore!

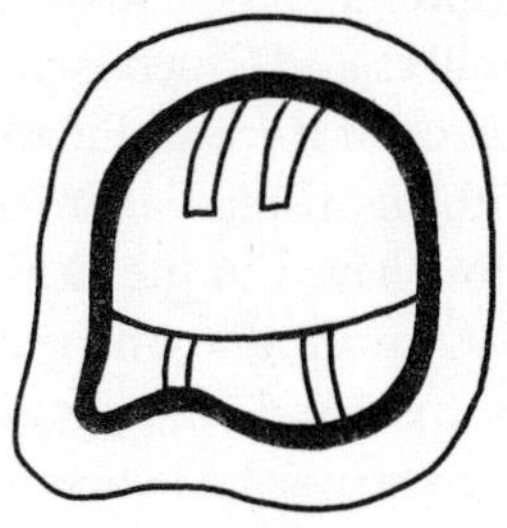

Corn

BEN

[This] is the name of the day of one's destiny.

—Chichicastenango

The meaning of the Yucatec word *ben* remains a mystery, as does the significance of the Mayan glyph that represents this day-sign; nevertheless, this day—variously known as Reed or Cane but symbolically related to Corn—is one of the most important of all. The Aztecs counted it as one of their Year Bearers, and there was a prophecy to the effect that the god-king Feathered Serpent or Quetzalcoatl would return to humanity in the year they called 1 Reed. The year 1 Reed corresponded to the year 1519 in the Gregorian Calendar, and it was in that year that Cortez arrived in Mexico. The emperor Montezuma suspected that Cortez's advent represented the fulfillment of the old prophecy, and this apprehension on the part of the Aztec emperor played a major role in the fall of ancient Mexico.

We have already met Quetzalcoatl in his incarnation as the god of the wind (see The Wind). He was one of the most ancient of the gods of Mexico, and his image decorates many of the temples of Teotihuacán which flourished from the time of Christ until about A.D. 800. Quetzalcoatl may well be yet another manifestation of the Sky Serpent, that universal deity known all over Mesoamerica and who was of great importance in Mayan mythology.

Quetzalcoatl is best known, however, as a great priest-king of the "historic" Toltecs. According to the legend, he was a spiritual leader who was born in A.D. 935 and achieved some kind of transfiguration in 987 (note that these dates indicate a span of fifty-two years, a Calendar Round cycle). As ruler of the Toltec city of Tula he declared an end to human sacrifice. Instead he demanded that the gods should be worshipped with sacrifices of flowers, song, and meditation. The priests of Tezcatlipoca (tez-kah-tlee-PO-kah), god of the Smoking

Mirror, stood against him. They "showed him his face in the mirror" —which is to say, they awakened within him the dark side or Shadow, that primal force that Tezcatlipoca symbolizes and which is perceived within us only when we gaze into his mirror of the self. Finally these priests lured Quetzalcoatl into incest with his sister. Fallen and disgraced, the prophet left his people and journeyed to the Gulf Coast. What happened to him there is unclear. According to one version of the story, he cast himself onto a funeral pyre and rose again as the Morning Star, the planet Venus. In this form he was known as Ce Acatl (Kay Ah-KAHTLE), or One Reed. Another story affirms that he sailed to the east on a raft of serpents, promising to return. It was this version of the story that so deeply affected Montezuma.

If he did in fact sail away in the year A.D. 987, where did he go? Interestingly, the Mayan books of Chilam Balam record the arrival of a priest-king or leader called Kukulcan (Feathered Serpent) in precisely that year, 987. According to the Mayan books, he established his kingdom at the city of Chichén Itzá in Yucatán, and died in 999.

It is said that Quetzalcoatl erected a pillar in the city of Tula, the "Place of Reeds." This pillar is no doubt a kind of World Tree, a cosmic center. We may note that among some contemporary Mayan groups, this day of the Corn is symbolically linked with the staff of office, which is carried by the village leader, or *alcalde*, as an emblem of authority. Thus, the growing Corn may be regarded as another metaphor for the central pillar or universal World Tree, source of all inner power and authority.

Our sense of authority or inner power is the motive factor in our destiny as well. Hence this day is also symbolic of one's personal destiny as embodied in the nagual or power animal (see Chapter 4). If someone is ill—suffering from a loss of personal power—a Mayan shaman may begin a healing ceremony on 8 Corn, which is known as "the invocation of the destiny animal." The ceremony calls upon one's nagual or power animal to restore health in the individual.

The Jaguar

Ix

Ix is the name of the commemoration of the world.

—Chichicastenango

Almost all contemporary Daykeepers throughout the Mayan world know this day-sign as the Jaguar. Along with the eagle and the serpent, this stealthy jungle cat who hunts by night is one of the most important totem animals in the mythologies of ancient Mexico and Central America; he is the Earth Lord personified. Darkness is his domain.

The sun's daily journey was a central metaphor in Mesoamerican myth. It stood for the eternal journey of human consciousness and its transformations. The sun in its bright shining is like the light of individuated consciousness. Then it plunges below the horizon, just as we descend into our own inner darkness and, like the Hero Twins in the Underworld, face our inner demons so that we may arise transformed. If the sun at midday was compared to an eagle, flying into the brilliant light of zenith, the hidden sun of night was imagined as a jaguar whose spotted skin symbolized the stars glittering in the night sky. Thus the "jaguar sun" was an invisible sun, the sun traveling through the Underworld in its jaguar guise.

Like the lords of medieval Europe, the Aztecs had their orders of knighthood, their sacred warriors. There were two such orders: the knights of the Eagle and the knights of the Jaguar. The Eagle warriors were dedicated to the principle of the sun in its splendor, the sun at the noon zenith. The knights of the Jaguar, on the other hand, were dedicated to the principle of the Underworld sun, the sun passing through darkness at midnight. They were the spies and undercover agents; their work was that of silence and cunning.

This day-sign, then, is one of the many images from the Sacred Calendar that have to do with the experience of darkness. In many ways, it shares a number of attributes with the day-sign called Night. If the day-sign Night symbolizes those "houses of darkness" where the Hero Twins of the *Popol Vuh* faced their spiritual challenges, then the Jaguar symbolizes the lord and master of those dark houses. Among contemporary daykeepers, this is preeminently the day-sign of Santo Mundo or Holy World, the old pagan Earth Father who manifests himself as the divine rascal Maximon. Bearded and dressed in his black slouch hat, puffing a cigar (like the old Lords of the Mayan Underworld) and nipping at a bottle of booze, Maximon strides through the life of the modern Maya like a wise old jaguar on the prowl and, in true pagan style, perpetrates a sacrilegious homosexual union with Christ. He is clever, amoral, and eternal. He is the Earth Father.

There are other symbolic connections between the day-signs Jaguar and Night. According to the modern Maya, both of these days are connected with mountains and with animals. Night, as we have seen, is ruled by Tepeyollotl or Pacal Votan, the indwelling spirit who lives within mountains and bestows upon them their teyolia—their coyopa or spiritual power. This "heart of the mountain" is also a lord of animals. An earth god, he presides over the sacred power in the earth and the animals who live upon it. The force that resides within the mountains, which gives them their volcanic and transformative power, is the same underworld source of power and energy which is imaged as the jaguar sun.

The Eagle

MEN

[This] is the name of good luck in money.

—Chichicastenango

The cheerful and the rejoicing is your nagual.

—The Book of Chilam Balam of Kaua

The Eagle is one of the most powerful of all day-signs, for in it the symbolism of the sun and moon, yin and yang, are united in an archetype of wholeness.

The Classic Period ideogram for this day-sign depicts a face. Most commonly, this face is associated in Mayan texts with the moon. Among the Maya, as among many other peoples of the world, the moon was a goddess. She created the art of weaving, and was the patroness of agriculture and childbirth.

As we have seen on many occasions, everything in Mesoamerican myth has two aspects, two faces. There is a young moon goddess who is the representative of all the fruitfulness and promise of the budding earth, and there is an old moon goddess symbolic of the wisdom of age. The hieroglyph for this day-sign shows us the face of the old moon goddess, and the Yucatec word for this day, *men*, literally means "the wise one." It remains a potent word unto this day, for it is the generic term for a shaman, a "knower." A man who takes such a path is a *h-men* (huh-MEN), while a woman is called a *x-men* (shuh-MEN). The Old Moon Goddess was the original knower, the first wise one. In central Mexico, this lunar goddess was often called Eagle Woman; she wore a headdress of eagle feathers and obsidian knives. Her title and the eagle feathers connect her with the Aztec day-sign Eagle, which is more often linked with the sun, while the knives suggest the Aztec rituals of human sacrifice. Thus sun and moon, male and female, combine in one archetype: When the sun rises, he is "soaring eagle"; when the sun sets, he is "falling eagle." The moon wears the sun in her hair.

As we have seen, there were two orders of knighthood among the Aztecs. Eagle Knights were the champions of the sun in his brightness, in his daytime shining. Jaguar Knights were the champions of the midnight sun. These Eagle Knights must have derived from some older order in Toltec times, one wherein the members of the order were seen as genuine spiritual warriors, fighting for the strong directive power of truth symbolized by the sun.

Physically, the day-sign of the Eagle corresponds to the right arm, symbolic of the warrior's strength; it contrasts with Monkey, the artist and trickster who is represented by the left hand. The Eagle is the sign of the spiritual warrior, whose heart is pure like the heart of the sun; but underneath the bright and shining glory of the daytime sun lies an older, subtler archetype of quiet wisdom: First Mother, the moon, the crone of wisdom.

The Maya of today, however, have forgotten the aged moon goddess and call this sign *tz'ikin* (tsee-KEEN), which literally means "bird" but usually designates the eagle. They still remember the powerful sense of motivation and focus that gave this day-sign its link to the most powerful of all the predatory birds. This is the day-sign that "cries out" for whatever it desires—whether money, or wisdom, or both. This is the sign of directed warrior energy and focused purpose.

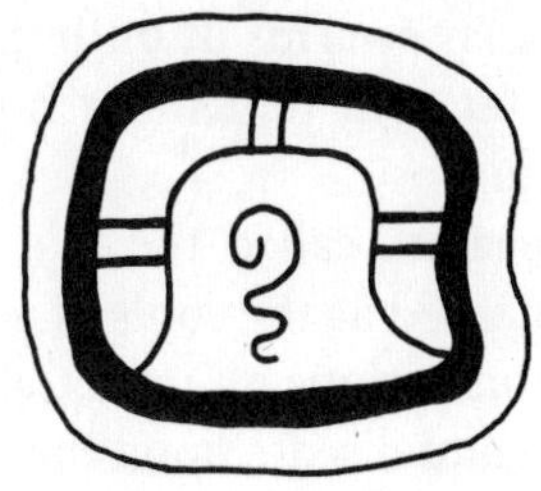

The Vulture

CIB

In...Cib the first candle was made, and thus it was that light was created where there had been neither sun nor moon.

—The Book of Chilam Balam of Chumayel

A day to ask for forgiveness....

—Chichicastenango

The Yucatec word *cib* literally means "wax," and the *Book of Chilam Balam of Chumayel* tells us that upon this day God lit the first candle; the first light was made to shine in the darkness.

Though candles are an important part of contemporary Mayan ritual, there were no candles in pre-Columbian days; the passage in the *Chumayel* dates from after the Spanish Conquest, and candles are an adaptation to Christian ways rather than a custom surviving from antiquity. Nevertheless, the association between wax and the day known as Cib, or Vulture, is ancient indeed. The wax symbolized by Cib in pre-Columbian times was beeswax. The Yucatec Maya recognized four divine figures who held up the four corners of the world—another variation on that all-important symbol, the four directions of time. They were called the Bacabs (Bah-KAHBS), and their appearance was that of four gigantic bees. On their heads they wore conch shells—the ideogram associated with the day-sign Cib. The conch shell symbolized emergence and rebirth because of its spiral shape; like the spirals of Anasazi and Hopi art, it told the story of humankind's emergence from earlier worlds as well as defining the whole process of death and rebirth which takes place eternally within the human soul.

The conch is also linked with the Underworld, the place from which the human race ultimately emerged and the place to which we must return if we are to experience the death and rebirth process.

According to the Maya, the spirits of the departed may sometimes return as butterflies or bees. We may think of Vulture as the day-sign of those departed souls who return to us as swarms of butterflies or bees. Those who have traveled in Yucatán will remember how the graveyards literally swarm with butterflies.

The Aztecs recognized four world-bearers called the *tzitzimime* (tsee-tsee-MEE-may), who were also regarded as the souls of women who had died in childbirth and who, upon various unlucky Calendar days, came down to earth to inflict death and disease upon the world. It is no wonder, then, that the Aztecs gave this day-sign to the vulture, who swoops down to feed on the remains of the dead.

If the vulture feeds on the remains of the dead, it also cleans away the decaying remnants of the past (in the 1930s, vultures were protected birds in the Mexican city of Veracruz because of their efficiency in cleaning the streets). The spiral conch worn by the four Bacabs suggests a similar function for this day-sign; after all, the spiral is the symbol of re-emergence and rebirth. The Aztecs—and probably the Toltecs before them—placed great emphasis on the confession of sins. It was believed that when a man confessed, his sins were "eaten" by Tlazolteotl (Tlah-zohl-TAY-otle), the goddess of sex and witchcraft, also known as Filth Eater because of her confessional role. This fierce goddess—reminiscent of the destructive female deities of Hindu or Buddhist Tantra—was the patroness of witches and sorcerers and her sexuality was a rampant, uncontrolled force. (The day-sign Cib is also sometimes called the Owl—in the American Southwest, witches, or *brujas*, are believed to take on the shapes of owls.) It was to her that dying Aztecs confessed their sins—their karma (or filth) was consumed (eaten) by the goddess, who thereby redeemed them. Thus the Aztecs paid homage to the transforming power of darkness—even as the similar Hindu goddess Durga Kali may ultimately be made manifest not as the horrible dancer decorated with skulls but as the beautiful, divine mother of the universe. Vulture is the day-sign in which the remnants of our karmic patterns are purged and cleared away.

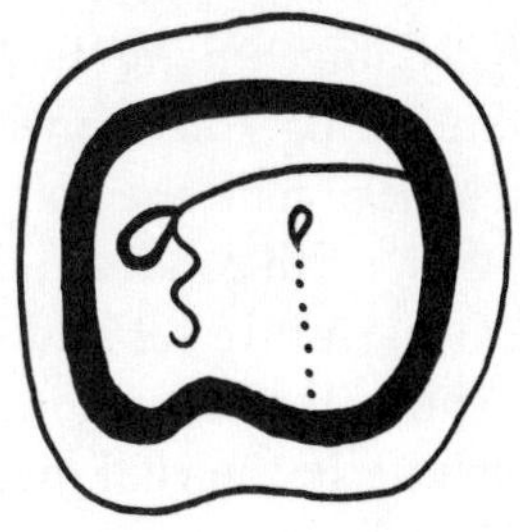

Incense

CABAN

Wise and prudent....

—The Book of Chilam Balam of Kaua

This is the name of our thoughts or manner or customary mode of behavior.

—Chichicastenango

Running like a constant through all the mythologies of Mesoamerica, as well as the American Southwest, is the theme of emergence. Humankind is perpetually emerging—or perhaps we should say evolving—through successive worlds, successive eras of cosmic time. The *Popol Vuh* records several "worlds" prior to this one, as the gods try unsuccessfully to fashion a humankind that will remember the rituals and live in harmony with the rest of the universe. In Aztec myth, each world is named after a day in the Sacred Calendar, preceded by the number 4. The first world was 4 Jaguar; this was the day upon which that world was created, and it ended when all its inhabitants were eaten by wild beasts. Next came 4 Wind, which was destroyed by violent windstorms; then 4 Storm, destroyed by a rain of fire; and after that 4 Water, destroyed by a flood. Then the present world was created. Called 4 Earthquake, which corresponds to the Mayan day-sign Caban, it will, at some unknown date in the future (or perhaps on the Mayan end-date of December 21, 2012), be destroyed by tremendous earthquakes.

The Aztec word *ollin* (ohl-yeen), which signifies "earthquake," also means simply "movement" or "motion." The Aztecs taught that their language, Nahuatl, was a kind of spiritual code, and that many of the religious or mystical terms in that tongue were filled with inner meanings. The words for "life" and "heart" are both derived from the word *ollin*. Hence the "earthquake" symbolized by the day-sign Caban is not merely a geological phenomenon, but a metaphor for the pulsating rhythm or movement of life itself.

When we look at the lore of the day-sign Caban among the Mayan peoples, we find still other dimensions of meaning. *Caban* means literally "earth," and its ideogram depicts a lock of hair, the hair of the young moon goddess who is also corn mother, earth goddess, and creative spirit. Again we meet First Mother, that universal goddess of beginnings. Caban represents the creative spirit (the moon goddess or First Mother) that lies inherent in the earth itself; the vital force that manifests in the human body as teyolia, a soul substance centered in the heart, is believed to reside in the earth. The upsurging motion or movement of this vital force, the source of creative activity, is analogous to the surging motion of the blood in human terms, or, to use a metaphor from the natural world, to an earthquake.

At least initially, the contemporary meaning of this day-sign would seem to be very different. Most Mayan daykeepers call this day "Incense," and associate it with the thinking process. This link between incense and the mind is ancient, for the *Chilam Balam of Chumayel* tells us that "incense is the brains of heaven." Incense smoke rises to heaven—and so should our thoughts when we are thinking correctly and intelligently. In the physical body, this day-sign corresponds to the mouth, from which our inspired thoughts flow forth in the form of speech. The connecting link between earthquakes, incense, speech, and the thinking process gives us one more important clue as to this day-sign's ultimate meaning: it symbolizes the creative force that, manifesting as the surging of heart's blood or the power of an earthquake, may also be compared to the force of inspiration, the spark of creative thought that brings all things into being.

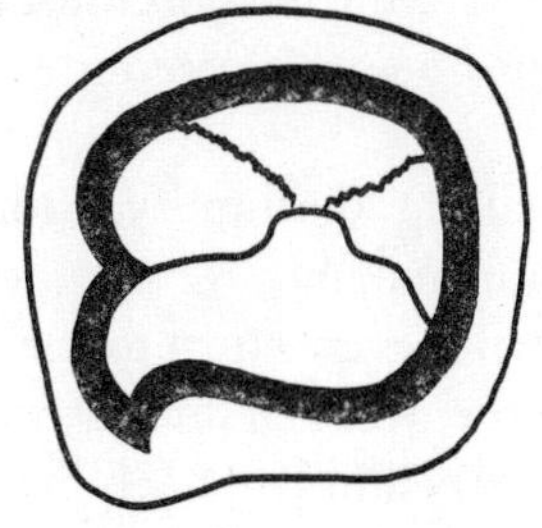

Flint

ETZNAB

A healer...a curandero.... Also very valiant.

—The Book of Chilam Balam of Kaua

All sources agree that this day-sign represents the sacrificial knife, and this reminds us uncomfortably of the Aztec passion for human sacrifice. It is a regrettable truth that almost all traditional societies and hieratic civilizations have practiced some form of human sacrifice. This is as true of the Druid groves or the Hindu practice of suttee as it is of ancient Mexico and Peru. However, the civilizations of Mexico seem to have gone overboard, and surviving sources tell of massive sacrifices involving thousands of people during the last days of the Aztec Empire. Yet this is true only of the final years of Aztec rule. As empire builders, the Aztecs cynically manipulated the ancient spiritual traditions of Mexico for their own imperial and political ends, thereby giving rise to an orgy of slaughter. They paid the price themselves in an equally bloody orgy of destruction.

Because they had such a fascination with the act of sacrifice, the Aztecs reverenced Flint or Etznab as a most fortunate day. Ultimately, this is not so much a day-sign of conflict and violence as it is a sign of human pain or the consciousness of suffering.

Symbolically, the sacrificial knife represented by the day-sign is not substantially different from the symbol of the sword in other traditions, including Christian ("I come not to bring peace, but a sword"). The knife divides human consciousness into a painful duality of right and wrong, yes and no—hence Flint was at one time associated with the number 2 in ancient Mayan numerology. To lose our innate unity, our consciousness of wholeness, is to become aware of opposites—which is always painful. This consciousness of opposites is necessary—it is a sacrifice that we must make in order to attain a certain level of moral consciousness. All spiritual traditions postulate an original, paradisal unity that is lost when consciousness of duality, of right and wrong, emerges from the primordial womb of the unconscious. It is in this world of opposites that we act—opposites are a precondition for our actions in the world.

We all seek to re-establish that original paradisal unity, and, if we devote our lives to the hard work of "soul-making," we may actually achieve this to some degree, though we will never return to the child-like unity of the womb. We have lived in the world of duality, we have sacrificed our state of childhood innocence, and if we achieve unity with the cosmos once again we shall do so on a different level entirely. We have grown up and have lived in the world of yes and no, the world of the sword that slashed our primordial womb in two. We may, like the Buddha, transcend suffering and sacrifice, but we will always remain conscious of the fact that it exists. This is the lesson of the day-sign Flint.

A knife may be wielded by a warrior or by a healer—it is the instrument of the surgeon as well as of the fighter. Thus the *Chilam Balam of Kaua* tells us that this day-sign symbolizes the healer, the curandero whose knife cuts away infection. Indeed, it is only when we have become aware of the duality of human existence that we are in fact awakened to the healing potential that lies within all of us. If the sword of consciousness that makes us aware of duality can wound us, it can also heal.

Storm

CAUAC

The quetzal is your nagual...very imaginative.

—The Book of Chilam Balam of Kaua

The glyph for Cauac contains a curious symbol which seems, to some, to resemble a bunch of grapes. But these are not grapes—these are clouds, pregnant with rain.

The same motif is found among Navajo and Pueblo peoples in the American Southwest, a probable inheritance from the Anasazi who were deeply influenced by ancient Mexico. Here, however, the rain clouds appear in a pyramidal shape that the Indians call "cloud terraces." The appearance of the pyramid in association with rain is significant. As we have seen, the pyramid is a symbol for the World Mountain and, by extension, the vital force of the earth. It signifies the power called teyolia which sleeps "in the heart of the mountain." Time itself is another pyramid, based on the structure of the universe, the pyramid of the thirteen heavens. Rain holds such a preeminent place in Mesoamerican and Southwestern spiritual traditions as to constitute yet another pyramid, another expression of that vital power that underlies and structures the whole universe. Rain is the source of life.

The day-sign Muluc, representing water, is analogous to jade. The jade and the water are both blue-green, a hue that may be regarded as equivalent to the green of the World Tree itself. Green is the color of the center of the directional cross; in fact, the Mayan word for center, *yaxkin*, contains the word for green, *yax*. This day-sign is linked symbolically with the green-plumed quetzal bird, which is the most precious of birds, just as jade is the most precious of stones. The Aztecs called this day-sign Rain, for the fertilizing power of rain is part and parcel of the "greening" that is at the center of the universe.

Cauac is not simply the rain; it is the rainstorm. The collected clouds (Water or Muluc) brought forth by Wind (Ik) are now ready to pour out (Storm or Cauac) to produce the flower (Ancestors or Ahau). Storm's ruling deities are the rain serpents who also govern Serpent (Chicchan), and who appear in various forms throughout Mesoamerica and the Southwest. Chac, the Mayan rain god, has his lesser chacs, just as Tlaloc, the rain god of highland Mexico, has his tlaloques. These same rain spirits appear as the kachinas of Hopi and Pueblo myth. The kachinas may not be serpentine or reptilian in form but the connection with reptiles in general and snakes in particular is still strong. The famous Hopi Snake Dance is essentially a rain dance, for the rattlers are the emissaries who will carry messages to the rain kachinas, who will tell the spirits how greatly the Hopis have honored them in the dance. In return, the kachinas will send rain to the Hopi.

When the storm begins, lightning strikes. Serpent is associated with lightning as well as with rain, and this same link with the lightning occurs in Storm. This day-sign represents that moment, repeated thoughout the world but always powerful, when the clouds gather, lightning strikes, and rain bursts forth—a quintessentially creative moment. The Navajo Night Chant expresses it beautifully:

With the far darkness made of the dark cloud over your head, come to us soaring

With the far darkness made of the rain and mist over your head, come to us soaring

With the zigzag lightning flung out high over your head

With the rainbow hanging high over your head, come to us soaring

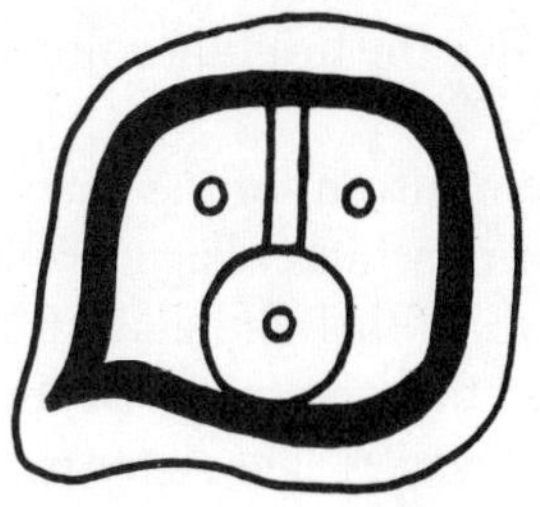

The Ancestors

AHAU

The day of the Ancestors.... The Ancestors already know.

—Momostenango

This, the final day-sign of the Calendar, was the most sacred of all to the Classic Maya. Their city-states were ruled by powerful kings called ahauob (literally "lords"), rulers who were sacred as well as secular. They were incarnations of the gods, conduits of energy and power who symbolized the life and health of the whole community. When the ahau mounted to the top of the pyramid to perform the rituals that sustained his kingdom, he stood symbolically at the apex of the World Mountain. He became the mountain, the tree at the center of the world, the energy or power that informed all things. Religious traditions the world over have used the symbol of the World Tree or World Mountain as a metaphor for the vital power that sleeps coiled at the base of the spinal column and which, when awakened, travels up the spine to the brain. The fasts and prayers that preceded Mayan ritual were no doubt intended to awaken this power within the king; by mounting the World Tree or World Mountain, he was making himself a shamanic channel for the entire quantum of energy vested in the kingdom. He was spiritually and psychically linked to the ancestors, also called ahauob—all the women and men of power and of spirit who had gone before, and whose collective energy constituted the sustaining spiritual reservoir of the people. In a sense, time itself was a lord, an ahau, for each katun, or twenty-year period, that marked vast changes in history and politics was called an ahau.

This is the day-sign of all things lordly and complete, including the world of the Ancestors that lies behind our present moment, linking us with times past in an endless revolution of days. In Guatemala, traditional Mayans who still keep the Calendar often decorate their cemeteries on these days. In so doing, they reinforce their connection with the spirits of their ancestors. (As we have seen, the Ancestors often take the shape of insects or butterflies—like the brightly colored butterflies that frequent Mayan cemeteries.)

This veneration of the Ancestors is reminiscent of the Days of the Dead, celebrated throughout Mexico, during which villagers lay a path of yellow marigolds leading from the graves of their fathers and grandfathers to their own homes. It is believed that the spirits of the dead will follow this trail of flowers to their old homes. The Aztec name for this day was Flower, and it is possible that, on one level, the "flower" referred to is the yellow marigold (yellow for the sun) which leads the Ancestors back to our own world. There is another shade of meaning as well—the Maya believed that the souls of the Ancestors blossomed again as flowers on the great World Tree.

In the metaphorical sense, we may well regard this final flower of the Calendar as a symbol of higher consciousness, for the flower has been used to represent enlightenment by many spiritual traditions, including Tantric Hinduism and both Chinese and Western alchemy. To link one's individual consciousness with that of all the Ancestors, to establish a continuum between personal consciousness and the collective unconscious, may well constitute the ancient Mesoamerican definition of enlightenment. Quetzalcoatl, the Feathered Serpent, taught that "flowers" were the most appropriate sacrifice to the gods. The Aztec poets who spoke out against human sacrifice believed that these flowers of Quetzalcoatl were a metaphor for poems and songs—the best offering to the gods was one that consisted of both physical flowers and one's deepest, most poetic prayers or spiritual chants. Indeed, the Aztecs regarded this as the day-sign of singers and poets.

Whether we consider this day the symbol of kings, of flowers, of poetry, or the Ancestors, it is clear that it represents that ecstatic process that connects us to the collective mind and to the cyclic flow of time itself.

6

Mayan Astrology

During the Classic Period, Mayan astrology was an enormously complex art. Not only did Mayan astronomers chart the motions of the planets with great accuracy but they perceived their entire creation myth as an event that was re-created eternally in the sky.

Major events such as coronations, battles, and ceremonial handball games were timed by planetary conjunctions as well as by the cycles of the Sacred Calendar—a conjunction of Venus and Jupiter, for instance, was considered a very powerful time to march forth to war. Because celestial events were believed to have significance for the destinies of people living on the earth, it is proper to refer to Mayan star-watching as astrology rather than astronomy.

The astrology of the Classic Period is a lost art. In those days, a child's horoscope would have included many factors—the day-sign, the significance of the fortnightly cycle, the movements of the planets, a consideration of the Mayan Zodiac (which was comprised of thirteen signs rather than twelve), and so on. But today...?

Contemporary Mayan astrology which, from a technical point of view, isn't really "astrology," since it has nothing to do with planets and constellations—is based on the day-signs of the Sacred Calendar.

Martin Prechtel says: "You can find diviners and astrologers on every street corner in Guatemala. They use all kinds of methods, some of which have nothing to do with the Calendar, like the guys who divine with two pieces of magnetized iron. Then there are the guys who have these little birds that peck at certain seeds—although the truth is, that's really a very old method that reaches all the way back to the origins of the Calendar itself. Then there are the astrologers, who do various mathematical calculations based on your basic day-sign and come up with something like a horoscope."

The method that follows is a common one among contemporary Mayan astrologers. It is called a Tree of Life reading. Though the day-signs of the four directions are based solidly on the traditional cosmic orientation of Quiché shamans, and I have used traditional meanings for the day-signs in my interpretation, I do not claim that what is written here would be identical—or even very similar—to the kind of reading you would receive from one of these "street-corner diviners" in Guatemala. Rather, I have tried to show the infinite possibilities, the versatility and universality inherent in the archetypes of the Sacred Calendar.

- Begin by using the Mayan Calendar Tables at the back of this book to find your basic day-sign. For example, let us assume that you wish to find the day-sign for an individual born August 18, 1961. Begin by finding the year 1961 in the Mayan Calendar Tables. Running your finger down the list of dates, you will note that August 9 was 1 Flint, while August 22 was 1 Monkey.
- Next, consult the Calendar Board diagram, found in various places throughout this book and reproduced in Figure 10 on the next page. Locate 1 Flint and count forward: August 9 is 1 Flint, August 10 is 2 Storm, and so on until you reach August 18, which will be 10 Deer. If you were born in late February or early March of an even-numbered year, be alert for leap year days! They can throw off your count. (Leap years are marked with an asterisk in the Mayan Calendar Tables at the back of the book.)

  10 Deer is the day-sign for any individual born on August 18, 1961. This is the single most important factor in the Mayan Tree of Life reading, for the day that one is born imparts its own energy and power—or, in Native terms, its nagual—to all those born under its influence.

  The day-signs of the Sacred Calendar are named after animals and forces of nature. As we have noted (Chapter 3), a person born on the day Crocodile will, in some sense, have the crocodile as a nagual. A person born on Storm will have a force of

CROCODILE	1	8	2	9	3	10	4	11	5	12	6	13	7
WIND	2	9	3	10	4	11	5	12	6	3	7	1	8
NIGHT	3	10	4	11	5	12	6	13	7	1	8	2	9
LIZARD	4	11	5	12	6	13	7	1	8	2	9	3	10
SERPENT	5	12	6	13	7	1	8	2	9	3	10	4	11
DEATH	6	13	7	1	8	2	9	3	10	4	11	5	12
DEER	7	1	8	2	9	3	10	4	11	5	12	6	13
RABBIT	8	2	9	3	10	4	11	5	12	6	13	7	1
WATER	9	3	10	4	11	5	12	6	13	7	1	8	2
DOG	10	4	11	5	12	6	13	7	1	8	2	9	3
MONKEY	11	5	12	6	13	7	1	8	2	9	3	10	4
ROAD	12	6	13	7	1	8	2	9	3	10	4	11	5
CORN	13	7	1	8	2	9	3	10	4	11	5	12	6
JAGUAR	1	8	2	9	3	10	4	11	5	12	6	13	7
EAGLE	2	9	3	10	4	11	5	12	6	13	7	1	8
VULTURE	3	10	4	11	5	12	6	13	7	1	8	2	9
INCENSE	4	11	5	12	6	13	7	1	8	2	9	3	10
FLINT	5	12	6	13	7	1	8	2	9	3	10	4	11
STORM	6	13	7	1	8	2	9	3	10	4	11	5	12
ANCESTORS	7	1	8	2	9	3	10	4	11	5	12	6	13

FIGURE 10 ***Calendar Board***

nature—a cloudburst or lightning bolt—as his or her totem. The tzolkin day that we are born determines the indwelling spirit that acts as our guardian. The tzolkin day of our birth gives us its "face."

Now that you have discovered the basic day-sign ruling your destiny, you will want to find the other four day-signs that make up your Mayan Tree of Life. A Tree of Life reading is based on the same fundamental principles we have already encountered in studying the shamanic world view of the Maya.

Your basic day-sign is the center point of a cross, medicine wheel, or Tree of Life that includes five signs, one for each of the four directions and one for the center. The day-sign of your birth is, of course, the center. A simple mental exercise will illustrate this concept.

Exercise: The Tree of Life

1. In Chapter 3, we learned to orient ourselves to the four directions. Now, stand and once again face East, both of your arms extended from your sides as in a cross. Imagine that your future lies before you in the East, along with your children, all your descendants, and all your lives to come. Behind you, in the West, are your ancestors and your own past existences. To your right, in the South, lie all your male qualities, as well as the men who cross your life's path. On your left, in the North, lie your female qualities, including the women you encounter in life.
2. Now, imagine that your heart center, the very core of your inner World Tree, is also occupied by one of the day-signs, such as 10 Deer in the above example.
3. Behind you (West) is another day-sign, symbolic of your past.
4. Ahead of you (East) lies a day-sign that is symbolic of your children and your future.
5. On your right (South) is the Power of the Right Hand, a day-sign symbolic of the masculine or yang energies of your psyche.
6. On your left (North) is one more day-sign, the Power of the Left Hand, representing your feminine or yin energies.

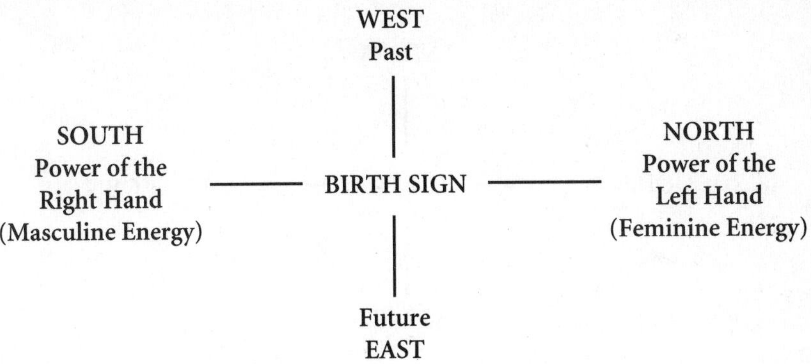

FIGURE 11 ***Diagram of the Mayan Tree of Life***

The various branches of the Tree of Life are illustrated in Figure 11. Now, we must discover which particular day-signs make up a personal Tree of Life.

The four directional day-signs that accompany you and your basic birth-sign through life are found by a magical-mathematical formula that makes use of the numbers 7 and 9. Let's continue with our example, that of an individual born on 10 Deer.

- Use the Calendar Board diagram to count backwards nine days from the day-sign, 10 Deer, until you reach 2 Storm, which is your Past Sign.
- Count forward nine days from 10 Deer. This brings you to 5 Eagle, which is your Future Sign.
- Now, count backwards seven days from 10 Deer. This will bring you to 4 Crocodile. This is the Power of the Right Hand, symbolic of your masculine or yang energies.
- Count forwards seven days from 10 Deer to 3 Corn, the Power of the Left Hand, symbolic of feminine or yin energies. You now have a complete Personal Tree of Life (see Figure 12).
- A few guidelines about how to interpret a Mayan Tree of Life reading can now be established. Basic descriptions for each day-sign will be provided in this chapter, but we can learn to read a Tree of Life in more detail by taking the numbers into account.

With a little bit of mathematical calculation you can see that, in terms of day-signs, the basic cross or Tree of Life for a person born on any Deer day will always be made up of the same elements: Crocodile

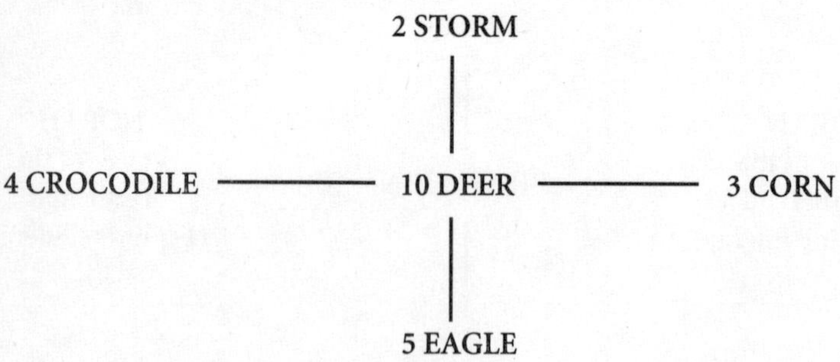

FIGURE 12 ***A Personal Tree of Life—for an individual born on 10 Deer***

will always be on the right, Corn on the left, and so on. We know from our study of symbolic, mythic, and divinatory meanings for Deer that individuals born on this day are bound to be powerful characters, whether in the magical sense or in more worldly terms. We may also suspect that such a person might be more positive, more reliable and less likely to abuse power by relying on "feminine" intuition rather than on "masculine" force. Why? Because Corn is a much less tricky energy to work with than that of the Crocodile, which tends to go overboard if left unchecked. By the same token, such an individual may often encounter women who are strong, like a "staff of life," and men who are creative, phantasmagorical, but perhaps a bit treacherous or even crazy. We can also see that Deer people, as well as being strongly empowered in the present, are moving towards an equally powerful destiny, as represented by the soaring Eagle (which also symbolizes their children). Storm, their Past Sign, is said to represent difficult, perhaps overpowering family karma. So if a Deer person is failing to manifest his potential, we might suspect that the pull of the karmic past is too strong. How do we know for sure?

The numbers give variation and depth to a reading, providing a total of 260 possible combinations. For a person born on 10 Deer, the Future Sign (5 Eagle) holds a higher number than the Past Sign (2 Storm). The power of the future appears stronger than that of the past. For an individual born on 8 Deer, the Past Sign would be 13 Storm, the Future Sign 1 Corn. In such a case, we might very well suspect that the past calls more loudly than the future. In the same way, we may check the balance of masculine and feminine energies.

Mayan Tree of Life readings may not have quite as much complexity as a Western style horoscope, with its ten planets, twelve signs, and twelve houses, but it is a reading that is meant to be used. In a shamanic universe, nothing is ever static or fixed. Everything is a tool.

For instance, if you were born on the day of the Dog, you might be a bit concerned about your fate. Dog itself represents a sensual energy so powerful as to be frequently ungovernable, as does Lizard, your Power of the Right Hand. Flint, your Future Sign, is likewise a difficult sign to use properly, for it takes a lot of wisdom to transform Flint from a sign of anger and dispute into a sign of healing—especially when the fierce sign Wind, governing your karmic past, indicates that you have an inheritance of rage at the soul level. Anyone born on Dog might wish to concentrate on building up his or her female energies that lie on the left hand—Vulture is a sign of easy-going tolerance, a state of mind that ensures that many of your blunders will be forgiven by the universe around you.

Remember, Mayan Astrology is shamanic practice. It is meant to be used, not just blindly accepted.

The Crocodile

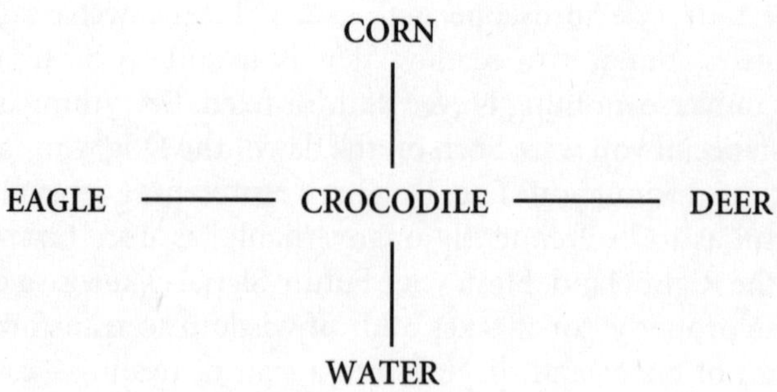

At the beginning of any phase of consciousness, the ego or sense of individuality is still weak. Not yet fully separated from the deep waters of the collective mind, this emerging ego or self-consciousness is easily influenced by the prevailing spirit of the times. Because the Crocodile represents that primordial energy that sleeps at the base of all things, those who were born under Crocodile's power may find that their feeling for dreams, magic, and mystery is a great deal stronger than their sense of self or individuality—Orson Welles (4 Crocodile), though best known for his prodigious achievements in film, also had the reputation of being clairvoyant, and Walt Disney's (5 Crocodile) entire career was based on vision and dreams, as was that of the surrealistic Italian director Federico Fellini (8 Crocodile).

The Maya say that Crocodiles are "easily dominated by the Year Lord"—which means that they are easily influenced by the spirit of the times, in the form of every type of stimulus or media imagery around them. Sometimes this domination by the time spirit may be beneficial, for Crocodiles may become positive carriers for all that is best in the time spirit—as with Welles and Disney. This is why *The Book of Chilam Balam of Kaua* calls them "the maize of the bread," the substance of the matter. Crocodiles can easily reflect everything that is valuable in the spirit of the society in which they live. This is especially true when they draw on their strong, positive family or ancestral/cultural roots, represented by Corn, their Past Sign. The same positive spirit will manifest itself when they call upon Eagle, their Right Hand Power, in order to act with strength and purpose in the outside world and increase their own sense of prosperity and authority. They can also draw upon the Deer, an equally intense but somewhat more mystical and mysterious (let's say intuitive) source of energy that constitutes their Left Hand Power (Welles had an especially strong Eagle and Deer).

While the primal Crocodile can reflect what is best in society, it can also reflect what is worst. Fascinated by the magic play of images arising from the collective mind (movies, TV, and advertising in our own culture), they may easily be drawn into a psychic dreamworld. They are all too likely to get lost and drown in the depths—their Future Sign is Water, a notoriously difficult sign that points out the dangers of such a muddy, psychic, emotional immersion. Billionaire Howard Hughes (3 Crocodile) spent his last years immersed in such a dark psychic netherworld, endlessly watching *Ice Station Zebra* and brooding about germs.

In many cases, only a sense of dedication towards the spiritual side of life will keep the Crocodile from slipping back into the primordial depths; if they make proper use of the strong positive forces which lie to their right and left and that are represented by the Eagle and the Deer, Crocodiles can learn to reflect the beauty and splendor that shine in that Otherworldy lake where the primal Crocodile swims. In doing so, they can reach the most positive destiny implied by the day-sign Water—that of the poet and mystic who reflects the pure and untroubled surface of the watery cosmic depths.

Notable Crocodile Natives:

Mircea Eliade (1)
Howard Hughes (3)
Orson Welles (4)
Walt Disney (5)
Federico Fellini, Woody Allen (8)

The Wind

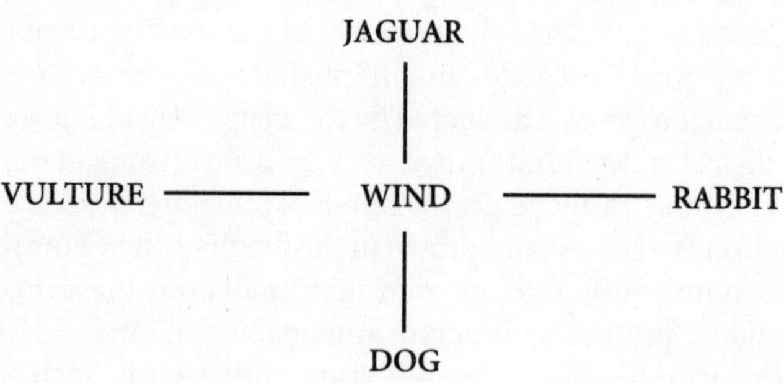

The Wind is symbolic of the vital spirit that gives life to and animates us all, but too much vital spirit may lead to excessive arrogance or pride. This takes place when an individual sees oneself—which, in this case, simply means one's ego—as the source of all the power and inspiration that flows through oneself in such great abundance. Perceiving all power and vitality as vested in ego, misuse of that creativity and power is all too likely. This is why the Daykeepers associate this birth-sign with dictators and military despots of the standard Latin American variety.

Those born on the day of the Wind must always recognize that the "divine breath" or vital spirit that fills them with so much energy is not their individual ego. Rather, it is their connection to the source of all life. If they can remember this fact, they can become capable of an almost infinite power to make things happen in the world, for they have an abundance of energy at their disposal. They can use the deep, underground wisdom of the Jaguar, their Past Sign, to stay awake and aware of their debt to the spiritual world. To accomplish all of this, they will have to learn to control their anger more than anything else. Wind people tend to blow like human hurricanes; they can really bring down the house. Think of Elizabeth Taylor's (9 Wind) notorious fits of temper, or Billy Graham's (11 Wind) sermons.

Traditional Daykeepers often tell parents to punish their angry Wind children not with blows, but with applications of the *xibirib* plant, which is so gentle that its leaves fold up and withdraw whenever anything brushes against them; thus the soft nature of the plant becomes part of the wild, raging Wind individual.

Fortunately, the Right Hand and Left Hand Powers of Wind natives are both quiet, relatively gentle signs. Vulture is good-natured (though sometimes lazy), while Rabbit is sensual and in love with the good things of this world. Wind people can draw upon both these powers in order to help themselves become more appreciative of all that is quiet, loving, and kind.

Their Future Sign is the Dog, and in this symbol we can see the dual possibilities that lie ahead of Wind natives. If they follow their innate tendency to be one of life's warriors, using all their energy and power to seek what makes the "little you" of the ego happy (at least for the moment), then they may well wind up embodying the worst qualities of the day-sign Dog—which is pretty bad indeed, indicative of a life of sensual dissipation and quarreling. But Dog, much like Vulture and Rabbit, is also a sign that can learn to take wise and tranquil joy in the ordinary beauties and rewards of daily life, seeing the inner spiritual light that shines through all our ordinary pursuits. If Wind people can learn to control their inner hurricane, they too can come to blow like a gentle breeze on a warm summer's day in the glory of a life well lived.

Notable Wind Natives:

Michael Jackson (4)
Elizabeth Taylor, Hillary Clinton (9)
Billy Graham (11)

The Night

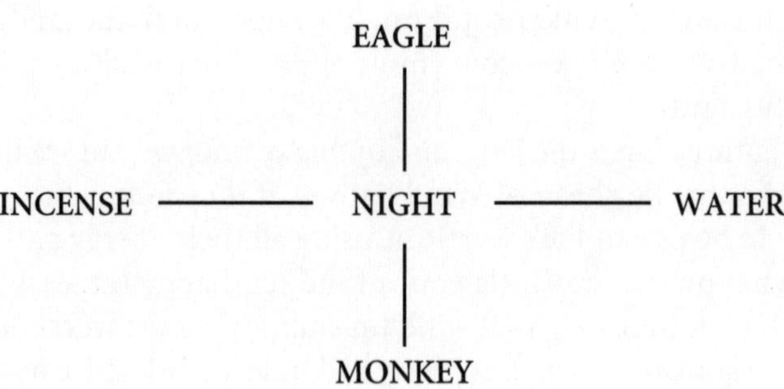

The Mayans say that there is a feminine softness about the people of the Night, whether they be male or female. Those who were born on this day have the wisdom of both yin and yang all around them. They speak and write well, and have a shimmering verbal talent—as we might well expect with Incense, sign of the thinker, as their Right Hand Power, and Water, a dreamy and poetic sign, as their Left Hand Power. Jack Kerouac, the literary firebrand of the Beat Generation, was born on 10 Night, and the mythologist Joseph Campbell, whose eloquence was as legendary as his knowledge, was born on 2 Night.

Campbell's career illustrates the fact that the depths that lie beneath the typical Night person's glittering speech and soft face are considerable—these natives have one foot in the Otherworld, and it shows. Sometimes this may manifest as a negative quality; Night people can spin webs of deceitful fantasy as easily as they can speak words of wisdom and truth. Their words can cut and wound as easily as they can inspire and heal. Sometimes they may be gloomy or tearful, and some truly unhappy Night people become addicted to gambling or sink to thievery, for their Incense minds and their Monkey trickery give them the diabolical cleverness of the professional thief. They sometimes combine spiritual wisdom with animal sensuality as intensely as any other sign. Behind them lies the Eagle, which cries out powerfully for whatever it wants—whether that be material wealth or spiritual wisdom. Night people will certainly use their Otherworldly charm, as well as the clever mind typical of their Right Hand Power (Incense) and the even more clever spirit of their Future Sign (Monkey) to seek what they desire.

What do they desire? The choice is theirs, and someday they will be tested in this regard, just as the Hero Twins were tested when they passed through the Night phase of human experience and spent time in the cold, treacherous houses of the Underworld. If it is their genuine destiny to work primarily in what we call the "real world," then good fortune is usually theirs, for the Maya say that Night people are likely to become wealthy. After all, they have a mysterious connection with the old earth god called Pacal Votan, whose precious jade lies hidden beneath the earth.

Night is one of the signs that endows its natives with "body lightning." According to the Quiché Maya, they make excellent shamans and diviners, as we might expect from those whose spiritual destiny it is to travel the nether regions in search of wisdom. Campbell, in fact, has acquired the reputation of a contemporary wise man in Western civilization. Specifically, Night people are said to be talented with the kind of spiritual artistry that relies on words—singing the old songs of marriage and love, or creating elegant prayers to the old spirits—Jack Kerouac brought an incantatory, almost shamanic quality to his writing. If Night people wish to seek for knowledge—as opposed to mere worldly substance—they will be able to develop some very powerful and unusual psychic abilities. They are also likely to develop a number of artistic talents. Not only do they have Incense and Water to help them on the right and left, but they are moving towards a destiny represented by Monkey, the master craftsman and artist *par excellence.*

NOTABLE NIGHTS:

Joseph Campbell (2)
Jack Kerouac (10)
Kevin Costner (11)

The Lizard

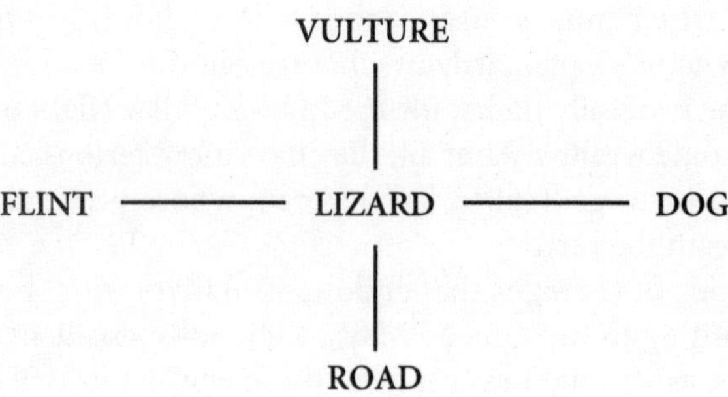

The *Chilam Balam of Kaua* asserts that those born under the day-sign Lizard will be both rich and wise, "masters of all the arts." It asserts that "the precious singing birds are your birds"—an apt prophecy for those born on the day that, above all others, is associated with fertility and growth. Indeed, all these benefits can be theirs if they keep their attention always on their true path, looking ahead to their ultimate goal, which is represented by the day-sign Road. After all, the Road of Life is the path, and some Lizards, like Martin Luther King, Jr. (2 Lizard) and Henry Kissinger (9 Lizard), have shown a suitably strong sense of destiny in all their worldly works.

At their best, Lizards are earthy individuals blessed with good health, for all these things are part of the Lizard's native abundance. A typical Lizard is also likely to be overwhelmingly sexual—among the Classic Maya, Lizard was associated with the South, and today's patroness of the South is Mary Magdalene! In the Aztec system, Lizard ruled the pelvic region of the human body, seat of sexual power. Lizards often have poor control over their passions—especially with the lazy and sensual Vulture as their Past Sign and the sexy Dog as their Left Hand Power. The sensual appetites of rock star Jim Morrison (4 Lizard) were legendary, and even King, who was obviously a very highly developed Lizard, had a reputation as a "womanizer."

Like all other day-signs, Lizard has its strengths—though these are more often strengths of this earth rather than of the world beyond. Lizard people make good workers, especially if they work outdoors in nature. Let them take up a hammer and some nails, tend their gardens, seek the healthful light of nature and avoid the darkly lit recesses of nightclubs and bars. Lizard is potentially a sign of good health, which is a blessing indeed. These natives need light, nature, and fresh air to make them truly healthy and prosperous.

Their weaknesses are as earthy as their strengths; in addition to their sensuality, they may also be prone to incur debts because they have as little control over their spending as they do over their sexual passions. The Vulture in their past and the Dog to their left both lean as strongly toward financial as sensual indulgences. Some Lizard people will go to the ultimate limits of sensual gluttony, like Morrison (who called himself "the Lizard King").

Those born on this day may always be struggling to avoid promiscuous, even adulterous, behavior. Not only is such behavior inappropriate, it can also activate the dangerous Flint power on their right hand and provoke genuine strife. If they channel their vital energies into some kind of work, they will live up to the promise of the *Chilam Balam*—they will master their chosen art, grow rich and prosperous, and "the precious singing birds" will indeed be their birds. If they give in to their love of sensual pleasure, they will be constantly in debt—as well as in trouble.

Notable Lizard Natives:

Martin Luther King, Jr. (2)
Queen Elizabeth II (3)
Jim Morrison (4)
Bill Cosby (8)
Henry Kissinger (9)
Israel Regardie (11)

The Serpent

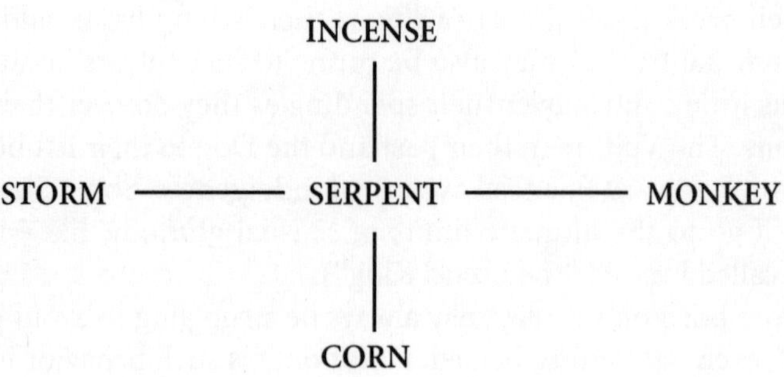

The Quiché Maya believe that Serpent people are extremely powerful and especially endowed with coyopa or body lightning. Serpent is one of the days that a Calendar shaman is likely to be born; in fact, the natives of this sign often become "spiritualists" or mediums, the most powerful and deeply feared specialists among the practitioners of the Sacred Calendar.

This underscores the ambivalence of the serpent power and the natives of the day-sign Serpent. Serpents possess an energy that is both highly magical and intensely sexual—Clint Eastwood (9 Serpent) and Marilyn Monroe (5 Serpent) both constitute good examples. Natives of this day-sign see beneath the surface of things, into the dark heart of reality; they have a connection with what many cultures have aptly termed "the wisdom of the serpent." The cognitive power and deep thinking of Incense (their Past Sign) and the cleverness of Monkey (their Left Hand Power) have blossomed into a subtle, knowing wisdom. This wisdom has an amoral quality to it; by itself it is neither good nor evil. It is a wisdom beyond opposites, wherein everything is reduced to the common ground of its being.

Without spiritual development, the serpent wisdom may twist and turn towards its dark and sinister side; Hindu teachers continually reiterate the fact that the kundalini can have both destructive and creative aspects. With the brooding day-sign called Storm as their Right Hand Power, the rage of Serpent natives is a terrible thing to see, and their despair knows no limits. No wonder, then, that Serpents are both respected for their wisdom and feared for their innate magic. The vital power within is intimately connected with sexuality, and Serpents may easily become slaves to their passions, motivated solely by their desires. In the case of Marilyn Monroe, the projection of the serpent power was so intense that she was overwhelmed by it. From a magical point of view, it helped to bring about her death. Another danger inherent in this day-sign is that, as with the mediums who are so deeply feared by the Maya, Serpents may use their insight and acumen for self-aggrandizement rather than inner development.

The great necessity for all those born under this day-sign is to obtain control of their inner powers. All yogic and magical disciplines come naturally to them and should be pursued, so that the "body lightning" may be brought under conscious control. Many of them will achieve this control—if not through actual spiritual practice, then at least through learning to live a balanced, compassionate life. After all, their Future Sign, the manifestation towards which they are moving, is Corn, and this is one of the most positive and fulfilling day-signs of all. Corn is the staff of life, and the day-sign Corn implies a concern for one's family and community. This points the way for the subtle Serpent—even if he is a mechanic rather than a magician. Compassion for others is the necessary key that unlocks a gentler, more sound existence for these knowers of the deep wisdom.

Notable Serpent Natives:

Marilyn Monroe (5)
Clint Eastwood (9)
Nancy Kerrigan (11)

Death

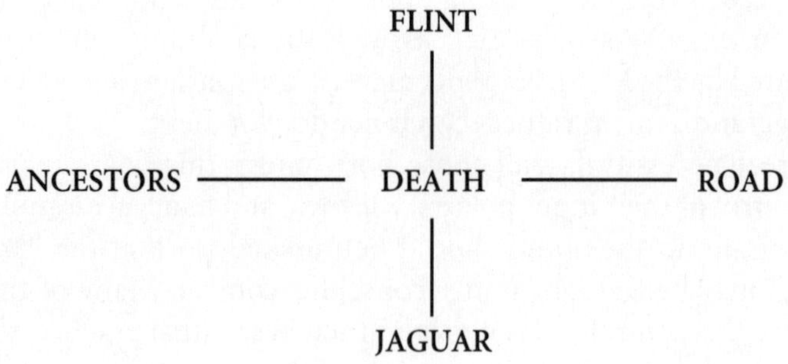

FLINT

ANCESTORS — DEATH — ROAD

JAGUAR

Those born on this "day of death" are fortunate indeed, for this is one of the luckiest birthdays in the entire Calendar. These natives share many traits with those born under Night which, like Death, is associated with the Underworld. To the Maya, the Underworld is Santo Mundo, the Holy Earth and underground source from which all power and growth emerge. It is not a place of terror and torment, like the Christian Hell. Those born under the day-sign Death may well receive the blessings of Santo Mundo. In the Tarot, the card called Death is sometimes more appropriately called Transformation. This sign needs to be understood in similar fashion. It is in the realm of the death gods that the hero twins of the Maya undergo their cosmic transformation and take their place among the stars—they have been metamorphosed from men into gods. The potential for such transformation is implicit within all human beings—in fact, spiritual transformation forms the basis of Mesoamerican mythology and prophecy. For those who were born on the day of Death, transformations will be smooth and lasting.

Death natives are said to have a certain softness or feminine streak about them whether they be male or female, which can be a very advantageous thing—Beatle Paul McCartney's (3 Death) boyish looks certainly didn't hurt his rise to stardom. There is a magnetic quality in their gentleness that draws prosperity—after all, Santo Mundo is the source of all wealth, and it is said that Death natives are born to get rich. Like natives of Night, those who were born on the day of Death often have a great deal of verbal skill—they may well be expert word-spinners, writers, and communicators. They are a little less likely than

Night people to slip into the darker waters of the Underworld—a quick look at our list of Death natives reveals a number of the entertainment industry's most endurable and prosperous survivors, including McCartney, Jane Fonda (1 Death) and Candice Bergen (6 Death). Though quarrelsome Flint lies behind all Death natives as their Past Sign, this echo from the karmic past seldom controls their lives. As their Left Hand Power, the Road endows them with an intuitive understanding of the rightness of things. Ahead of them, as their Future Sign, lies the wise and wealthy Jaguar, incarnation of Santo Mundo himself. No wonder wealth often lies in their future!

There is an uncanny feeling about natives of this day-sign. After all, their true home is in the pool of souls with the Ancestors lingering nearby as their Right Hand Power. Thus their male soul favors dreams rather than logic. Swedish filmmaker Ingmar Bergman (12 Death), for example, has proven to be one of the great modern explorers of the dreams and darker visions that make up our collective pool of souls. Death people often have psychic gifts, including a potent quantity of the "body lightning," and according to the Quiché, Death natives traditionally make good shamans. As Daykeepers in tradtional Guatemalan society, they are likely to specialize as "marriage spokesmen." Turning their verbal skills toward matchmaking, they are as romantic as they are clever and may be inveterate matchmakers, always involving themselves in the romantic lives of their friends.

NOTABLE DEATH NATIVES:

George Bush, Jane Fonda (1)
Paul McCartney (3)
Candice Bergen (6)
Ingmar Bergman (12)

The Deer

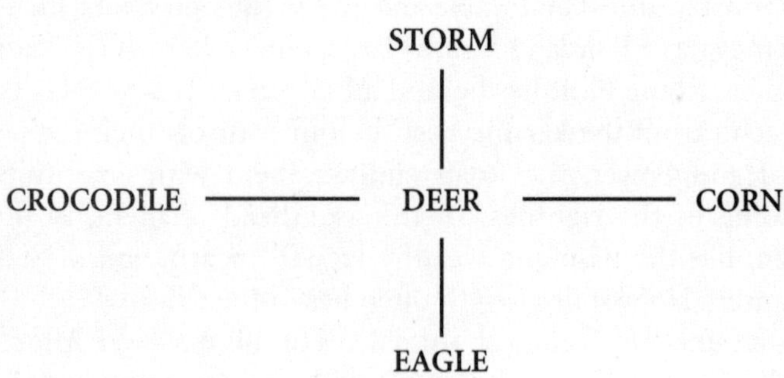

Those born on the day of the Deer have a special ability to embody and express a sense of the holiness of life. They may, however, express themselves with so much power that they come on like a locomotive.

It should be remembered that the Deer is one of the four Lords of the Year. Two of these Year Lords, Incense and the Road, are considered gentle, whereas the Wind and the Deer are intrinsically powerful and intense. Most Deer natives express their power quite forcefully and directly and bear absolutely no resemblance to the stereotype of the timid, gentle deer. Rather, they are like the powerful stag who is the "lord of the forest," and tend to dominate most situations. Their power is both spiritual and worldly (this is a day of the earth gods). In Guatemala, a Deer native may well become a powerful shaman or civic leader, the latter role equally applicable in our own society. One of the planet's current spiritual leaders, Pope John Paul II, is a Deer (10 Deer), and though many East European Catholics regard him as a heroic figure (a typical role for Deer to play), there are many others, especially women, who find the Pope more than a little domineering—a trait equally typical of the Deer.

For Deer natives, the primary issue in life is most likely to be use of power. With Storm as their Past Sign, many Deer people have had a difficult childhood or troubled family. If the past overshadows them and clouds their spirit, they may find their wild and ungovernable Right Hand Power, the Crocodile, acquiring too much influence in their lives and urging them to seek power and dominate others purely for the sake of power. Their future is represented by the Eagle, the sign of wisdom and success, and if they lean towards their Left Hand

Power, the auspicious day-sign of the Corn, they will be able to grow in wisdom as well as in power.

How does one lean towards the day-sign called Corn? The Corn represents the benevolent power of authority, whether in one's family or in one's community. According to Mayan thinking (indeed, all tribal thinking), authority is benevolent when it is dedicated to the common good. It is important for Deer natives to always question their goals. Are they truly using their tremendous inner resources for the good of others, or do they have their own hidden, selfish agendas?

Deer people are called to spiritual leadership as often as to more worldly pursuits. In some Guatemalan communities, 8 Deer is the most sacred day of all, the day shamans are initiated. One of contemporary Western society's best-known "shamans" is a native of this day-sign—Carlos Castaneda was born on 3 Deer. In divination, the day-sign Deer may often indicate the involvement of a shaman or, in our own culture, some other exceptionally powerful individual. It is one of the day-signs believed to be specially endowed with "body lightning." When Deer people suspect that they have unusual psychic talents and abilities, they're usually right—but these abilities, like all facets of the Deer's power, must be used with care.

NOTABLE DEER NATIVES:

Carlos Castaneda (3)
Prince Charles (4)
Allen Ginsberg (7)
Pope John Paul II (10)

The Rabbit

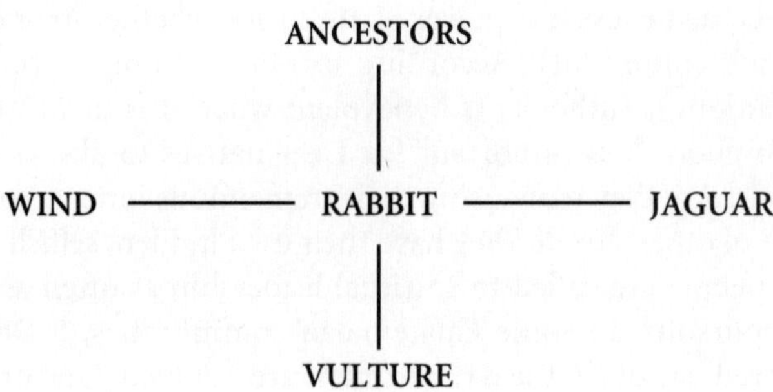

Those who were born on a Rabbit day are likely to have a fortunate destiny, for Rabbit is considered a very positive birth-sign. The Native peoples of Mesoamerica, like the Chinese, "saw" a rabbit (rather than a man) in the moon. Indeed, the Chinese and Mesoamerican moon rabbits would seem to be one and the same critter, for those born in the Chinese year of the Rabbit share many similarities with those born on the Mayan day of the Rabbit, notably a feeling of ease and comfort with the "real" world. Rabbit people can easily become successful, and among the Quiché Maya Rabbit natives are known for their gifts as farmers; they usually have "green thumbs." To the Maya, Rabbit is pre-eminently the sign of the harvest. This talent for creating abundance should not surprise us, since Rabbit also signifies the "greening" or "ripening" of the earth. For urban Westerners, that green thumb may translate into a talent for making money—especially since the Jaguar, a very potent "money" sign, is their Left Hand Power. Jaguar is a slippery, magical, seductive sign, and the Left Hand Power works through intuition and the subconscious. This day-sign's talent for making money and acquiring the "good things" of life is an inborn art rather than a carefully acquired skill.

Rabbit natives are considered to have a fair quantity of "body lightning" since the day-sign of the Ancestors, symbolic of spiritual communication, is the Past Sign for all Rabbit natives. Even for those Rabbit natives who are not particularly psychic, the influence of the Ancestors will still make itself known in terms of strong family ties. Their links with their family, culture, or heritage are strong—and, if the number associated with the day-sign Ancestors is too high, they may be overpowering. Fortunately, Rabbit people have the Wind as their Right Hand Power, which allows them to overcome the past by drawing on a strong sense of individuality.

If Rabbit is productive, it is also sensual. This runaway sensuality can lead Rabbit people into drug and alcohol abuse. Among the Aztecs, the day 2 Rabbit was especially notorious for alcoholism, so much so that a person's addiction was referred to idiomatically as his "rabbit"—much as we would refer to a "monkey on his back." Elvis Presley (2 Rabbit) and Jimi Hendrix (9 Rabbit), though embodying typical Rabbit generosity, were both notorious for their substance abuse problems. All Rabbit people, even those who have never experienced such difficulties in their own lives, must channel their energies into productive work. Boredom, frustration, or simply too little to do may easily lead them into overindulgence. Their Future Sign, Vulture, like Rabbit itself, is very self-indulgent and fond of all pleasure. This day-sign increases their desire to acquire and enjoy beautiful things (think of Elvis' Cadillacs!), and as the sign of their future, it virtually ensures that they will achieve what they desire. Rabbit natives must beware of "too much of a good thing," for laziness and excess can cause all their abundance to slip down the drain.

One of the meanings of Vulture is "pardon" or "forgiveness." Thanks to Rabbit's essential good nature and jovial temperament, their lapses into self-indulgence will most often be forgiven, and pardon from the gods, the ancestral spirits, or the depths of their own souls lies at the end of their road.

Notable Rabbit Natives:

Elvis Presley (2)
Jimi Hendrix (9)
Toni Morrison (12)
David Carradine (13)

Water

CROCODILE

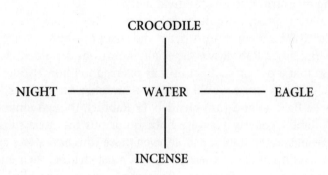

NIGHT —— WATER —— EAGLE

INCENSE

Mayan Daykeepers regard this as a very difficult birth-sign. Those who were born on a Water day may well have a heavy debt to pay to the Sacred Earth or Santo Mundo—in the popular metaphysics of our own time and place, we would say that they come into the world carrying "heavy karma."

Some, but by no means all, Water natives have health issues at stake. The Maya believe that many of these individuals are prone to chronic illnesses of all kinds, and it is said that they require the constant assistance of Native healers and Daykeepers in order to help them live a normal life. Oprah Winfrey (8 Water), who has waged a life-long struggle with her weight, illustrates the fact that Water people, far from being doomed by fate, can overcome their difficulties in tremendously successful fashion.

Health issues are only one aspect of this day-sign, just like sexuality is only one aspect of the zodiacal sign Scorpio. Water natives Mick Jagger (3 Water) and John Lennon (10 Water) were by no means sickly—though Lennon was certainly subject to a great deal of very heavy karma. Health need not be the only kind of karmic headache imposed on Water natives—President Clinton (5 Water) was afflicted with a firestorm of bad press from the moment he entered the White House.

On a deeper level, Water natives have Crocodile as their Past Sign, representing a phase in the cycle of life wherein consciousness is still emerging from the primal energy of the unconscious, the netherworld of Santo Mundo. Thus, consciousness is fragile, still subject to the regressive pull from the unconscious. The "waters" in which Water people drown are often the waters of their own past.

Consciousness emerging from the primeval Underworld is fragile and precious. The Mayan glyph for this day-sign may have represented either a drop of water or a circle of jade, both of which were held to be supremely precious. The day-sign Water carries with it the sense of wonder that all newborn entities feel in the presence of a magical, still unknown world. These Water people may sometimes be tenuous and tentative, but they are capable of tremendous artistic vision. A look at our list of Water natives reveals an unexpectedly strong showing for this day-sign among rock stars—Jagger, Lennon, and Madonna (4 Water) are all Water natives.

The day-signs that support Water are strong and favorable. Night as their Right Hand Power endows them with the clever, cunning wisdom of the Otherworld, allowing them to navigate the deep waters of the soul with superb intuition. However, it is usually the Left Hand Power that symbolizes one's intuitive gifts. Here they have Eagle, the sign that "cries out" for everything it wants—and often gets it.

Though the road laid out for Water people may be difficult and stormy at times, it has a good end in sight, for their Future Sign is Incense, the symbol of the thinker. If they use their intuition to steer through the dark places, they will sharpen their intellect and powers of discrimination. Their minds will become vital, powerful instruments for the realization of their goals.

NOTABLE WATER NATIVES:

Mick Jagger (3)
Madonna (4)
President Bill Clinton (5)
Oprah Winfrey (8)
John Lennon (10)

The Dog

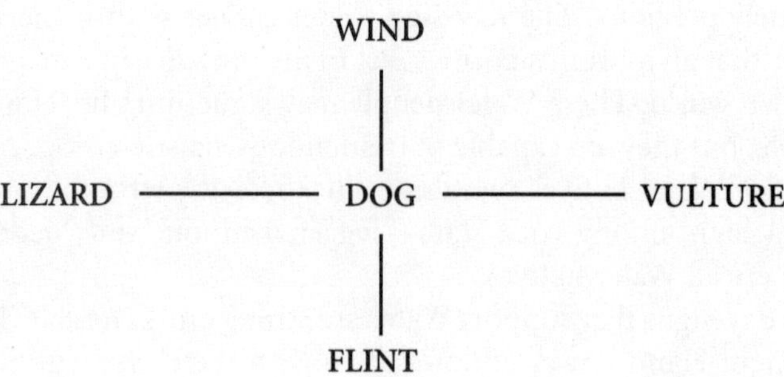

Of all the day-signs, Dog has perhaps the most questionable reputation. Its natives are said to be extremely sexual in nature; they are sometimes even called "fornicators and adulterers."

Observe for a short time the behavior of dogs to see why these individuals are believed to be so libidinous. Their totem, the dog, is a creature whose sensual instincts overflow in every direction without inhibition. According to tradition, the same is true with people born under this day-sign. Of course, there are any number of day-signs that have a similar love for such worldly pleasures, but only Dog has the distinction of owning pleasure-loving Lizard as its Right Hand Power and lazy, sensual Vulture as its Left Hand Power. Dog's lust for love, life, and sensory delight hems it in on all sides.

Sensuality also means a love for, and consequently a friendship with, the world of the senses. The *Book of Chilam Balam of Kaua* refers to a native of this day-sign as "the adorned one, of the easy life." Dog people are frequently able to surround themselves with the pleasures they crave so much—country singer Willie Nelson's (8 Dog) life was so easy and adorned that it attracted the unwanted interest of the IRS!

Dog's unbridled love of luxury is, at worst, motivated by a selfish hunger to consume everything in sight. Dog natives have the blustery Wind as their Past Sign, and the Wind's hurricane of ego combined with Dog's dreams of pleasure can lead to some fairly greedy scenarios. It can also lead Dog into the midst of conflict, as indicated by the day Flint, which is the Future Sign for these natives.

A cursory look at the day-signs that make up Dog's personal Tree of Life might lead some of these natives to doubt whether there's any hope at all. Are they condemned to reel from one sensual thrill to the next, always seeking more? (Some Dogs, of course, will think this is a great way to live!) Many Dog natives doubt themselves almost constantly, but doubt—one of the negative meanings of this day-sign when it appears in a divination—is the opposite of certainty or faith. This duality of doubt and faith reveals the most positive aspect of the day-sign Dog.

In Mayan and Aztec myth, the dog was the creature who, carrying a torch to light the way, guided souls through the Underworld. The dog is a universal symbol of unquestioned loyalty, and in this particular instance, of unquestioned faith. Whenever we journey through the darkness of our private underworld, we take a path upon which logic and intellect are of no help. Only an unquestioning faith can light our way through the interior darkness so, like the sun, we may emerge upon some other dawn. Dog natives have this quality of faith. It is their greatest asset.

Clearly, these people live close to their instincts. The unconscious force that endows them with their notorious sensuality is the same power that gives them that most precious of all human qualities: the faith to prevail.

Notable Dog Natives:

Robert Bly (2)
Willie Nelson (8)

The Monkey

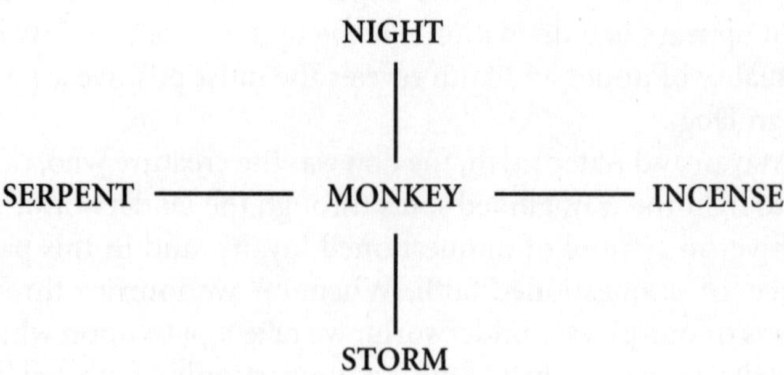

This is one of the most fortunate day-signs. Those born under Monkey are believed to be lucky in all things: marriage, children, business, and money. Ronald Reagan (1 Monkey), with his day-sign's typically lackadaisical luck, grinned and quipped his way from Hollywood stardom to the governorship of California, then to two terms as president of the United States. Monkeys win without even trying.

They know things without needing to learn, too. The Maya say that there is no need to train Monkey natives in the Daykeeper's art, because these people just know; they don't need to be taught (not surprising, with mystical Night as their Past Sign). In this sense, Monkey natives are like their mythic progenitors, One Batz and One Chouen, two characters in the *Popol Vuh* described as "great knowers" responsible for the invention of the fine arts. Monkey people are the natural artists and craftsmen of the world. They often have the best qualities of the "artistic temperament"—they are friendly and well liked because of their vitality and liveliness, but the ego problems of artists are well known. One Batz and One Chouen grew so arrogant that they neglected the care of their brothers, the hero twins. They were, in fact, so cruel to their brothers that the gods changed them into chattering monkeys as a fitting punishment.

Monkey natives can become so absorbed in their own creativity, so vain over their skill and luck, that they neglect to think of others. On occasion, they may even be purposefully cruel to those who lack their own creative spark. Egotism is the dark side of this most favorable of day-signs.

Even though many Monkeys—like Reagan, Dustin Hoffman (9), or Barbra Streisand (13 Monkey)—have stellar careers and seem to be successful at anything they do, the fact remains that Monkey's Tree of Life is comprised of some fairly difficult day-signs that occasionally make their influence known. Their Past Sign is the Night, and they travel into this world bearing with them the deep knowing wisdom of the Otherworld. This power can be used for good or for ill, and Monkey, for all its cleverness, sometimes has difficulty distinguishing right from wrong. Charles Manson (10 Monkey) had that Night knowledge in abundance, and made use of the sexual, magical force of Monkey's Right Hand Power (Serpent) and the strategic gifts of its Left Hand Power (Incense) to raise a wild Storm (Future Sign) in the world. Newspaper heiress Patricia Hearst (4 Monkey) raised a similar Storm with her foray into the dark world (Night) of the Symbionese Liberation Army, living a tale of sex and violence (Serpent) that captured America's imagination during the middle 1970s. Though she served time in prison for bank robbery, she got out early with typical Monkey good luck, and, playing the Trickster as only a Monkey can do, went on to enjoy an occasional career in the movies playing supporting roles in the films of the controversial and eccentric director John Waters. Monkeys usually land on their feet.

Notable Monkey Natives:

Ronald Reagan (1)
Patty Hearst (4)
Jacques Cousteau (8)
Dustin Hoffman (9)
Charles Manson (10)
Barbra Streisand (13)

The Road

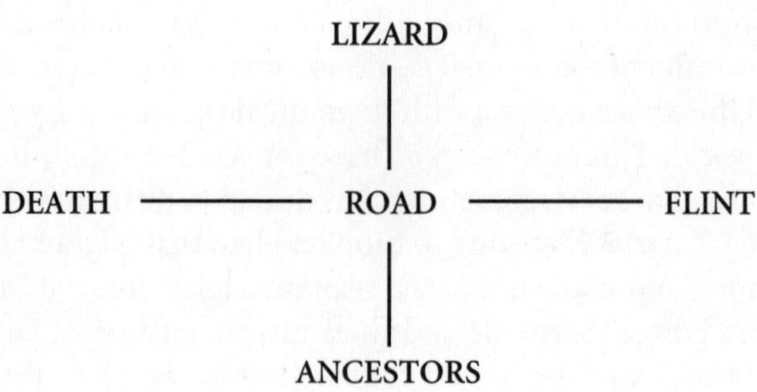

This day-sign represents the sacred spiral of life which goes by many names: to the Classic Maya it was itz, "the dew of heaven," to the Aztecs it was malinalli (their name for this day-sign), and to contemporary Daykeepers it is "the lightning in the blood." It is the sacred path of energy that descends from heaven and travels down our spinal column, but also rises from the earth up that same internal World Tree. That path of energy is the Road of Life.

There is no question that natives of this day-sign are especially endowed with power. Why, then, do so few celebrities appear as natives of the Road of Life?

In most cases, the power vested in natives of this sign is employed in quiet ways; these people are often too busy helping their communities to worry much about seeking the limelight. Their Future Sign is the Ancestors, and their principal concern is for the vast masses of people who will come after them—as in the old Native American saying, they act "for the benefit of seven generations." Many—perhaps most—Road natives lead lives of quiet service to others.

Those who find themselves born on the Road of Life have a naturally spiritual destiny and their task is to walk that road in beauty and balance. In Guatemala, it is said that these people are fortunate in matters of health—no doubt because the life-force itself flows through them with special vitality. Because of their innate destiny to walk the Road of Life, they are considered excellent candidates for all kinds of shamanic work. This is logical—after all, this day-sign is a symbol of the "lightning in the blood," a shaman's principal tool. Men born under the sign of the Road are believed to make excellent Calendar priests with a natural talent for ritual—not surprisingly, since the Otherworldly sign of Death (and transformation) constitutes their Right Hand Power. Road women often become midwives—again no surprise since Flint, the sign of the surgeon's knife, is their Left Hand Power. In modern Western society, this energy can help women to become skilled doctors or healers.

One way or another, Road natives are usually involved with spiritual service to their society. On occasion, one may encounter a Road native like Hugh Hefner (4 Road), publisher of *Playboy* magazine, who leans strongly back towards the sensual Lizard of his karmic past. However, a more typical traveler on the Road of Life was Margaret Mead (3 Road), the renowned anthropologist whose researches raised profound questions about what good health in a society really means. In some cases, she shocked her contemporaries by discussing the sexual lives (Lizard) of traditional societies. Her work with cultures that were still organized along shamanic lines (Death on her Right Hand) led her to speculate and philosophize about the meaning of the human condition itself, producing a body of work that is likely to resonate through "seven generations" (Ancestors as her Future Sign).

Notable Road Natives:

Margaret Mead (3)
Hugh Hefner (4)
H. Ross Perot (10)

The Corn

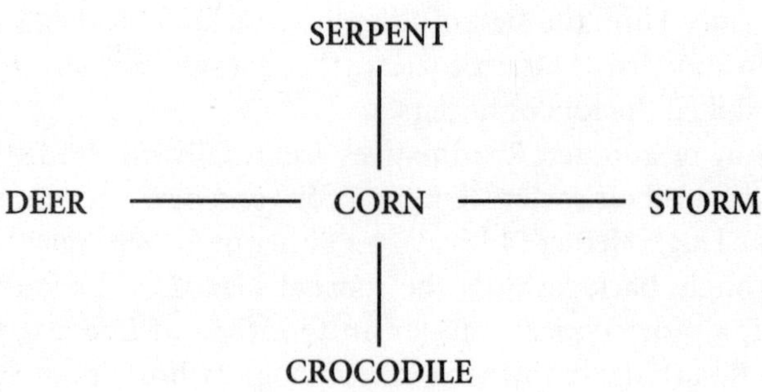

To be born on the day of the Corn is a very fortunate occurrence. In the mythology of ancient Mexico, this was the birth-sign of Feathered Serpent, bringer of light, and a day the gods come down to earth.

These natives are productive. As community members they are leaders, and as parents they are alleged to be both fortunate and wise. *The Book of Chilam Balam of Kaua* insists that Corn natives tend to have many children. They also may play a parental role for their extended families or entire communities. They function like the staff of office (one of the principal symbols of this day-sign), the supportive pillar of the world. Sigmund Freud and Carl Jung, two of the founders of modern psychology—pillars of the modern world, by any standards—were both born on the day 10 Corn.

In general, these people are practical, earthy, and nurturing. Their good fortune and joy in ordinary life may cause Corn natives to be a bit conservative or complacent—they have no need to rock a boat that carries them so gracefully. This is why our list of well-known Corn natives includes only a few names. It is a quiet day-sign that has little desire to seek the limelight.

Even the most fortunate day-sign has a dark side, and Corn's Tree of Life includes a number of challenging influences. The presence of Serpent as the Past Sign suggests that many of these natives bring a great deal of sexual karma with them into this life—Freud, for example, devoted his entire life to dealing with deeply hidden sexual issues. Storm on the Left Hand generates a great deal of emotional turbulence, especially regarding women—Jung attracted very creative women into his life, as befits the day-sign Storm, but his extramarital affairs strained his home life considerably. While the Deer on the Right Hand may sometimes function as a symbol of strength and inner power, the presence of Crocodile as the Future Sign shows that Corn natives face progressively more challenges as they develop along their path—challenges that may include madness, illusion, and anger. Crocodile may also describe the native's children; both Freud and Jung had daughters who followed in their footsteps—Jung's daughter Greta took a typically mystical Crocodile path and became an astrologer.

The Chilam Balam of Kaua also notes that in some cases children may be the only wealth of these natives, and that they may be otherwise of very modest means, perhaps even poor. Diana Ross (13 Corn), like O. J. Simpson, emerged from poverty to enjoy Corn's traditional abundance, while Mia Farrow (8 Corn) may indeed have been blessed in terms of children, but suffered the emotional pain of Storm and the sexual karma of Serpent when her husband Woody Allen—a Crocodile—was accused of molesting them.

Despite their sometimes wild ups and downs, Corn people often possess a spirituality that goes beyond the confines of purely conventional religion; this is one of the birth-signs that is considered favorable for prospective Calendar shamans.

Notable Corn Natives:

O. J. Simpson (4)
Mia Farrow (8)
Sigmund Freud, Carl Jung (10)
Diana Ross (13)

The Jaguar

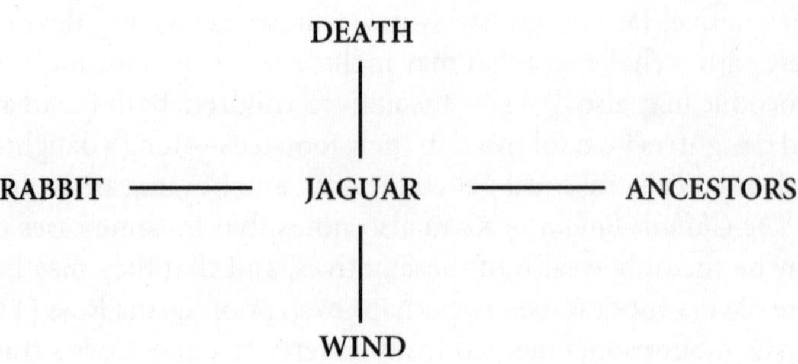

To the Classic Maya, the jaguar was a symbol of the night sky. When the solar eagle plunged below the horizon and the sun traveled through the Underworld, it traveled as a jaguar. Today, the day-sign Jaguar is said to be the sign of that old Underworld god who currently goes by the name of Santo Mundo the Earth Father, or Maximon.

Jaguar natives share a certain slippery, Otherworldly glitter with the natives of Night, Death, and Ancestors, the other Underworld signs. Death, in fact, is their Past Sign and the Ancestors constitutes their Left Hand Power, so it may truly be said that they emerge from the Otherworld with their time in the pool of souls still predominant in their personalities. It's no wonder that former President Richard M. Nixon (2 Jaguar) was called "Tricky Dick." Like a true native of the Underworld, he slipped through crisis after crisis, always emerging with a grin and a fair share of power. One of the Jaguar's challenges, however, is that he is always headed towards the Wind, which generally blows conflict and contention into his life. Nixon may have slipped out of the net many times, but Watergate finally proved to be too much of a windstorm even for him. Similarly, Lech Walesa (3 Jaguar), though born into humble circumstances, possessed enough Jaguar cunning to stay one step ahead of such masters of Underworld treachery as the KGB.

According to contemporary Daykeepers, Jaguar natives are likely to become wealthy. The Maya think of wealth in terms such as gold, silver, and crops—all of which are either found in the earth or emerge from it. Since Jaguar is an Underworld sign closely linked to Santo Mundo, it follows that wealth is an adjunct of this day-sign. A close parallel exists in Greco-Roman myth. Pluto, the fearsome god of the dead, was also a god of wealth because the source of wealth (i.e., gold, silver, and precious metals) lay hidden under the earth. This, in fact, is the origin of our word "plutocrat." Jaguar natives are the plutocrats of the Mayan world.

The wealth that falls to the natives of this day-sign has a price. It is said that those born on the day Jaguar are likely to be afflicted with all manner of illness. This is because the vital and transforming power of the Underworld, the Santo Mundo, is always pushing the Jaguar native towards transformation. We all resist change and the conflict manifests as illness.

There is, of course, one solution to this: to accept change and embrace inner transformation. Many Jaguar natives are to be found engaged in current spiritual practices and workshops that stress inner transformation, and this is as it should be. The Jaguar native who accepts the need for transmutation can become an especially powerful shamanic figure. Among the Quiché Maya this person is considered a good candidate for initiation into the ancient ways and the knowledge of the Sacred Calendar. Whatever one's cultural or spiritual background may be, however, the Jaguar who transforms night-world cunning and cleverness into true magic and wisdom can reach great heights indeed.

NOTABLE JAGUAR NATIVES:

Richard Nixon (2)
Lech Walesa (3)
Arnold Schwarzenegger (12)

The Eagle

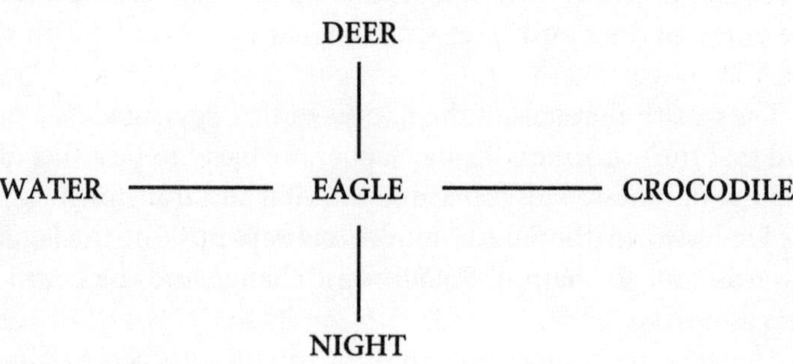

The Eagle is a day-sign of special power in both the material and spiritual realms. It is said that the natives of this sign will cry out like eagles, asking Santo Mundo, the Earth Father, for wealth, power, and the benefits of the spirit. In general, they will get what they ask for because their spirits are strong and their motivation is high. President John F. Kennedy was an Eagle.

The Eagle is a sign of passion and desire. These people expect the best out of life and seek to soar above the crowd. A great deal of their passion for life is devoted to the material attributes of human existence, which is why it is said they are likely to become wealthy. They achieve their material eminence not through mere luck, but through skill. They usually make assertive and powerful business people.

There is a spiritual side to this day-sign as well. In ancient Mexico, the eagle was the symbol of the daytime sun (in contrast to the jaguar, which was the totem of the night). Thus this day-sign represents the light of conscious thought, as opposed to the intuitive perceptions of more Otherworldly signs like Jaguar or Death. Putting it all together, we may say that the Eagle is, at least potentially, the magician of light. If Eagles soar to the top of the worldly heap, they are equally likely to soar to the summit of consciousness. The eagle is the totem bird for shamans all over the world, and this is a sign believed to be endowed with "body lightning." Therefore, the Quiché Maya say that Eagle natives are as likely to shine as shamans or religious professionals as they are to occupy a prominent position in business or society.

The Eagle is a sign of wholeness and completeness. It represents the striving for perfection on all levels of human existence. In order to achieve the heights, Eagle people must remain balanced in the very center of their beings. The central pole of their personal Tree of Life shows Eagles have Deer for their Past Sign and Night for their Future Sign. Both of these signs exemplify wisdom, power, cunning, and the lightning in the blood. These natives also have Water and Crocodile as their Right Hand and Left Hand Powers, respectively. These are turbulent signs, and when Eagles leave the straight path of motivation, focus, and achievement by leaning too far towards either the male or the female polarity, they are certain to run into difficulties. Kennedy was known for his extramarital affairs (the wild and intractable side of Crocodile) but he also suffered from Addison's Disease (Water's penchant for illness). Ringo Starr of the Beatles (7 Eagle) has undergone treatment for alcoholism—a problem that partakes of both day-signs, Crocodile and Water.

Let the natives of the day-sign Eagle, therefore, learn to identify the true goal of their hearts and strive always towards that goal with clear and focused power. Let them learn to control their turbulent emotions and be guided by the light of conscious awareness.

Notable Eagle Natives:

John F. Kennedy (4)
Ringo Starr (7)

The Vulture

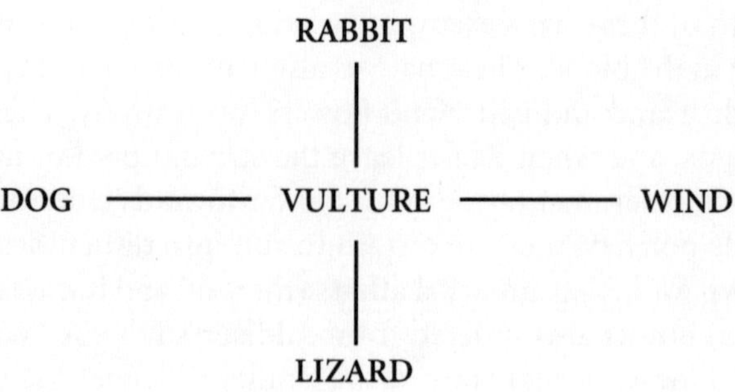

Those born on the day of the Vulture are highly sensual people. They have a deep inner connection with the earth and the vitalizing power that flows from the Underworld, connections that assure a sensitivity to the world of the flesh. As their Past Sign they have the fertile and self-indulgent Rabbit, while the sexy Dog constitutes their Right Hand Power. What is the end of their road, their Future Sign? Lizard, the ultimate sensualist!

Despite so much temptation, Vulture people will be forgiven for their lapses—or so the Daykeepers assure us. We may remember that Vulture is essentially a sign of "karmic clean-out," symbolized by the carrion-eating vulture itself and by the "descending goddesses" who, in ancient times, were associated with this day. These goddesses were, in a sense, the spirits of the dead who have come back to jar their descendants into awareness by making their lives temporarily miserable. Moments of misery and darkness purify our souls—begetting new life and a greater degree of compassion—as symbolized by the votive candle that "burns away our sins," another attribute of this day-sign. When the Daykeepers speak of sins, they are referring primarily to sins of the flesh, especially those involving sexuality.

The vulture still enjoys a prominent role in the folklore of the modern-day Maya. He is generally represented as a slow, easy-going creature, though other animals avoid him because he smells of carrion and appears lacking in intelligence. He is nevertheless a useful bird and, in his own lazy way, a good fellow. In Mayan animal stories, he often gets tricked, but he may also play the final trick himself; he is not as dumb as he looks. It is believed that Vulture people, like their totem bird, will be generally irresponsible but often lucky.

The Vulture attitude towards parenting is sometimes slipshod; though affectionate with their children, they tend to be overly permissive and irresponsible. Neither are they the most faithful of spouses. The stormy marital history of rock star Bob Dylan (3 Vulture) is a case in point, though Dylan, with true Vulture good luck, goes on and on. Perhaps his karma really is being resolved in the process. In Dylan's life, however, the Wind as his Left Hand Power plays a greater than usual role. It is 9 Wind, a very high number, which stresses conflict and angry scenes, especially in the "female" realm of marriage.

There is a certain good-natured laziness about Vulture people which is as charming as it is annoying. Despite their lapses and their seeming lack of motivation, they do well in business, accumulate money, and their families usually prosper. Why not? Their karma is being cleaned up and placed in order for them even as they journey through their daily lives. The day-sign Lizard lies at the end of their road, signifying that their rewards, like their relatively simple joys and desires, are to be found in the material world and its pleasures.

Notable Vulture Natives:

Bob Dylan (3)
Robert Redford (5)

Incense

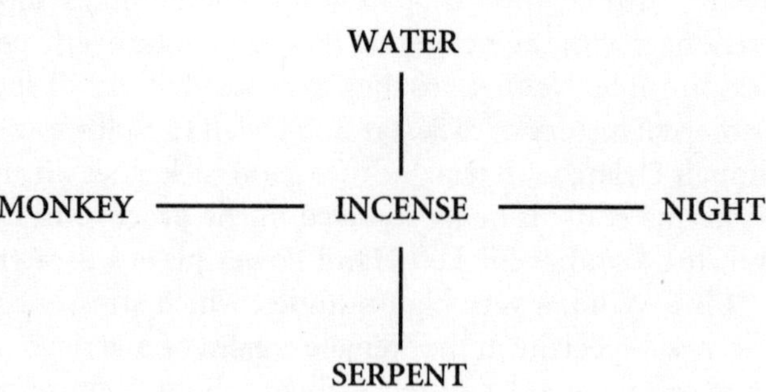

The contemporary Mayan image of this day-sign is the thinker, and most of the meanings attached to it in divination are concerned with the process of thought. Incense people, however, are both reflective and active—their reflective mode, symbolized by the day-sign Night, constitutes their intuitive Left Hand Power. Their active mode, symbolized by Monkey, lies on the more assertive Right Hand. Their thoughts give birth to activity, and their activities give birth to reflection, in an endless cycle.

It is said that Incense people, whether male or female, will have a distinctly masculine "tone"—even Shirley Temple (8 Incense) grew up to be a United States ambassador. The Mayans, like so many other peoples, conceive of the process of thinking as essentially masculine; to use the Chinese term, it is a yang activity. The thought gives birth to the deed. Hence Incense people are doers, and often emerge as leaders in their community. This day-sign's talent for directed action functions on the spiritual as well as the material plane; Incense is regarded as a favorable sign for shamans and Daykeepers.

Flashes of inspiration may be just as erratic as they are creative. Incense is a Year Lord, and sometimes a rather capricious one. There is no way to know beforehand whether the newest ideas devised in the clever brains of Incense people will be of benefit to the world or merely pipe dreams. The mental rollercoaster upon which Incense people often find themselves is exemplified by Timothy Leary (11 Incense), whose early work as a Harvard psychiatrist embodied the mental power of his day-sign. His career as the counter-cultural guru of LSD evoked an intellectual but utopian dreamworld which captured the imagination of a generation. After his release from prison, he began a new career as a New Age philosopher, returning to the heady, erratic Incense world of ideas!

Incense people are just as likely to be argumentative, quarrelsome, or confused as they are to be meditative and visionary—the subtle Serpent, often too clever for its own good, is the power that lies at the end of their road. Our thoughts are like sparks of energy surging forth out of the earth, and it is no wonder that so many of the peoples of ancient Mexico knew this day-sign as Earthquake. Like an earthquake, the flash of inspiration strikes with a random hand. This erratic side of Incense is especially noticeable whenever Water, sign of the karmic past, is overly strong.

Incense people need to focus their considerable mental powers in one direction to avoid becoming scattered, frazzled, or just plain spaced out. Considering their potential magical and spiritual gifts, meditation is of the greatest benefit to them, for it helps to awaken those gifts—the Maya used to call incense "the brains of heaven."

NOTABLE INCENSE NATIVES:

Hank Williams (5)
Shirley Temple-Black (8)
Timothy Leary (11)

Flint

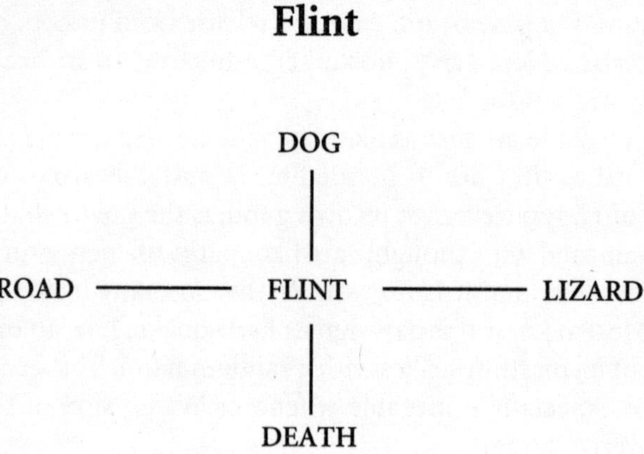

To become conscious of duality is to see the world as an arena of conflict. To choose between two realities is to enter that conflict, to become a warrior or crusader. It is this painful awareness of the opposites that makes Flint a potentially difficult birth-sign. These natives are all too likely to see the world in terms of black and white. Their natural warrior spirit (1 Flint was the feast day of the Aztec war god) leads them to take sides and to take action, and Flint people can frequently be found in the front ranks of any battle—or at the forefront of any brawl. Flint's physical correspondence is the mouth, just like the day-sign Incense. Perhaps we may see in this a suggestion that the words we utter are subject to duality, capable of expressing inspiration (Incense) or causing quarrels (Flint).

The Maya consider natives of Flint to be contentious and argumentative, which is another way of saying that they take the opposites too seriously. If they become totally caught up in their own loves and hates, they may stop at nothing to fight for their own side—consequently they may slander others and become untruthful in order to get what they want.

President Lyndon Johnson (5 Flint) conducted the war in Vietnam with true Flint style—his words were as cutting and fierce as his military policies. And only a Flint person like Senator Jesse Helms (8 Flint) would have blundered into uttering statements that appeared to be death threats against President Clinton! More often than not, it is the Flint person himself who becomes the real victim of his own quarrelsome nature.

The Book of Chilam Balam of Kaua, however, equates Flint with "the healing condition" and calls Flint natives "healers." It is part of this day-sign's inherent duality that its natives may also become renowned healers. The knife that kills may also be the surgeon's scalpel, and an awareness of conflict may lead to the desire for harmony.

Harmony is the key word. Those born under Flint need, above all, to struggle for harmony and learn to use their discrimination as a gift, instead of as a knife, to sunder the bonds of illusion and untruthfulness rather than becoming lost in and exhausted by wild crusades. If they can do this, they may well become the healers of the community rather than its troublemakers. To accomplish this, they must set their sights toward the future rather than the past and call upon the transformational energy of the day-sign Death that lies ahead of them, rather than troublesome and uncertain Dog, the symbol of their karmic past. They can gain assistance by calling on the energy of Road, their Right Hand Power, as well.

Flint women are often exceptionally beautiful. Jacqueline Kennedy Onassis, Goldie Hawn, and Sophia Loren were all born on the day Flint, on 1, 7, and 9 respectively. Yet all of them have found it necessary, at times, to use the hard-edged scalpel of truth in their lives, for they have all faced conflict and strife—sometimes on a genuinely grandiose scale.

Notable Flint Natives:

Jacqueline Kennedy Onassis (1)
Paul Simon (2)
Lyndon Baines Johnson (5)
Goldie Hawn (7)
Marcel Marceau, George Harrison, U.S. Senator Jesse Helms (8)
Sophia Loren (9)

Storm

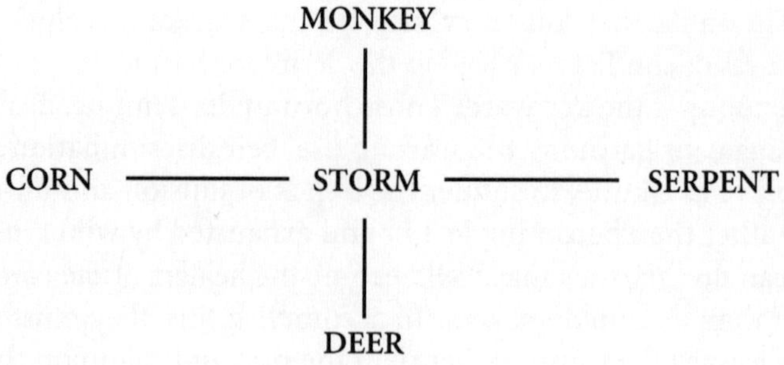

MONKEY

CORN —— STORM —— SERPENT

DEER

Those born on the day of the Storm may often feel as if their lives are but one long tempest. The Daykeepers say that Storm natives are often visited with trouble and turmoil by the Ancestors—which is to say that they come into this life with a great deal of karma to work through, and consequently are subject to more than ordinary amounts of harassment and sorrow. Despite this turbulent relationship with the karmic past, however, their more immediate antecedents are often fortunate, as shown by the auspicious Monkey in their past. Several of the Storm natives listed here have been at the center of such karmic turbulence. Lady (formerly Princess) Diana (1 Storm) spent several unpleasant years in the midst of emotional storms that shook the British royal family, while Yoko Ono (2 Storm), widely believed to have been responsible for the arguments that ended the Beatles, later saw her husband shot to death in front of her eyes.

This predilection for finding themselves at the center of any conflict is a shame, for Storm individuals are typically sensitive and compassionate beings. *The Book of Chilam Balam of Kaua* calls them "very imaginative" and "noble." Their sensitive temperaments may turn them into artists or world-servers, and we must remember that one of the divinatory phrases linked with this day-sign is "a table set for the gods." This refers to the table of offerings that Daykeepers make to the gods—a metaphor for service and surrender. Thus, Storm natives may find release from their karmic burdens by dedicating themselves to a higher cause.

The sensitivity of these natives tends to leave them thin-skinned. It is no wonder they are so susceptible to the storms of life; the gentle and yielding nature of water is part of their psychology and is responsible for their intense compassion as well as their sorrow and difficulties. Their sensitivity may not be immediately apparent, however, for they often mask it with a hard-edged attitude reminiscent of their left-hand power, the Serpent. Ono and Marlene Dietrich (5 Storm), for example, are better known for their sharp tongues than for their gentleness. Lady Diana, more typically, often gave way to sadness and despair during the emotional storms that raged all around her.

Their hypersensitivity sometimes manifests as illness; like Water people, Storm natives are often fragile. *The Chilam Balam of Kaua* asserts that Storm natives are prone to experience illness whenever a new year picks up his burden. Storm people should take care to avoid the colds and flus that often come during the change of seasons—late February and early March in North America—for this is when the Mayan year changes and the new Year Bearer hoists his burden.

Despite the karmic burdens they bear, Storm natives look forward to a powerful and positive resolution of their difficulties. The magical and deeply empowered Deer lies ahead of them, a symbol of the courage and strength gained when they "set a table for the gods" and dedicate their compassionate energies to a higher cause.

Notable Storm Natives:

Lady Diana (1)
Little Richard, Yoko Ono (2)
Manley Palmer Hall (3)
Marlene Dietrich (5)

The Ancestors

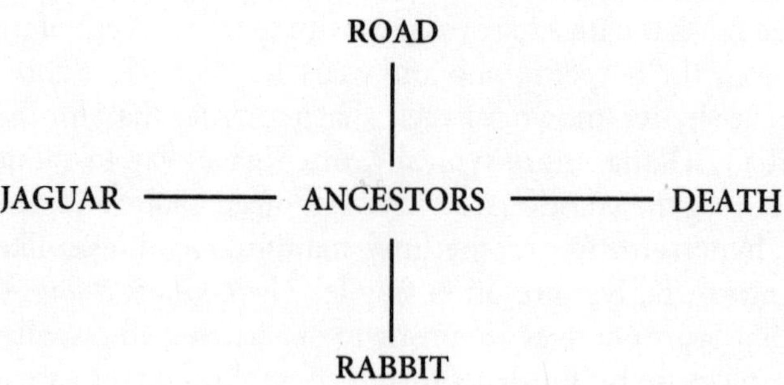

Considering the primary importance of this day-sign, one might expect an augury of unblemished good fortune for all those born on this day. In fact, the character of the Ancestor native is typically quite complex. According to Sahagún, the Aztecs regarded this as the day-sign of poets and singers, of dancers and creative artists. This day-sign may have a flavor of self-indulgence as well, for Sahagún tells us that these natives are also prone to slip into extremes of sensuality.

The poetic or artistic vocation was, to the Aztecs, primarily a spiritual vocation—creating poems and songs was to offer one's "flowers" to the gods. Most creative artists feel some sort of inner connection to a higher force or power and it is rare in creative circles to find the complete atheist without any allegiance to some mystery, some numen in the heart of things. The symbolism of the day-sign Ancestors informs us that this creative source or numen is rooted in the collective unconscious, the continuity between ourselves and all those who have gone before.

If the collective mind enlightens us, it may also drag us into a world of illusion, as noted when considering the day-sign Crocodile. Natives of the day of the Ancestors are equally likely to be enticed by the depths. They may suffer from some of the delusions that Jung tells us are characteristic of those who venture too deeply into the collective ocean of consciousness without keeping a firm grip on ordinary reality. Daykeepers say that while Ancestor natives are mediumistic and may be able to communicate with the dead, this communion with the ancestral world may be too close, too immediate, and therefore unhealthy. Too great an immersion in the realm of collective visions and dreams is the danger inherent in the sign Ancestors. Nothing better illustrates this uneasy relationship with the dead than the career of Elisabeth Kubler-Ross (8 Ancestors), the Swiss-born psychologist who pioneered the development of hospices dedicated to the practice of "conscious dying." She then went on to lose most of her money and a great deal of her reputation to a group of shady "trance mediums" in southern California who claimed to be in communication with the spirits of the departed.

If these natives can avoid giving way to excessive sensuality or excessive involvement in the unhealthy side of mysticism, they are likely to become wealthy and wise, enriched rather than crippled by their artists' grasp on the Otherworldly. Their personal Tree of Life certainly provides them with the ability to achieve such a balance, thanks to the presence of the day-sign Road behind them. Their ancestral karma is strong and positive, while Jaguar on their Right Hand and Death on their Left Hand endow them with the strongest (and most clever) aspects of their Otherworldly heritage. Their future is governed by the fertile and prosperous Rabbit, holding forth the promise of ultimate success and enjoyment in life.

Notable Ancestor Natives:

Tonya Harding (3)
Bruce Springsteen (5)
Elisabeth Kubler-Ross (8)

7

Mayan Divination

The Sacred Calendar has always been an instrument of divination as well as a measure of time. Among the present-day Maya divination is probably the most common use of the Sacred Calendar.

Martin Prechtel believes that the uninitiated ought not to attempt divination with the Sacred Calendar on any level. The gods become angry with those who trifle with their mysteries—yet the techniques of Mayan Calendar divination have been published and are a matter of public record. The American anthropologist Ruth Bunzel recorded one method at Chichicastenango in the 1930s,[1] while two more anthropologists, Dennis and Barbara Tedlock, apprenticed themselves to a Calendar diviner named Andres Xiloj in Guatemala during the 1970s.[2] Therefore, I do not believe there is much point in preserving a secrecy that no longer exists.

There is, however, a need to warn the reader that divination with the Sacred Calendar is not a game, and should never be treated as such. The technique outlined here omits many of the magical and ritual actions involved with traditional divination. What remains is a method of working applicable to any oracle, whether it be the Tarot, the runes, or the Mayan Calendar. Nevertheless, the casual reader who may be familiar with the work of Bunzel or the Tedlocks is urged to avoid the prayers, candle-burnings, and censings that accompany the art of divination in Guatemala. Particularly, one should avoid pronouncing the names of the days in Maya (especially Quiché Maya) or awakening the "lightning in the blood," as is often done in traditional shamanic divinations in Guatemala.

Most American readers, if they are familiar with Mayan divination techniques at all, have learned what they know by way of Barbara Tedlock's book, which is the only one readily available. Though the Tedlocks learned a very ritualized way of doing divination, most diviners work with much less ceremony. In terms of prayers, rituals, or the number of times the seeds are laid out, one client's divination may be entirely different from that performed for the next querent. The model used here should not be regarded as "the one and only way" to perform divination. You should feel free to experiment.

Performing Mayan Divination

The first thing you will need is a bag of divining seeds. The diviner's bag is essentially a medicine pouch, and not unlike the kind of pouch in which one might carry runes. Medicine pouches are easy to come by in any New Age store; in fact, any cloth or leather bag will do. The best pouch, of course, is the one you make yourself.

Once you have a pouch, you need divining seeds. In Guatemala, many shamans use the seeds of the ceiba or tz'ite tree, which was the World Tree of Mayan myth. Martin uses beans—of what sort I do not know. He remarks: "The beans are very toxic. It takes a lot out of me just to open my divining bag."

What he means, presumably, is that the beans or seeds used in divination acquire various "difficult" magical energies—whether from the stormy gods and spirits who watch over divination, from the energies of clients who have sickness or other problems, or maybe from all these sources. Again, it is best to avoid putting yourself in a situation involving powers of which you know but little. Divination, in the broadest sense of the word, works on any level—for example, you don't need to put your psycho-energetic system in danger in order to use the *I Ching*, an oracle in which the traditional Chinese prayers are dispensed with and in which pennies often substitute for the traditional yarrow stalks. You can just go to the supermarket, buy a bag of popcorn kernels, and use these instead. In fact, many apprentice diviners use corn kernels in Guatemala today, and it is probable that corn kernels were used for divination by Calendar priests in the pre-Columbian era.

How many seeds or kernels should be included in your diviner's pouch? That is a matter of individual preference. An appropriate number is 260, since that is the number of days in the Sacred Calendar. However, in Momostenango a bag of 150 is considered standard.

Most Mayan shamans include a number of crystals or other magical stones in their divining bags. If the stones are small enough, they may actually be mixed with the seeds and used in the divination. For the most part, however, you will probably wish to use your crystals or other stones in a "layout." It is common practice among Calendar shamans to lay out groups or arrangements of stones on the divining table as they begin work. The selection of crystals or other precious stones to fill out your medicine bag should be, as it is among the Maya, a matter of personal choice. Choose those stones with which you feel a special affinity.

Having acquired your pouch, your seeds, and your stones, you may now wish to keep these things in a special place. They are your divining tools. Treat them with honor and respect.

During divination, sit across a table from the querent. Traditional diviners often have a special table in their home, used only for divination. You can use any table—your kitchen table, the coffee table in your living room—of course, if you go to someone else's house to perform the divination, use whatever is available.

Your first act is to set the table. This can be done simply or with as much ceremony as you please. Most diviners use a cloth to spread out their seeds. Small rugs or shawls from Mexico and Central America make very nice divining cloths, though you can use whatever you please. After you have spread out your cloth, you may wish to light a few candles.

Shake the corn kernels out of your pouch and place them in a pile on the divining cloth, or you may place a small bowl on the cloth and shake the seeds into the bowl instead, which will make them easier to grasp during the divinatory process.

Next, lay out your stones and crystals. Many Mayan diviners create a layout of stones around the divining space. Sometimes, as in conservative Momostenango where the Tedlocks were trained, the layout is traditional and proceeds according to established rules. However, layouts vary from village to village and even among individuals, so suit yourself. You may use as few as two or three stones or as many as ten. Place them in front of you or to one side, in patterns that seem meaningful to you. I usually place my layout to my upper left, with my large seeing crystal in the center and four other stones surrounding it to symbolize Santo Mundo and the Four Directions.

Traditional shamans begin their divinations with a prayer, customarily invoking the Mayan trinity, the Lord of the Year, and the Four Directions, as well as a veritable host of saints and spirits. Large quantities of copal are burnt, summoning the Ancestors and driving away evil spirits. This is one area of practice where it is best *not* to follow custom. Take particular care to avoid summoning the Ancestors or spirits who watch over the Sacred Calendar or calling on the day-names in the Mayan language—which is equivalent to calling on the gods. If you want to open your divination with a prayer, make one up yourself. Keep it universal in tone.

Have the querent formulate a question. Then reach randomly into the heap of kernels you've placed beside you either in a bowl or on your cloth. As you grasp the kernels, try to keep your mind open, receptive, and empty. Don't think about what you're doing, just reach into the kernels and grab some.

Place the handful of kernels in front of you, arranging them in groups of four. After you have placed about four or five such groups of four in a line, start another line just below it and continue until all the kernels are placed. When you are finished, you will have a spread that looks something like the diagram given on the next page (Figure 14).

As you examine the kernels, it is important to note how things end. The final group of kernels in your spread can provide subtle shades of meaning about the course of the divination.

- If the series ends in a nice even group of four, the results of the divination will be clear and certain.
- If there are only two kernels in the final group, this is still a good sign, indicating at least relative clarity.
- A remainder of three kernels makes the results of the divination more uncertain.
- A remainder of one seed renders the issue even more uncertain. In fact, a remainder of only one kernel may even cause a traditional diviner to call off the operation and wait for another time.

Beginning with the first group of four kernels, count off the days of the tzolkin, regarding each little group of four as a separate Calendar day. Readers who are familiar with the work of Barbara Tedlock will have read that the kernels should be counted from the day upon which

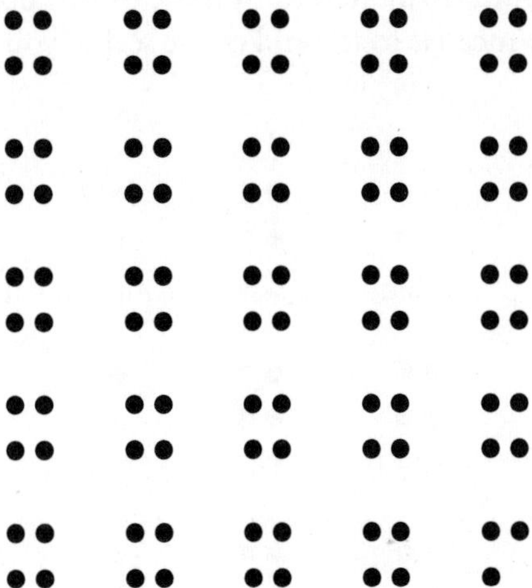

FIGURE 14 ***Arranging the Divining Seeds***

the divination occurs, but Martin disagrees. Beginning one's count with the day in question, he says, should only be used for specific issues. Ruth Bunzel recorded a similar practice in Chichicastenango in the 1930s, noting that, when divining about an illness, Quiché shamans often began their count from the day the querent became ill.

Martin asserts that one should always begin a count with the day-sign upon which the querent was born. I have found that this is indeed the best way to read for another person—especially if you are simply exploring the general circumstances surrounding the querent. If you are reading for someone born on 3 Incense, for instance, then the first group of kernels will be called 3 Incense, and so on until the end.

Count each group of four kernels as if you were counting off the successive days of the tzolkin. Quiché diviners count quickly and rhythmically as if chanting—the intonation of the sacred words carries a great deal of magical force with it. For you, this will hardly be possible, and, as stated before, it is definitely not recommended under any circumstances. Keep a Calendar Board diagram with you to help you count. When you reach the final group of kernels, take special note of the day and number it represents. Each day-sign has a special divinatory meaning, which we shall explore later on in this chapter.

In the example given here (Figure 15), we have assumed that you are performing your divination for someone born upon 3 Incense. So, counting from 3 Incense to the end of the series, you will end up with 1 Crocodile.

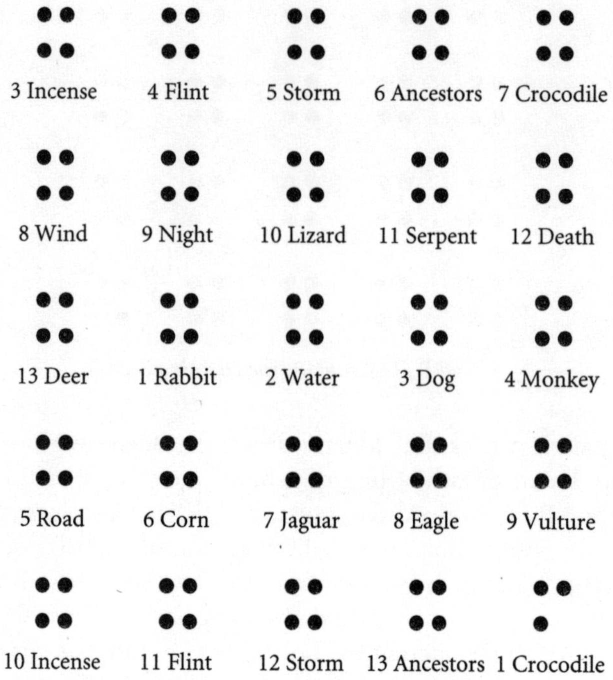

3 Incense 4 Flint 5 Storm 6 Ancestors 7 Crocodile

8 Wind 9 Night 10 Lizard 11 Serpent 12 Death

13 Deer 1 Rabbit 2 Water 3 Dog 4 Monkey

5 Road 6 Corn 7 Jaguar 8 Eagle 9 Vulture

10 Incense 11 Flint 12 Storm 13 Ancestors 1 Crocodile

FIGURE 15 ***Reading the Days: First Count***

In divination, Crocodile indicates that there is a mystery involved. Exactly what that mystery is may not be too clear, especially since the final group of kernels contains only three units, indicating uncertainty. However, if we consult the divinatory meanings for Crocodile given later in this chapter, we may guess that the mystery involves an enemy, or a psychic and mystical experience that leaves the querent feeling slightly crazy, perhaps doubting his or her sanity. We can see that the situation is not serious, however, because 1 is the lowest possible number. In general, read the numbers according to the guidelines established in Chapter 4. Briefly, these are as follows:

- The numbers 1 through 4 are considered relatively weak. In the case of a positive day-sign, the low number weakens its potential for good. In the case of a challenging day-sign, its power to do harm is similarly weakened.
- The numbers 5 through 9, as middle numbers, are regarded as being in a state of balance and constitute the most harmonious numbers you can receive in a divinatory spread. Helpful day-signs are even more helpful by virtue of being in balance. Challenging or difficult day-signs reach their most positive potential when the numbers are in balance.
- The numbers 10 through 13 are generally considered *too* high. They represent an excess of the energy connected with that day-sign, which can be very difficult in the case of day-signs that are challenging to begin with. In some cases, too high a number can spoil the energy of a positive day-sign by creating "too much of a good thing," though in other cases a higher number can simply mean more positive energy. Check the "Divinatory Meanings" at the end of this chapter for sign-by-sign details.

At this point, you have noted 1 Crocodile as a result. However, the day-signs are often read in pairs; reading two day-signs helps to create a complete image or "tell a story." The second day-sign can be obtained in one of two ways:

- The simplest method is to read the last two day-signs in your layout as a pair. In the example given here, we would match 13 Ancestors with 1 Crocodile. So, if we examine the divinatory meanings for Ancestors, we may guess that a very powerful figure—someone skilled in magical matters—is involved. This person's wisdom and knowledge is making the client feel uneasy or uncomfortable, a little bit "crazy." This individual has opened the querent's mind to the great mysteries of life. However, the situation is not negative, because Crocodile—which can sometimes be a dangerous sign—is represented by the number 1, a very low number that indicates that it really isn't much of a problem.

  Of course, all oracles speak in symbols, and symbols by their very nature open the doors to numerous possibilities. Maybe the querent is a very ordinary person who doesn't know any powerful individuals involved with occult matters. So we might consider the possibility that in this reading Ancestors indicates home and family, and we might suspect that some matter in the domestic situation is making the querent "crazy."

3 Incense 2 Wind	4 Flint 3 Night	5 Storm 4 Lizard	6 Ancestors 5 Serpent	7 Crocodile 6 Death
8 Wind 7 Deer	9 Night 8 Rabbit	10 Lizard 9 Water	11 Serpent 10 Dog	12 Death 11 Monkey
13 Deer 12 Road	1 Rabbit 13 Corn	2 Water 1 Wind	3 Dog 2 Eagle	4 Monkey 3 Vulture
5 Road 4 Incense	6 Corn 5 Flint	7 Jaguar 6 Storm	8 Eagle 7 Ancestors	9 Vulture 8 Crocodile
10 Incense 9 Wind	11 Flint 10 Night	12 Storm 11 Lizard	13 Ancestors 12 Serpent	1 Crocodile 13 Death

FIGURE 16 ***Reading the Days: Second Count***

- There is another method of deriving pairs of day-signs. This is the method taught to the Tedlocks in Momostenango and shown in the diagram above (Figure 16).

After you have reached 1 Crocodile at the end of the series, go back to the beginning of the layout, still counting the days in order. If your first count ended with 1 Crocodile, then you will begin at the top again with 2 Wind. This gives a different day and number, 13 Death, when you again reach the end of the count. Note the significance of that day as well.

In this case, combine the meanings of 1 Crocodile and 13 Death. We can see from studying the divinatory meanings that Death is a very favorable sign. The querent may be feeling a bit crazy about an impending marriage or budding romance. If so, it will all work out for the best, thanks to the overwhelmingly positive nature of Death. If we choose to employ the more mythic or esoteric meanings for the day-signs given in Chapter 5, we may suspect the querent is feeling distressed due to a spiritual transformation in the unconscious.

Mayan shamans usually talk to their clients while they work, asking questions meant to explore the possibilities indicated by the oracle. Using the example given above, we might ask the querent: Are you involved in a romance? Is it making you feel stressed out and crazy?

In many cases, one layout will not be enough, as you will quickly see once you get a "feel" for the reading and begin exploring its ramifications with the querent. Continuing with the above example, you may discover, through the day-signs and careful questioning, that the querent, a woman, is in love with a very handsome and wealthy man. Now you know why Death is a 13—the fact that this day-sign is represented by the highest possible number symbolizes that this romance seems to have everything going for it. So why is she distressed, as indicated by Crocodile? Does she suspect the man of seeing other women on the side?

Let us assume she does. Whether or not the man in question is "fooling around" is not clear from the first layout—Death is stronger than Crocodile, which suggests that everything is probably just fine. The answer, however, is none too definite since the series ends with an uneven number of kernels. You will want to place the kernels back in the bowl and keep dipping in again and again, doing layouts until you have completely explored the question and all its attendant issues. Never regard a question as completely answered until the day-signs actually give some advice on how to deal with the issue at hand.

When the divination process is finally complete, end with another prayer, this time thanking the powers for helping you in your efforts.

Divinatory Meanings of the Day-Signs

In Mayan society, divinatory readings often take on magical dimensions. When a client comes to a diviner and asks a question, the answer might be found in ordinary circumstances, such as a quarrel with a spouse or neighbor. It is equally possible that the source of the problem will be found to lie in something "magical." The client might be in disharmony with an ancestral spirit, or someone might have placed a spell on him or her. In order to ascertain whether this is the case, a Calendar diviner—who is also a shaman—will make use of a technique called the "Speaking of the Blood." As he counts the seeds of the sacred tz'ite, he may find his finger drawn unaccountably to a particular group of seeds. The "body lightning" will become activated, causing the diviner's blood to "speak" by way of a trembling in the hand or thigh. The diviner will then take note of the day-sign represented by the group of seeds to which his hands have been drawn, for this particular day-sign has its own spiritual message for the client, one that may support or confirm the rest of the reading—but is equally likely to open a whole new (and usually magical) doorway.

If the source of the client's problem is found to be rooted in the spirit world, then ordinary, everyday solutions will be inadequate. A magical solution is required for a magical problem, and at this point the diviner begins to function primarily as a shaman, instituting a program of prayers and rituals on behalf of the client.

It should be clear, from all of this, that there is an inner or "initiated" teaching regarding the meanings of the day-signs. We shall not attempt to deal with this level in these pages—working directly with the body lightning is very dangerous and should never be attempted without the guidance of a teacher. The techniques and meanings given in this chapter function well enough, according to the same universal principles that govern all oracles and systems of divination, whether the vehicle is the Tarot, the *I Ching*, or the Sacred Calendar. If approached in this spirit, the Sacred Calendar can give you results equal in depth and intelligence to any of these other oracles.

In an earlier chapter, we have discussed some of the symbolism and mythology associated with each day-sign. These symbolic meanings should always be kept in mind when performing a divination. Each day-sign also has specific divinatory meanings, and the skilled reader is one who can intuitively synthesize the worldly meanings of the signs with their more symbolic dimensions.

To illustrate this point, let's take an example from the Tarot. At the symbolic level, the card known as the Fool is a complex metaphor for liberation, enlightenment, and "sacred chaos." In actual divinatory practice, it may indicate either an experience of cosmic freedom or hasty, unconsidered, and foolish action. The Tarot reader must use intuition to "feel" his way into the truth of the matter and blend all the possible interpretations into a meaningful whole. The Sacred Calendar works in precisely the same fashion. Like any oracle, it may speak of the ordinary events in our lives, but it also reveals deeper and more spiritual meanings behind those events. The following is an outline of the divinatory meanings which Mayan shamans commonly associate with each day-sign.

Crocodile

Key Words: all things secret, hidden, or mysterious; insanity, craziness; humility; that Great Mystery that drives mortals to vision or madness

If Crocodile figures as the result in a question about love or marriage, you may be about to enter into a relationship with someone who will drive you "crazy"—someone who will fill your life with headaches and distraction. If the question has to do with a journey, it will be the kind of trip where everything goes wrong—lost luggage, planes missed, and so on. In a business question, a Crocodile result indicates too many problems to make the deal worthwhile, and in a question regarding illness, Crocodile may show that you are responding to the negative energies of someone who wishes you ill—though if the number of the day is low (from 1 to 4), the illness will not be serious. In fact, the only context in which Crocodile is useful is a spiritual one, for here it symbolizes that you may be about to dive deep into the mystery of life itself. All the same, take care—the waters of life are very deep and dark!

Wind

Key Words: raw power, especially expressed through anger, strength, wildness, violence, frenzy, or fury; an enemy; the destructive powers of the universe

If the question concerns business, be careful! A Wind answer means that the deal will be nothing but trouble, and the same meaning applies in regard to questions about travel. If this is a question about love and marriage, the object of your affections might even turn out to be an enemy—certainly he or she is too willful and intense to be a cooperative partner. If Wind appears in a question about health, you may be affected negatively by your own anger or that of others. If 9 Wind is the final result of any question, you have offended the very spirit of the cosmos as embodied in the Mayan concept of the Ancestors, probably by way of your anger. Make amends.

Night

Key Words: darkness and dawn; the opening of things closed; slander, lies, and trickery

A divination ending in a low-numbered Night day is generally favorable and stresses the positive aspect of this day-sign. With regard to success, relationships, or travel, any Night day between 1 and 9 may be regarded as a positive answer. Higher numbers, 10 through 13, are "too powerful" and stress the treacherous Underworld aspect of Night—they must be regarded as essentially negative answers, showing lies, trickery, or unexpected difficulties. Like the two previous days, Night as an answer to a question involving health may mean that your problem is the result of someone's negative influence.

Lizard

Key Words: payment of debts; sexual desire

If Lizard appears as the result in a reading, you owe somebody something, and consequently you are carrying "a heavy net" of debts. These may be to other people or to your inner self, but in any event you must make amends. If the result is a low number, such as 2 Lizard, then the debt is recent and not too serious. If it's 12 or 13 Lizard, you may be dealing with an old karmic debt of major consequence. Keep Lizard's powerful sexual connotations in mind as well; in a question regarding love or relationships, Lizard symbolizes that wild passions are afoot.

Serpent

Key Words: an enemy; sorcery or witchcraft; sickness; the sweeping of the curandera's broom (i.e., healing)

"Beware of enemies" can be taken as the essence of any divinatory sequence ending with a Serpent day. If the question involves love or relationships, the one you love may actually be acting as your secret foe; the same applies to business partners. The Maya also apply this principle to questions involving illness, and assume that the sufferer has been bewitched. Since this happens very rarely in our own society, this judgment should be seen in context. If Serpent appears in a question involving health, it should be taken as a warning and the querent should see a doctor immediately. If Serpent is found in combination with very positive day-signs, it may indicate the healing of an illness, for Serpent is the day-sign associated with healers and curanderas.

Death

Key Words: the ultimate dissolution of all polarities; marriage (and the female side of life generally); asking for good, asking for pardon; the Ancestors

A divination ending in Death is very favorable for all matters: health, business, travel, and especially love. If the number is low the answer is only moderately favorable, though you should still regard it as a positive sign. A high-numbered Death day is very fortunate: the patient will recover, the journey or business deal will bring exceptional good fortune, the marriage or relationship is a very good one. If the divinatory process begins to indicate a specific individual, Death suggests that the individual is female.

Deer

Key Words: a priest or shaman; a powerful person in general; to overwhelm an individual with one's personal power; divination

The presence of the day-sign Deer in a divination most often indicates an actual person—one of great spiritual or temporal power. This may be a teacher or guru, a healer, or simply someone possessed of great inner intensity. Sometimes, because Deer's power is both worldly and otherworldly, it may represent an individual whose power is more temporal—perhaps a civic leader, banker, or politician. In any event, this person is powerful enough to wield great, perhaps overwhelming influence. Whether this influence is for good or for evil will depend on the other day-signs with which Deer is linked in the reading. If another individual is not indicated, then the querent is the person who wields power and influence.

Rabbit

Key Words: rebirth, regeneration, ripening, harvest, abundance

In general, Rabbit is a good sign in any reading. If the question involves love, the romance is now "ripe," and marriage may very well be the result. Business questions that yield a Rabbit ending also indicate ripeness; the deal is ready to be sealed, especially if Rabbit appears in combination with Eagle, which signifies money.

Water

Key Words: payment of karmic debts; suffering; illness

Appearing as the result of a divination, Water is primarily an indicator of some karmic debt that must be paid. This might mean that the querent actually owes money or service to another person, or it may mean that the querent has offended the customs of the Ancestors (i.e., his own socio-spiritual values) and must make amends. If the question concerns an illness, then it is some debt—whether to an individual or to the collective—that has caused this sense of "dis-ease" in the individual. The seriousness or intensity of the debt is dependent on the strength of the number—low numbers indicate a fairly easy debt, while higher numbers indicate a debt that is either of long standing or somehow "karmic."

Dog

Key Words: sex, especially when it's slightly illicit; domestic quarrels; uncertainty

In general, the presence of Dog as a divinatory result means sex is involved. This is especially true of the middle and high numbers (from 6 through 13). If the question involves a relationship, it can often mean the querent's partner is seeing someone else. If the question involves beginning a relationship or entering into marriage, a Dog result should be taken as a negative indicator. If 9 Dog appears with regard to an illness, it is believed that one's own sensual indulgences (or inner turmoil caused by those indulgences) lie at the root of the problem. Low-numbered results (1 through 5) or the appearance of Dog in a context that has nothing to do with sex indicate that the querent is indecisive. Other results in the series may indicate the cause of the querent's indecision, but the presence of low-numbered Dog days is a clue that uncertainty is uppermost in the querent's mind.

Monkey

Key Words: to spin the thread of life; to weave the good things of the world; marriage; divination; continuity with the past

Monkey indicates a resounding "yes" answer, whether the question concerns love, money, or travel. The higher the number, the more positive the outlook. Monkey represents the thread on the weaver's shuttle; this answer means that whatever you want—be it romance or wealth—will be rolled up or spun into a beautiful tapestry, as in the art of weaving. Even in questions of illness, Monkey has a somewhat positive connotation; the illness is simply a lack of harmony with one's own nature, and if not serious it can be alleviated by inner work.

The Road

Key Words: the road of life, good fortune, and personal destiny

The presence of Road in a reading tells us how we are faring on the Road of Life. Sometimes this may be a warning: for instance, if Road and Crocodile appear together as two consecutive results in a series, then one has "lost the road." Even if one is sorely troubled, the presence of Road means that one need only "ask for pardon" and it will be granted. If Road comes up repeatedly in the course of a reading, or if it appears in combination with the day-sign Deer, the querent is being called to some special spiritual destiny.

Corn

Key Words: one's spiritual destiny or totem animal; home and family (especially the father's family); the male side of life generally

Corn, like Road, has a strong connection with personal destiny. A strong appearance from this day-sign can mean that the querent's destiny is calling him or her to some specific task, some quantum leap in inner or outer growth. If the querent is ill, then Corn suggests the illness is a result of failing to live up to one's destiny, and that this destiny must be consciously sought out. In other contexts, a Corn result may alert the diviner that the answer lies "within the family." Other results in the reading must be studied carefully, for it may be either the problem or the solution that is to be found in the family circle.

Jaguar

Key Words: the Earth Father as universal creative force; the earth or the world in general; property; healing

A Jaguar result is excellent, especially if one seeks land or a home; the querent will find the home he longs for. However, if the surrounding day-signs are unfavorable, or if the associated number is very high, there may be a problem involving land or property, and in this context Jaguar means that the querent has not rendered proper thanks to

Santo Mundo, the Sacred Earth—in some fashion he or she has fallen out of harmony with nature. This matter of giving thanks to the earth spirit extends to questions of illness as well. If a low-numbered Jaguar day appears, the illness is not serious and the client will soon recover. A higher number again means that the client is out of harmony with the earth. He or she must make amends in order to place him or herself back in balance with Santo Mundo. An offering may be required.

EAGLE

KEY WORDS: good luck in worldly affairs: money; crying out (like an eagle) for what one desires

Eagle is a very good sign when it appears as a divinatory result. If one is asking a question regarding travel or business, Eagle means that the outcome will be favorable—the higher the number, the better the outcome. If Eagle appears in other contexts, it suggests that land or money is involved, and it may well indicate that such benefits are about to accrue to the client. Eagle has a spiritual meaning as well—it may mean that the querent cries out like the eagle, asking for wisdom.

VULTURE

KEY WORDS: pardon; the family; the power of forgiveness (especially in family matters)

In divination, a Vulture outcome is generally favorable. Whatever the problem, pardon and forgiveness are not far off. The spirit of compassion and tolerance is powerful when this day-sign appears. If the question involves business, money or travel, Vulture bodes well for success—the higher the number, the more successful the venture. With regard to relationships, Vulture signifies that the lover or potential marriage partner about whom the client is inquiring will become "like one of the family." In questions involving an illness, Vulture places the responsibility for the problem on the querent's relationships with his or her family. Something is out of harmony here, and must be healed so that long-term recovery and total health are possible.

INCENSE

KEY WORDS: one's thoughts and habits (both good and bad); the ambivalent nature of the human mind; the thinking process in general; meditation, argument, resolution, conclusion, worry

Incense is a very mutable day-sign, and everything depends on the other day-signs that appear with it in the same series. By itself, Incense simply tells us to think. Determining what we need to think about is established by examining the other days in the same reading. If Incense appears along with Vulture, we must think about what karmic issues need to be cleaned out. If it appears with Eagle, we may need to think more about money and material things, or if it appears with Monkey we might need to meditate about how to express our inherent creativity.

FLINT

KEY WORDS: the force of divisiveness and conflict as expressed through quarrels and fights; lies and slander; hidden matters or deception

This day-sign means there's a fight in the making. If the number is very high (10, 11, 12, or 13) someone might even end up spending the night in jail. Flint can mean (in the proper context) that your spouse suspects you of cheating and is angry. If you are inquiring about a relationship, a journey, or a business deal, beware of the possibility that quarrels and arguments may ruin the show.

STORM

KEY WORDS: gossip, trouble, harrassment; the destructive power of the karmic past, but also an offering to the divine

Because of its association with illness in general, Storm tends to be a bad sign if the question involves health. It may, however, be good in other instances, especially questions involving business. In particular, 8 Storm may show that someone—most often the querent—is being drawn into a negative lifestyle because of karmic forces from the past.

THE ANCESTORS

KEY WORDS: the power of the Ancestors (or the deceased, or even death in general); houses and the building of houses

The Ancestors have a strong connection with one's home, and it is this aspect of the day-sign Ancestors that often appears in divination. There may be a quarrel brewing with someone in your home—most frequently your spouse, though it may also indicate a quarrel with siblings or other relatives concerning some family property. In questions involving illness, Ancestors has a very specific set of associations. Take note of the client's age: babies and children are indicated by the numbers 1 through 4, young adults by 5 and 6, middle-aged people in their prime by the sacred numbers 7 and 8, older people by 9, and wise elders or spiritual practitioners by 10 through 13 (though 13 may often signify an occultist, especially one whose spiritual practices carry a hint of danger or imbalance). If the number of the Ancestors day in the reading matches the client's age group, the illness may be serious and a doctor should be consulted immediately. These guidelines concerning the ages of various people can, in fact, be used in any reading wherein Ancestors appears and the identity of some individual is part of the question.

ENDNOTES

1. Bunzel, Ruth. *Chichicastenango* (Seattle: University of Washington Press, 1959).
2. Tedlock, *Time and the Highland Maya*, 153–71.

8

Mayan Historical Prophecy

Mayan historical prophecy—the Mayan concept of the shape of history—has become not only a controversial topic, but a somewhat embarrassing one. Associated in the minds of the general public with the wilder fringes of New Age millennialism, it includes a scenario that goes something like this:

The earth will be destroyed, except for the "spiritually evolved" New Agers, who will be spirited away from the difficulties (i.e., blood, death, and reality) by benevolent beings from outer space. Afterwards, these blissed-out survivors will return to build a new world based on earth-centered cybernetics, channeled babblings from "masters" with weird names, and a resurgence of the tofu industry.

I am absolutely convinced that this is not the scenario that was propounded through historical prophecy during the Classic and Post-Classic eras of Mayan civilization.

But what, then, does the Mayan prophetic tradition actually tell us?

The Long Count

The Maya used the Sacred Calendar to compute large cosmic and historical cycles. These vast computations were accomplished by the use of a system of reckoning called the Long Count.

The Long Count is perhaps the greatest achievement of Mayan civilization. It was based in part on the institution of sacred kingship. It helped the scribes make careful computations of the genealogies of the ahauob and enabled them to calculate vast cycles of history that were endowed with prophetic meaning.

Where did the Long Count come from, and when was it developed? It does not seem to be as old as the Sacred Calendar. To the best of our current knowledge, the tzolkin had been revolving slowly in its fifty-two year rounds for almost a millennium before the Long Count first appeared. The earliest Long Count date yet found is on a vertical column from the state of Chiapas in southern Mexico and reads 7.16.3.2.13, corresponding to December 7, 36 B.C. A stela from Tres Zapotes in Olmec country reads 7.16.6.16.18, or September 3, 32 B.C. Another early Long Count date comes from El Baul in Guatemala, with an inscription indicating a date in A.D. 36.[1] These early dates come from outside the Mayan area. Tres Zapotes is in the lowlands of Veracruz, and El Baul is in the vicinity of Izapa. The earliest date, from Chiapas, comes from a site midway between the two.

The early Long Count date from Tres Zapotes has led some scholars to theorize that the Long Count was yet one more invention of the prodigious Olmecs. However, by the time the first Long Count inscriptions appear, Olmec civilization had declined to a mere shadow of itself. Perhaps this unique method of reckoning time is indeed one of the last achievements of a declining civilization, conceived when the vital Olmec energy had turned cerebral and contemplative.

The Long Count endowed the Maya with a sense of cosmic vision that made them unique. Though all Mesoamerican civilizations made use of the Sacred Calendar, only the Maya practiced the Long Count. Whether or not they "invented" it, they adapted it as their own and made it a foundation stone of their culture. In a way, it is a measure of their unique mathematical and philosophical gifts.

Based on the Sacred Calendar, the Long Count adds a new level of complexity to the concept of ritual time. Its most basic unit is the *kin* (KEEN), which literally means "sun" and signifies a day (one day is "one sun"). Twenty days (the number of day-signs in the tzolkin) equals one *uinal* (wee-NAHL), and eighteen uinals is equal to one *tun* (TOON). The word *tun* literally means "stone," and is comprised of 360 days. This quantity of time, rather than the 365-day haab (solar year), constitutes the real starting point for computing historical cycles. A *katun* (kah-TOON) is comprised of twenty tuns; twenty katuns equal one *baktun* (bahk-TOON)—144,000 days—a period of approximately 395 years. Thirteen baktuns is equal to 5,125 years. The relationship between these units of time is presented in Figure 17.

		1 kin	=	1 day
20 kins	=	1 uinal	=	20 days
18 uinals	=	1 tun	=	360 days
20 tuns	=	1 katun (20 tuns)	=	7,200 days
20 katuns	=	1 baktun (400 tuns)	=	144,000 days
13 baktuns	=	1 Great Cycle (5,200 tuns)	=	1,872,000 days

FIGURE 17 ***The Long Count***

This comprises the highly publicized "Great Cycle" that inspired the "New Age event" called the Harmonic Convergence. The Great Cycle in which we are now living began on August 13, 3114 B.C., when First Mother and First Father brought the present world into being, as the Palenque Creation Myth tells us. It will end on December 21, 2012.

The Long Count dates all events from the initial beginning of the Great Cycle in 3114 B.C., a date written as 0.0.0.0.0. The numerical positions stand for baktuns, katuns, tuns, uinals, and kins respectively. For example, our date May 27, 1983, would be written as 12.18.9.17.19, indicating that twelve baktuns, eighteen katuns, nine tuns, seventeen uinals, and nineteen kins have passed since the beginning of the Great Cycle. Note that here, as in the solar calendar, the number series begins with 0. The twenty kins within a uinal are numbered 0 through 19, the eighteen uinals are numbered 0 through 17, and so on.

The two most important subdivisions of the Great Cycle are the baktuns and the katuns. Each baktun lasts about 395 years. Each katun lasts for approximately 20 years, and it was the katuns which the Maya used to predict the course of political events.

The Katun Cycle

Almost everything we know about the katun cycle is contained in the *Books of Chilam Balam.*[2] These prophetic works and divinatory almanacs have a somewhat complex and mysterious history. They originated in the utterances of one or more individuals known as Chilam Balam, the "jaguar prophet." This person or persons, who lived in Yucatán at sometime before the Spanish Conquest, produced a series of prophecies, based on the katuns, which actually predicted the Spanish invasion and conquest of Yucatán. Though the Maya had been conquered politically, there were many who maintained their spiritual liberty for years afterwards, practicing the old rites and keeping the Sacred Calendar. For these traditionalists, the prophecies of the Jaguar Prophet became a kind of Bible or sacred text. Written copies were kept in various towns and villages around the Yucatán peninsula. Over the centuries, the keepers of the books inserted other material into their own copies, so that the *Book of Chilam Balam of Chumayel* is now different in many ways from the *Book of Chilam Balam of Tizimin,* or any other version of these books.

The books of Chilam Balam based the meaning of each katun on the numbers rather than the day-signs. Each katun is an ahau, a "lord" who rules over that span of time. Each katun ends on the day Ahau in the Sacred Calendar, though always on a different number. The entire katun is given the number of the Ahau day on which it ended.[3]

As with everything else pertaining to the Sacred Calendar, a special rhythm was set up. The katuns always progressed in the same ineluctable order, as follows:

11 Ahau
9 Ahau
7 Ahau
5 Ahau
3 Ahau
1 Ahau
12 Ahau
10 Ahau
8 Ahau
6 Ahau
4 Ahau
2 Ahau
13 Ahau
11 Ahau

This rhythm of the katuns sets up an orderly sequence that can be applied to the entire Great Cycle and diagramed on a Calendar Board framework. It shows us the template of history as the Classic Mayan scribes understood it (Figure 18).

The element of prediction or prophecy—or, in more contemporary terms, of assessing socio-political trends—is based on the numbers of the katuns.[4] Each katun or twenty-year period will have a distinct character or quality that, to some degree, determines the kinds of events that will take place during that period of time. Of course there were other factors, such as the cycle of individual Year Lords or the conjunctions and stations of planets in the sky, which colored the situation. History never repeated itself exactly; rather, it could best be understood in terms of general historical themes that remained constant while being subject to modification by other concurrent cycles.

To make matters more complex (as they always are when working with the Sacred Calendar), the thirteen numbers had very distinct and specific meanings when applied to the cycle of katuns. The prophecies of Chilam Balam allow us at least a glimpse of these meanings, and those who have an interest in such matters may check the beginning and ending dates of all the katuns for this century in the Calendar Tables at the back of this book.

11 Ahau—A time of misery and of little rainfall; a harsh and ungenerous katun.

9 Ahau—A time of "excessive adultery" and widespread lasciviousness; also a time of drought or poor harvests.

7 Ahau—A time of political chicanery; the lascivious or carnal tendencies of the previous katun remain in force.

5 Ahau—The word usually applied to this cycle by the *Chilam Balam* books is "harsh."

3 Ahau—A time of drought, pestilence, and war.

1 Ahau—This was simply known as "the evil katun."

12 Ahau—This katun was believed to be exceptionally positive.

10 Ahau—A time of drought.

8 Ahau—Though this is marked as a time of conflict or war, it also signifies an end to "greed and vexation"; this rather ambiguous meaning suggests harmony or peace struggling to emerge in a time of conflict.

6 Ahau—Another period of general moral turpitude and sensual indulgence.

4 Ahau—During this time, the *Chilam Balam* announces the return of Kukulcan or "the quetzal." This, of course, is the Toltec prophet and avatar Feathered Serpent or Quetzalcoatl.

BAKTUN:

0	1	2	3	4	5	6	7	8	9	10	11	12
2	1	13	12	11	10	9	8	7	6	5	4	3
13	12	11	10	9	8	7	6	5	4	3	2	1
11	10	9	8	7	6	5	4	3	2	1	13	12
9	8	7	6	5	4	3	2	1	13	12	11	10
7	6	5	4	3	2	1	13	12	11	10	9	8
5	4	3	2	1	13	12	11	10	9	8	7	6
3	2	1	13	12	11	10	9	8	7	6	5	4
1	13	12	11	10	9	8	7	6	5	4	3	2
12	11	10	9	8	7	6	5	4	3	2	1	13
10	9	8	7	6	5	4	3	2	1	13	12	11
8	7	6	5	4	3	2	1	13	12	11	10	9
6	5	4	3	2	1	13	12	11	10	9	8	7
4	3	2	1	13	12	11	10	9	8	7	6	5
2	1	13	12	11	10	9	8	7	6	5	4	3
13	12	11	10	9	8	7	6	5	4	3	2	1
11	10	9	8	7	6	5	4	3	2	1	13	12
9	8	7	6	5	4	3	2	1	13	12	11	10
7	6	5	4	3	2	1	13	12	11	10	9	8
5	4	3	2	1	13	12	11	10	9	8	7	6
3	2	1	13	12	11	10	9	8	7	6	5	4

Figure 18 ***The Katun Cycle***

The prophecy for Katun 4 Ahau is one of spiritual regeneration and messianic expectation.

2 Ahau—An unstable period, characterized by fluctuations in the availability of goods.

13 Ahau—An unlucky period generally.

It will be apparent from the data given above that the Maya were pessimists about the course of human history. The Sacred Calendar tells us, by way of the day-signs, that each individual has the possibility to perfect himself through inner transformation—but humanity as a whole was obviously perceived as a much less hopeful case.

April 5, 1993, was the beginning of the final katun of the entire Great Cycle. This katun, ending December 21, 2012, is numbered 4—4 Ahau is the katun of the return of the great avatar Feathered Serpent.

Make of it what you will.

The End of the Great Cycle

Those who know the Mayan Calendar primarily through New Age sources, and particularly through the highly publicized Harmonic Convergence event, may wonder: Wasn't the Mayan Great Cycle—and perhaps the world as we know it—supposed to end on August 17, 1987, rather than December 21, 2012?

Harmonic Convergence theorist Jose Arguelles derived the 1987 date from the writings of Tony Shearer, a Sioux Indian from Colorado who has written on the subject of the Aztec (not the Mayan) version of the Sacred Calendar.[5] The surviving Aztec codices speak of four previous eras, worlds or "suns" that have come and gone before the advent of our present world, the "fifth sun." Various ancient sources attribute different sequences or durations of these previous "suns." The best known version, contained in the *Aztec Legend of the Suns*, gives the following dates for the successive "suns," each named for a day-sign and given the number 4:

4 Jaguar 955—279 B.C.

4 Wind 279 B.C.—A.D. 85

4 Storm 85—A.D. 397

4 Water 397—A.D.1073

4 Earthquake (Incense) A.D. 1073—?

The Aztec text gives no terminal date to the fifth sun, the one in which we now live.[6]

Shearer's theory is based on a variant interpretation in which a "sun" or "world" lasts 1,144 years. This number is derived by adding the number of Heavens and Hells, which gives us 13+9=22. Then 22 is multiplied by 52, which represents a "bundle of years" or complete Calendar Round. Shearer argues that the present world, 4 Earthquake (4 Incense or 4 Caban), began in A.D. 843 and that the landing of Cortez on the shores of Mexico on April 21, 1519, represented the shift from the cycle of the 13 Heavens to that of the 9 Hells. Shearer postulates an ending to the "fifth sun" on August 17, 1987.

From a scholarly point of view, the 1987 date simply does not appear in any of the old Long Count inscriptions, and it is difficult to see why Shearer and Arguelles placed so much emphasis on it. After all, Arguelles was perfectly aware that the actual ending of the Great Cycle itself is in 2012. In fairness to the position taken by these Harmonic Convergence theorists, we must remember that the Sacred Calendar is a Native American system of myth and magic, and that a number of Native American spokespersons—notably the Cherokee medicine woman Dhyani Ywahoo and the Yucatec Mayan teacher Hunbatz Men—have agreed with Arguelles and with Shearer (who is also Native American) regarding the significance of the 1987 date.

Even more fascinating, however, is the actual end date of the Mayan Calendar, December 21, 2012. Scholars have always regarded this as a "derived" date, unrelated to any celestial phenomena—since even the Maya, with their prodigious mathematical abilities, could scarcely have looked that far into the future. They were certainly aware that the end date was also the winter solstice, but beyond that...?

Beyond that, there is actually a great deal. Astrologer John Jenkins has shown that December 21, 2012, is one of those rare days, occurring only once in thousands of years, when the sun stands at the actual (as opposed to apparent) conjunction of the zodiac with the center of the Milky Way—the celestial equivalent of the Mayan World Tree. Therefore, it is fair to say that the sun is at the very center of all things on the final day of this Great Cycle.

Such an occurrence can hardly be accidental. Yet, as Jenkins shows, the Maya could only have computed such an end date if they were aware of the precession of the equinoxes. So at the very least, Jenkins' discovery establishes that the Maya were even more astronomically sophisticated than we believed.[7]

Whether we postulate 1987 or 2012 as indicating a quantum shift in the nature of time, we are still left with the question of whether the end of the current Great Cycle really signifies "the end of history."

Only the monotheistic religions such as Christianity and Islam insist on a linear model of time—one with a clear beginning and an equally clear, absolute, ending. Most traditional or tribal religions postulate a whole different world view. They see human history as a series of endlessly recurring cycles. We have no reason to suspect that the Mayans saw things differently.

Let us look back. A Great Cycle lasts 5,125 years. The last one began in 3114 B.C. Does that mean that there was a previous Great Cycle, one that ostensibly began in 8239 B.C.?

We must assume that there was. In fact, some of the Mayan glyphic texts record dates far back in the past, unbelievable millions of years ago.[8] Obviously, the Maya themselves believed that there had been previous Great Cycles. First Mother and First Father may have created "the world as we know it" in 3114 B.C., but that was surely a re-creation, one of a number of endless cyclic creations.

The end of the Great Cycle simply implies the beginning of a new Great Cycle. In fact, Pacal the Great of Palenque, optimistically projecting his own royal dynasty forward into eternity, recorded a Long Count date equivalent to October 23, A.D. 4772—some 2,760 years beyond the Great Cycle's "terminal date" of A.D. 2012.[9]

There is no doubt that a cyclic philosophy of history was part of Mayan tradition. At the beginning of this chapter, we listed the world cycles, which the Aztecs believed had led up to our own. The first was 4 Jaguar, and the primordial inhabitants of this world were torn to pieces by wild beasts. Next came 4 Wind; its inhabitants were blown away by fierce winds. The next two worlds were 4 Storm and 4 Water, which were destroyed by thunderstorms and floods respectively. Then came the fifth world, 4 Earthquake (Incense), which, according to the Aztecs, is the present world. Because ancient sources disagree on how long these successive worlds last, we have no way of knowing when 4 Earthquake is due to end or what is expected to follow it. Similarly, Pueblo tribes of the American Southwest, such as the Hopi and Zuñi, conceive of humanity as "emerging" through successive worlds—the goal is to evolve spiritually, though humankind slips backwards as often as not. The Southwestern tribes often place the drama of emergence in a purely mythic "time beyond time"—one that has only a tentative relationship to historical, chronological time.

The Mayan *Popol Vuh* records a similar progression of worlds. The gods make several attempts at creating human beings, but the first few attempts fail. The earliest effort results in howling, chattering creatures, which the gods transform into the animals. The next try results in a man of mud who dissolves in the rain. The third try produces men of wood who are able to function in a primitive fashion but cannot worship the gods properly—they are not yet spiritual beings. The gods destroy them in violent rains and floods, even sending the animals to attack them. Their descendants are the monkeys. Finally, on the fourth try, the gods create men.[10]

The analogies with the Aztec cycle and the Puebloan drama of emergence are obvious, and we shall be on firm ground if we suspect that the Mayan Great Cycle corresponds in some way to one of these "worlds" or "creations." The Maya, however, have placed a definite end date on this present world that some ancient Mesoamericans called 4 Earthquake—an end date of December 21, 2012.

What is important about the tale of the worlds in the *Popol Vuh* is that it presents us with a clear message: the early "men" are destroyed by fire, flood, and wild animals in order to facilitate an ongoing process of evolutionary development, as in the Southwestern myths. The intent of the gods is to create a human being who is fully realized. The concept of successive worlds records the progress of human spiritual evolution, and the changes in Great Cycles mark significant evolutionary leaps—moments when powerful transformations occur, when one world or level of consciousness goes through a kind of death in order that a higher level of development may take shape.

If the end of the Great Cycle means anything, it most emphatically does not mean the actual physical destruction of the planet. It heralds the death of an outmoded level of consciousness that no longer serves humanity's needs. The end of all our carefully cherished assumptions about life and the universe will surely be a painful experience, and is bound to have painful repercussions in the political or social world. However, the ancient prophecies are equally clear in promising the birth of a new, more enlightened field of consciousness.

ENDNOTES

1. Michael Coe, *Mexico* (New York: Thames and Hudson, 1984), 76–7, and *The Maya* (New York: Thames and Hudson, 1984), 48–9.

2. The various *Books of Chilam Balam* and their translations are as follows: *The Codex Perez* and the *Book of Chilam Balam of Mani* have been translated by Eugeme Craine and Reginald Reindorp (Norman: University of Oklahoma, 1979), while the day-sign auguries from the *Book of Chilam Balam of Kaua* have been translated into Spanish by Alfredo Barrera Vasquez as *Horoscopos Mayas* (Merida: Area Maya, 1986). Munro Edmonson has translated *The Ancient Future of the Itzá: The Book of Chilam Balam of Tizimin* (Austin: University of Texas, 1982) as well as *Heaven Born Merida and Its Destiny: The Book of Chilam Balam of Chumayel* (Austin: University of Texas, 1986). An older translation of the Chumayel manuscript is by Ralph L. Roys, *The Book of Chilam Balam of Chumayel* (Norman: University of Oklahoma, 1967), which in my opinion is sometimes superior to Edmonson's version.

3. This, at least, was how it was done in the Classic Period. Munro Edmonson, translator of two *Chilam Balam* manuscripts, believed that the Long Count system went through several major changes just before and after the Spanish Conquest. For reasons of clarity, however, we will stick to the Classic Period katun count in this book.

4. Jose Arguelles has created a somewhat different version of the Mayan Calendar's "structure of time" based on the idea that the katuns may be interpreted as day-signs rather than numbers. This is one of the more fascinating bits of "creative interpretation" to be found in his book *The Mayan Factor.*

5. Shearer, *Beneath the Moon and Under the Sun.*

6. Miguel Leon-Portilla, *Aztec Thought and Culture: A Study of the Ancient Nahuatl Mind* (Norman: University of Oklahoma, 1982), 38–9.

7. John Major Jenkins, "The How and Why of the Mayan End Date in 2012 A.D." *The Mountain Astrologer* 8:1 (Dec/Jan 1994–95): 52–7.

8. Schele and Freidel, *Forest of Kings*, 430, n. 39.

9. Ibid.

10. Dennis Tedlock, trans. *Popol Vuh: The Mayan Book of the Dawn of Life* (New York: Simon and Schuster, 1985), 76–86.

Appendix

Mayan Calendar Tables for the 20th Century

The Calendar Tables list the beginning of each fortnightly period from the beginning of the twentieth century until the end of the Great Cycle (December 21, 2012), and can be used to find any Mayan Calendar date within that period.

Some readers may note that the correlation between the Mayan and Western calendars given here is different from the one given in Jose Arguelles' well-known book *The Mayan Factor* and in his subsequent writings. Arguelles and his adherents keep their own version of the Sacred Calendar, with their own day-count; theirs is not the same as the traditional Mayan day count. In this book I have used the traditional Mayan count, as it has been kept since pre-Columbian times and as it is still kept today in various parts of Mesoamerica.

How to Use the Calendar Tables

Let us say you are attempting to find the Mayan equivalent for our date June 26, 1995. First, find the year 1995 in the Calendar Tables. Running your finger down the column, you note that the fortnight that began immediately before that date was 1 Crocodile, which began on June 15.

Now turn to the Calendar Board on page 183 of this appendix. Find the day 1 Crocodile. Then count down to the appropriate day in the following method:

June 15 = 1 Crocodile
June 16 = 2 Wind
June 17 = 3 Night
June 18 = 4 Lizard
June 19 = 5 Serpent
June 20 = 6 Death
June 21 = 7 Deer
June 22 = 8 Rabbit
June 23 = 9 Water
June 24 = 10 Dog

In essence, it really is that simple. (If you're feeling creative, you can count backwards, if it's quicker, from the 1 date *following* the date you're looking for.) However, be aware of leap years. They can throw off your count.

Leap Years are important in another respect, too. Note that in each column listing the Mayan dates, a Mayan New Year's day is listed along with the name of the year. The actual New Year date changes every four years. This is because the Maya did not honor the custom of leap years (though they were aware of the astronomical factors that have caused Westerners to develop the concept). In these tables, Leap Years have been marked with an asterisk.

Those with an interest in the cycles of history will also find the ending dates for the katuns or twenty-year periods included.

CROCODILE	1	8	2	9	3	10	4	11	5	12	6	13	7
WIND	2	9	3	10	4	11	5	12	6	13	7	1	8
NIGHT	3	10	4	11	5	12	6	13	7	1	8	2	9
LIZARD	4	11	5	12	6	13	7	1	8	2	9	3	10
SERPENT	5	12	6	13	7	1	8	2	9	3	10	4	11
DEATH	6	13	7	1	8	2	9	3	10	4	11	5	12
DEER	7	1	8	2	9	3	10	4	11	5	12	6	13
RABBIT	8	2	9	3	10	4	11	5	12	6	13	7	1
WATER	9	3	10	4	11	5	12	6	13	7	1	8	2
DOG	10	4	11	5	12	6	13	7	1	8	2	9	3
MONKEY	11	5	12	6	13	7	1	8	2	9	3	10	4
ROAD	12	6	13	7	1	8	2	9	3	10	4	11	5
CORN	13	7	1	8	2	9	3	10	4	11	5	12	6
JAGUAR	1	8	2	9	3	10	4	11	5	12	6	13	7
EAGLE	2	9	3	10	4	11	5	12	6	13	7	1	8
VULTURE	3	10	4	11	5	12	6	13	7	1	8	2	9
INCENSE	4	11	5	12	6	13	7	1	8	2	9	3	10
FLINT	5	12	6	13	7	1	8	2	9	3	10	4	11
STORM	6	13	7	1	8	2	9	3	10	4	11	5	12
ANCESTORS	7	1	8	2	9	3	10	4	11	5	12	6	13

The Mayan Calendar Board

Gregorian Date	Mayan Date
KATUN 1 AHAU (1894–1914)	
1900	
Jan 11	1 RABBIT
Jan 24	1 CROCODILE
Feb 6	1 JAGUAR
Feb 19	1 DEER
Mar 4	1 ANCESTORS
Mar 17	1 CORN
Mayan Year 5 INCENSE (Mar 21)	
Mar 30	1 DEATH
Apr 12	1 STORM
Apr 25	1 ROAD
May 8	1 SERPENT
May 21	1 FLINT
Jun 3	1 MONKEY
Jun 16	1 LIZARD
Jun 29	1 INCENSE
Jul 12	1 DOG
Jul 25	1 NIGHT
Aug 7	1 VULTURE
Aug 20	1 WATER
Sep 2	1 WIND
Sep 15	1 EAGLE
Sep 28	1 RABBIT
Oct 11	1 CROCODILE
Oct 24	1 JAGUAR
Nov 6	1 DEER
Nov 19	1 ANCESTORS
Dec 2	1 CORN
Dec 15	1 DEATH
Dec 28	1 STORM
1901	
Jan 10	1 ROAD
Jan 23	1 SERPENT
Feb 5	1 FLINT
Feb 18	1 MONKEY
Mar 3	1 LIZARD

Gregorian Date	Mayan Date
Mar 16	1 INCENSE
Mayan Year 6 WIND (Mar 21)	
Mar 29	1 DOG
Apr 11	1 NIGHT
Apr 24	1 VULTURE
May 7	1 WATER
May 20	1 WIND
Jun 2	1 EAGLE
Jun 15	1 RABBIT
Jun 28	1 CROCODILE
Jul 11	1 JAGUAR
Jul 24	1 DEER
Aug 6	1 ANCESTORS
Aug 19	1 CORN
Sep 1	1 DEATH
Sep 14	1 STORM
Sep 27	1 ROAD
Oct 10	1 SERPENT
Oct 23	1 FLINT
Nov 5	1 MONKEY
Nov 18	1 LIZARD
Dec 1	1 INCENSE
Dec 14	1 DOG
Dec 27	1 NIGHT
1902	
Jan 9	1 VULTURE
Jan 22	1 WATER
Feb 4	1 WIND
Feb 17	1 EAGLE
Mar 2	1 RABBIT
Mar 15	1 CROCODILE
Mayan Year 7 DEER (Mar 21)	
Mar 28	1 JAGUAR
Apr 10	1 DEER
Apr 23	1 ANCESTORS
May 6	1 CORN

*** indicates a leap year**

Gregorian Date	Mayan Date
May 19	1 DEATH
Jun 1	1 STORM
Jun 14	1 ROAD
Jun 27	1 SERPENT
Jul 10	1 FLINT
Jul 23	1 MONKEY
Aug 5	1 LIZARD
Aug 18	1 INCENSE
Aug 31	1 DOG
Sep 13	1 NIGHT
Sep 26	1 VULTURE
Oct 9	1 WATER
Oct 22	1 WIND
Nov 4	1 EAGLE
Nov 17	1 RABBIT
Nov 30	1 CROCODILE
Dec 13	1 JAGUAR
Dec 26	1 DEER
1903	
Jan 8	1 ANCESTORS
Jan 21	1 CORN
Feb 3	1 DEATH
Feb 16	1 STORM
Mar 1	1 ROAD
Mar 14	1 SERPENT
Mayan Year 8 ROAD (Mar 21)	
Mar 27	FLINT
Apr 9	1 MONKEY
Apr 22	LIZARD
May 5	1 INCENSE
May 18	1 DOG
May 31	1 NIGHT
Jun 13	1 VULTURE
Jun 26	1 WATER
Jul 9	1 WIND
Jul 22	1 EAGLE
Aug 4	1 RABBIT
Aug 17	1 CROCODILE
Aug 30	1 JAGUAR
Sep 12	1 DEER
Sep 25	1 ANCESTORS
Oct 8	1 CORN
Oct 21	1 DEATH
Nov 3	1 STORM
Nov 16	1 ROAD
Nov 29	1 SERPENT
Dec 12	1 FLINT
Dec 25	1 MONKEY
***1904**	
Jan 7	1 LIZARD
Jan 20	1 INCENSE
Feb 2	1 DOG
Feb 15	1 NIGHT
Feb 28	1 VULTURE
Mar 12	1 WATER
Mayan Year 9 INCENSE (Mar 20)	
Mar 25	1 WIND
Apr 7	1 EAGLE
Apr 20	1 RABBIT
May 3	1 CROCODILE
May 16	1 JAGUAR
May 29	1 DEER
Jun 11	1 ANCESTORS
Jun 24	1 CORN
Jul 7	1 DEATH
Jul 20	1 STORM
Aug 2	1 ROAD
Aug 15	1 SERPENT
Aug 28	1 FLINT
Sep 10	1 MONKEY
Sep 23	1 LIZARD
Oct 6	1 INCENSE
Oct 19	1 DOG
Nov 1	1 NIGHT

*** indicates a leap year**

Gregorian Date	Mayan Date
Nov 14	1 VULTURE
Nov 27	1 WATER
Dec 10	1 WIND
Dec 23	1 EAGLE

1905

Gregorian Date	Mayan Date
Jan 5	1 RABBIT
Jan 18	1 CROCODILE
Jan 31	1 JAGUAR
Feb 13	1 DEER
Feb 26	1 ANCESTORS
Mar 11	1 CORN

Mayan Year 10 WIND (Mar 20)

Gregorian Date	Mayan Date
Mar 24	1 DEATH
Apr 6	1 STORM
Apr 19	1 ROAD
May 2	1 SERPENT
May 15	1 FLINT
May 28	1 MONKEY
Jun 10	1 LIZARD
Jun 23	1 INCENSE
Jul 6	1 DOG
Jul 19	1 NIGHT
Aug 1	1 VULTURE
Aug 14	1 WATER
Aug 27	1 WIND
Sep 9	1 EAGLE
Sep 22	1 RABBIT
Oct 5	1 CROCODILE
Oct 18	1 JAGUAR
Oct 31	1 DEER
Nov 13	1 ANCESTORS
Nov 26	1 CORN
Dec 9	1 DEATH
Dec 22	1 STORM

1906

Gregorian Date	Mayan Date
Jan 4	1 ROAD
Jan 17	1 SERPENT
Jan 30	1 FLINT
Feb 12	1 MONKEY
Feb 25	1 LIZARD
Mar 10	1 INCENSE

Mayan Year 11 DEER (Mar 20)

Gregorian Date	Mayan Date
Mar 23	1 DOG
Apr 5	1 NIGHT
Apr 18	1 VULTURE
May 1	1 WATER
May 14	1 WIND
May 27	1 EAGLE
Jun 9	1 RABBIT
Jun 22	1 CROCODILE
Jul 5	1 JAGUAR
Jul 18	1 DEER
Jul 31	1 ANCESTORS
Aug 13	1 CORN
Aug 26	1 DEATH
Sep 8	1 STORM
Sep 21	1 ROAD
Oct 4	1 SERPENT
Oct 17	1 FLINT
Oct 30	1 MONKEY
Nov 12	1 LIZARD
Nov 25	1 INCENSE
Dec 8	1 DOG
Dec 21	1 NIGHT

1907

Gregorian Date	Mayan Date
Jan 3	1 VULTURE
Jan 16	1 WATER
Jan 29	1 WIND
Feb 11	1 EAGLE
Feb 24	1 RABBIT
Mar 9	1 CROCODILE

Mayan Year 12 ROAD (Mar 20)

Gregorian Date	Mayan Date
Mar 22	1 JAGUAR
Apr 4	1 DEER

*** indicates a leap year**

Gregorian Date	Mayan Date
Apr 17	1 ANCESTORS
Apr 30	1 CORN
May 13	1 DEATH
May 26	1 STORM
Jun 8	1 ROAD
Jun 21	1 SERPENT
Jul 4	1 FLINT
Jul 17	1 MONKEY
Jul 30	1 LIZARD
Aug 12	1 INCENSE
Aug 25	1 DOG
Sep 7	1 NIGHT
Sep 20	1 VULTURE
Oct 3	1 WATER
Oct 16	1 WIND
Oct 29	1 EAGLE
Nov 11	1 RABBIT
Nov 24	1 CROCODILE
Dec 7	1 JAGUAR
Dec 20	1 DEER

***1908**

Gregorian Date	Mayan Date
Jan 2	1 ANCESTORS
Jan 15	1 CORN
Jan 28	1 DEATH
Feb 10	1 STORM
Feb 23	1 ROAD
Mar 7	1 SERPENT

Mayan Year 13 INCENSE (Mar 19)

Gregorian Date	Mayan Date
Mar 20	1 FLINT
Apr 2	1 MONKEY
Apr 15	1 LIZARD
Apr 28	1 INCENSE
May 11	1 DOG
May 24	1 NIGHT
Jun 6	1 VULTURE
Jun 19	1 WATER
Jul 2	1 WIND
Jul 15	1 EAGLE
Jul 28	1 RABBIT
Aug 10	1 CROCODILE
Aug 23	1 JAGUAR
Sep 5	1 DEER
Sep 18	1 ANCESTORS
Oct 1	1 CORN
Oct 14	1 DEATH
Oct 27	1 STORM
Nov 9	1 ROAD
Nov 22	1 SERPENT
Dec 5	1 FLINT
Dec 18	1 MONKEY
Dec 31	1 LIZARD

1909

Gregorian Date	Mayan Date
Jan 13	1 INCENSE
Jan 26	1 DOG
Feb 8	1 NIGHT
Feb 21	1 VULTURE
Mar 6	1 WATER
Mar 19	1 WIND

Mayan Year 1 WIND (Mar 19)

Gregorian Date	Mayan Date
Apr 1	1 EAGLE
Apr 14	1 RABBIT
Apr 27	1 CROCODILE
May 10	1 JAGUAR
May 23	1 DEER
Jun 5	1 ANCESTORS
Jun 18	1 CORN
Jul 1	1 DEATH
Jul 14	1 STORM
Jul 27	1 ROAD
Aug 9	1 SERPENT
Aug 22	1 FLINT
Sep 4	1 MONKEY
Sep 17	1 LIZARD
Sep 30	1 INCENSE

*** indicates a leap year**

Gregorian Date	Mayan Date
Oct 13	1 DOG
Oct 26	1 NIGHT
Nov 8	1 VULTURE
Nov 21	1 WATER
Dec 4	1 WIND
Dec 17	1 EAGLE
Dec 30	1 RABBIT
1910	
Jan 12	1 CROCODILE
Jan 25	1 JAGUAR
Feb 7	1 DEER
Feb 20	1 ANCESTORS
Mar 5	1 CORN
Mar 18	1 DEATH
Mayan Year	**2 DEER (Mar 19)**
Mar 31	1 STORM
Apr 13	1 ROAD
Apr 26	1 SERPENT
May 9	1 FLINT
May 22	1 MONKEY
Jun 4	1 LIZARD
Jun 17	1 INCENSE
Jun 30	1 DOG
Jul 13	1 NIGHT
Jul 26	1 VULTURE
Aug 8	1 WATER
Aug 21	1 WIND
Sep 3	1 EAGLE
Sep 16	1 RABBIT
Sep 29	1 CROCODILE
Oct 12	1 JAGUAR
Oct 25	1 DEER
Nov 7	1 ANCESTORS
Nov 20	1 CORN
Dec 3	1 DEATH
Dec 16	1 STORM
Dec 29	1 ROAD

Gregorian Date	Mayan Date
1911	
Jan 11	1 SERPENT
Jan 24	1 FLINT
Feb 6	1 MONKEY
Feb 19	1 LIZARD
Mar 4	1 INCENSE
Mar 17	1 DOG
Mayan Year	**3 ROAD (Mar 19)**
Mar 30	1 NIGHT
Apr 12	1 VULTURE
Apr 25	1 WATER
May 8	1 WIND
May 21	1 EAGLE
Jun 3	1 RABBIT
Jun 16	1 CROCODILE
Jun 29	1 JAGUAR
Jul 12	1 DEER
Jul 25	1 ANCESTORS
Aug 7	1 CORN
Aug 20	1 DEATH
Sep 2	1 STORM
Sep 15	1 ROAD
Sep 28	1 SERPENT
Oct 11	1 FLINT
Oct 24	1 MONKEY
Nov 6	1 LIZARD
Nov 19	1 INCENSE
Dec 2	1 DOG
Dec 15	1 NIGHT
Dec 28	1 VULTURE
***1912**	
Jan 10	1 WATER
Jan 23	1 WIND
Feb 5	1 EAGLE
Feb 18	1 RABBIT
Mar 2	1 CROCODILE
Mar 15	1 JAGUAR

*** indicates a leap year**

Gregorian Date	Mayan Date
Mayan Year	**4 INCENSE (Mar 18)**
Mar 28	1 DEER
Apr 10	1 ANCESTORS
Apr 23	1 CORN
May 6	1 DEATH
May 19	1 STORM
Jun 1	1 ROAD
Jun 14	1 SERPENT
Jun 27	1 FLINT
Jul 10	1 MONKEY
Jul 23	1 LIZARD
Aug 5	1 INCENSE
Aug 18	1 DOG
Aug 31	1 NIGHT
Sep 13	1 VULTURE
Sep 26	1 WATER
Oct 9	1 WIND
Oct 22	1 EAGLE
Nov 4	1 RABBIT
Nov 17	1 CROCODILE
Nov 30	1 JAGUAR
Dec 13	1 DEER
Dec 26	1 ANCESTORS
1913	
Jan 8	1 CORN
Jan 21	1 DEATH
Feb 3	1 STORM
Feb 16	1 ROAD
Mar 1	1 SERPENT
Mar 14	1 FLINT
Mayan Year	**5 WIND (Mar 18)**
Mar 27	1 MONKEY
Apr 9	1 LIZARD
Apr 22	1 INCENSE
May 5	1 DOG
May 18	1 NIGHT
May 31	1 VULTURE
Jun 13	1 WATER
Jun 26	1 WIND
Jul 9	1 EAGLE
Jul 22	1 RABBIT
Aug 4	1 CROCODILE
Aug 17	1 JAGUAR
Aug 30	1 DEER
Sep 12	1 ANCESTORS
Sep 25	1 CORN
Oct 8	1 DEATH
Oct 21	1 STORM
Nov 3	1 ROAD
Nov 16	1 SERPENT
Nov 29	1 FLINT
Dec 12	1 MONKEY
Dec 25	1 LIZARD
1914	
Jan 7	1 INCENSE
Jan 20	1 DOG
Feb 2	1 NIGHT
Feb 15	1 VULTURE
Feb 28	1 WATER
Mar 13	1 WIND
Mayan Year	**6 DEER (Mar 18)**
Mar 26	1 EAGLE
Apr 8	1 RABBIT
Apr 21	1 CROCODILE
May 4	1 JAGUAR
May 17	1 DEER
May 30	1 ANCESTORS
END KATUN 1 AHAU (May 30)	
BEGIN KATUN 12 AHAU	
Jun 12	1 CORN
Jun 25	1 DEATH
Jul 8	1 STORM
Jul 21	1 ROAD
Aug 3	1 SERPENT

*** indicates a leap year**

Gregorian Date	Mayan Date
Aug 16	1 FLINT
Aug 29	1 MONKEY
Sep 11	1 LIZARD
Sep 24	1 INCENSE
Oct 7	1 DOG
Oct 20	1 NIGHT
Nov 2	1 VULTURE
Nov 15	1 WATER
Nov 28	1 WIND
Dec 11	1 EAGLE
Dec 24	1 RABBIT
1915	
Jan 6	1 CROCODILE
Jan 19	1 JAGUAR
Feb 1	1 DEER
Feb 14	1 ANCESTORS
Feb 27	1 CORN
Mar 12	1 DEATH
Mayan Year	**7 ROAD (Mar 18)**
Mar 25	1 STORM
Apr 7	1 ROAD
Apr 20	1 SERPENT
May 3	1 FLINT
May 16	1 MONKEY
May 29	1 LIZARD
Jun 11	1 INCENSE
Jun 24	1 DOG
Jul 7	1 NIGHT
Jul 20	1 VULTURE
Aug 2	1 WATER
Aug 15	1 WIND
Aug 28	1 EAGLE
Sep 10	1 RABBIT
Sep 23	1 CROCODILE
Oct 6	1 JAGUAR
Oct 19	1 DEER
Nov 1	1 ANCESTORS
Nov 14	1 CORN
Nov 27	1 DEATH
Dec 10	1 STORM
Dec 23	1 ROAD
***1916**	
Jan 5	1 SERPENT
Jan 18	1 FLINT
Jan 31	1 MONKEY
Feb 13	1 LIZARD
Feb 26	1 INCENSE
Mar 10	1 DOG
Mayan Year	**8 INCENSE (Mar 17)**
Mar 23	1 NIGHT
Apr 5	1 VULTURE
Apr 18	1 WATER
May 1	1 WIND
May 14	1 EAGLE
May 27	1 RABBIT
Jun 9	1 CROCODILE
Jun 22	1 JAGUAR
Jul 5	1 DEER
Jul 18	1 ANCESTORS
Jul 31	1 CORN
Aug 13	1 DEATH
Aug 26	1 STORM
Sep 8	1 ROAD
Sep 21	1 SERPENT
Oct 4	1 FLINT
Oct 17	1 MONKEY
Oct 30	1 LIZARD
Nov 12	1 INCENSE
Nov 25	1 DOG
Dec 8	1 NIGHT
Dec 21	1 VULTURE
1917	
Jan 3	1 WATER
Jan 16	1 WIND

*** indicates a leap year**

Gregorian Date	Mayan Date
Jan 29	1 EAGLE
Feb 11	1 RABBIT
Feb 24	1 CROCODILE
Mar 9	1 JAGUAR
Mayan Year	**9 WIND (Mar 17)**
Mar 22	1 DEER
Apr 4	1 ANCESTORS
Apr 17	1 CORN
Apr 30	1 DEATH
May 13	1 STORM
May 26	1 ROAD
Jun 8	1 SERPENT
Jun 21	1 FLINT
Jul 4	1 MONKEY
Jul 17	1 LIZARD
Jul 30	1 INCENSE
Aug 12	1 DOG
Aug 25	1 NIGHT
Sep 7	1 VULTURE
Sep 20	1 WATER
Oct 3	1 WIND
Oct 16	1 EAGLE
Oct 29	1 RABBIT
Nov 11	1 CROCODILE
Nov 24	1 JAGUAR
Dec 7	1 DEER
Dec 20	1 ANCESTORS
1918	
Jan 2	1 CORN
Jan 15	1 DEATH
Jan 28	1 STORM
Feb 10	1 ROAD
Feb 23	1 SERPENT
Mar 8	1 FLINT
Mayan Year	**10 DEER (Mar 17)**
Mar 21	1 MONKEY
Apr 3	1 LIZARD
Apr 16	1 INCENSE
Apr 29	1 DOG
May 12	1 NIGHT
May 25	1 VULTURE
Jun 7	1 WATER
Jun 20	1 WIND
Jul 3	1 EAGLE
Jul 16	1 RABBIT
Jul 29	1 CROCODILE
Aug 11	1 JAGUAR
Aug 24	1 DEER
Sep 6	1 ANCESTORS
Sep 19	1 CORN
Oct 2	1 DEATH
Oct 15	1 STORM
Oct 28	1 ROAD
Nov 10	1 SERPENT
Nov 23	1 FLINT
Dec 6	1 MONKEY
Dec 19	1 LIZARD
1919	
Jan 1	1 INCENSE
Jan 14	1 DOG
Jan 27	1 NIGHT
Feb 9	1 VULTURE
Feb 22	1 WATER
Mar 7	1 WIND
Mayan Year	**11 ROAD (Mar 17)**
Mar 20	1 EAGLE
Apr 2	1 RABBIT
Apr 15	1 CROCODILE
Apr 28	1 JAGUAR
May 11	1 DEER
May 24	1 ANCESTORS
Jun 6	1 CORN
Jun 19	1 DEATH
Jul 2	1 STORM

*** indicates a leap year**

Gregorian Date	Mayan Date
Jul 15	1 ROAD
Jul 28	1 SERPENT
Aug 10	1 FLINT
Aug 23	1 MONKEY
Sep 5	1 LIZARD
Sep 18	1 INCENSE
Oct 1	1 DOG
Oct 14	1 NIGHT
Oct 27	1 VULTURE
Nov 9	1 WATER
Nov 22	1 WIND
Dec 5	1 EAGLE
Dec 18	1 RABBIT
Dec 31	1 CROCODILE
***1920**	
Jan 13	1 JAGUAR
Jan 26	1 DEER
Feb 8	1 ANCESTORS
Feb 21	1 CORN
Mar 5	1 DEATH
Mayan Year	**12 INCENSE (Mar 16)**
Mar 18	1 STORM
Mar 31	1 ROAD
Apr 13	1 SERPENT
Apr 26	1 FLINT
May 9	1 MONKEY
May 22	1 LIZARD
Jun 4	1 INCENSE
Jun 17	1 DOG
Jun 30	1 NIGHT
Jul 13	1 VULTURE
Jul 26	1 WATER
Aug 8	1 WIND
Aug 21	1 EAGLE
Sep 3	1 RABBIT
Sep 16	1 CROCODILE
Sep 29	1 JAGUAR

Gregorian Date	Mayan Date
Oct 12	1 DEER
Oct 25	1 ANCESTORS
Nov 7	1 CORN
Nov 20	1 DEATH
Dec 3	1 STORM
Dec 16	1 ROAD
Dec 29	1 SERPENT
1921	
Jan 11	1 FLINT
Jan 24	1 MONKEY
Feb 6	1 LIZARD
Feb 19	1 INCENSE
Mar 4	1 DOG
Mayan Year	**13 WIND (Mar 16)**
Mar 17	1 NIGHT
Mar 30	1 VULTURE
Apr 12	1 WATER
Apr 25	1 WIND
May 8	1 EAGLE
May 21	1 RABBIT
Jun 3	1 CROCODILE
Jun 16	1 JAGUAR
Jun 29	1 DEER
Jul 12	1 ANCESTORS
Jul 25	1 CORN
Aug 7	1 DEATH
Aug 20	1 STORM
Sep 2	1 ROAD
Sep 15	1 SERPENT
Sep 28	1 FLINT
Oct 11	1 MONKEY
Oct 24	1 LIZARD
Nov 6	1 INCENSE
Nov 19	1 DOG
Dec 2	1 NIGHT
Dec 15	1 VULTURE
Dec 28	1 WATER

*** indicates a leap year**

Gregorian Date	Mayan Date
1922	
Jan 10	1 WIND
Jan 23	1 EAGLE
Feb 5	1 RABBIT
Feb 18	1 CROCODILE
Mar 3	1 JAGUAR
Mar 16	1 DEER
Mayan Year	**1 DEER (Mar 16)**
Mar 29	1 ANCESTORS
Apr 11	1 CORN
Apr 24	1 DEATH
May 7	1 STORM
May 20	1 ROAD
Jun 2	1 SERPENT
Jun 15	1 FLINT
Jun 28	1 MONKEY
Jul 11	1 LIZARD
Jul 24	1 INCENSE
Aug 6	1 DOG
Aug 19	1 NIGHT
Sep 1	1 VULTURE
Sep 14	1 WATER
Sep 27	1 WIND
Oct 10	1 EAGLE
Oct 23	1 RABBIT
Nov 5	1 CROCODILE
Nov 18	1 JAGUAR
Dec 1	1 DEER
Dec 14	1 ANCESTORS
Dec 27	1 CORN
1923	
Jan 9	1 DEATH
Jan 22	1 STORM
Feb 4	1 ROAD
Feb 17	1 SERPENT
Mar 2	1 FLINT
Mar 15	1 MONKEY

Gregorian Date	Mayan Date
Mayan Year	**2 ROAD (Mar 16)**
Mar 28	1 LIZARD
Apr 10	1 INCENSE
Apr 23	1 DOG
May 6	1 NIGHT
May 19	1 VULTURE
Jun 1	1 WATER
Jun 14	1 WIND
Jun 27	1 EAGLE
Jul 10	1 RABBIT
Jul 23	1 CROCODILE
Aug 5	1 JAGUAR
Aug 18	1 DEER
Aug 31	1 ANCESTORS
Sep 13	1 CORN
Sep 26	1 DEATH
Oct 9	1 STORM
Oct 22	1 ROAD
Nov 4	1 SERPENT
Nov 17	1 FLINT
Nov 30	1 MONKEY
Dec 13	1 LIZARD
Dec 26	1 INCENSE
***1924**	
Jan 8	1 DOG
Jan 21	1 NIGHT
Feb 3	1 VULTURE
Feb 16	1 WATER
Feb 29	1 WIND
Mar 13	1 EAGLE
Mayan Year	**3 INCENSE (Mar 15)**
Mar 26	1 RABBIT
Apr 8	1 CROCODILE
Apr 21	1 JAGUAR
May 4	1 DEER
May 17	1 ANCESTORS
May 30	1 CORN

*** indicates a leap year**

Gregorian Date	Mayan Date
Jun 12	1 DEATH
Jun 25	1 STORM
Jul 8	1 ROAD
Jul 21	1 SERPENT
Aug 3	1 FLINT
Aug 16	1 MONKEY
Aug 29	1 LIZARD
Sep 11	1 INCENSE
Sep 24	1 DOG
Oct 7	1 NIGHT
Oct 20	1 VULTURE
Nov 2	1 WATER
Nov 15	1 WIND
Nov 28	1 EAGLE
Dec 11	1 RABBIT
Dec 24	1 CROCODILE
1925	
Jan 6	1 JAGUAR
Jan 19	1 DEER
Feb 1	1 ANCESTORS
Feb 14	1 CORN
Feb 27	1 DEATH
Mar 12	1 STORM
Mayan Year 4 WIND (Mar 15)	
Mar 25	1 ROAD
Apr 7	1 SERPENT
Apr 20	1 FLINT
May 3	1 MONKEY
May 16	1 LIZARD
May 29	1 INCENSE
Jun 11	1 DOG
Jun 24	1 NIGHT
Jul 7	1 VULTURE
Jul 20	1 WATER
Aug 2	1 WIND
Aug 15	1 EAGLE
Aug 28	1 RABBIT

Gregorian Date	Mayan Date
Sep 10	1 CROCODILE
Sep 23	1 JAGUAR
Oct 6	1 DEER
Oct 19	1 ANCESTORS
Nov 1	1 CORN
Nov 14	1 DEATH
Nov 27	1 STORM
Dec 10	1 ROAD
Dec 23	1 SERPENT
1926	
Jan 5	1 FLINT
Jan 18	1 MONKEY
Jan 31	1 LIZARD
Feb 13	1 INCENSE
Feb 26	1 DOG
Mar 11	1 NIGHT
Mayan Year 5 DEER (Mar 15)	
Mar 24	1 VULTURE
Apr 6	1 WATER
Apr 19	1 WIND
May 2	1 EAGLE
May 15	1 RABBIT
May 28	1 CROCODILE
Jun 10	1 JAGUAR
Jun 23	1 DEER
Jul 6	1 ANCESTORS
Jul 19	1 CORN
Aug 1	1 DEATH
Aug 14	1 STORM
Aug 27	1 ROAD
Sep 9	1 SERPENT
Sep 22	1 FLINT
Oct 5	1 MONKEY
Oct 18	1 LIZARD
Oct 31	1 INCENSE
Nov 13	1 DOG
Nov 26	1 NIGHT

*** indicates a leap year**

Gregorian Date	Mayan Date
Dec 9	1 VULTURE
Dec 22	1 WATER
1927	
Jan 4	1 WIND
Jan 17	1 EAGLE
Jan 30	1 RABBIT
Feb 12	1 CROCODILE
Feb 25	1 JAGUAR
Mar 10	1 DEER
Mayan Year	**6 ROAD (Mar 15)**
Mar 23	1 ANCESTORS
Apr 5	1 CORN
Apr 18	1 DEATH
May 1	1 STORM
May 14	1 ROAD
May 27	1 SERPENT
Jun 9	1 FLINT
Jun 22	1 MONKEY
Jul 5	1 LIZARD
Jul 18	1 INCENSE
Jul 31	1 DOG
Aug 13	1 NIGHT
Aug 26	1 VULTURE
Sep 8	1 WATER
Sep 21	1 WIND
Oct 4	1 EAGLE
Oct 17	1 RABBIT
Oct 30	1 CROCODILE
Nov 12	1 JAGUAR
Nov 25	1 DEER
Dec 8	1 ANCESTORS
Dec 21	1 CORN
***1928**	
Jan 3	1 DEATH
Jan 16	1 STORM
Jan 29	1 ROAD
Feb 11	1 SERPENT

Gregorian Date	Mayan Date
Feb 24	1 FLINT
Mar 8	1 MONKEY
Mayan Year	**7 INCENSE (Mar 14)**
Mar 21	1 LIZARD
Apr 3	1 INCENSE
Apr 16	1 DOG
Apr 29	1 NIGHT
May 12	1 VULTURE
May 25	1 WATER
Jun 7	1 WIND
Jun 20	1 EAGLE
Jul 3	1 RABBIT
Jul 16	1 CROCODILE
Jul 29	1 JAGUAR
Aug 11	1 DEER
Aug 24	1 ANCESTORS
Sep 6	1 CORN
Sep 19	1 DEATH
Oct 2	1 STORM
Oct 15	1 ROAD
Oct 28	1 SERPENT
Nov 10	1 FLINT
Nov 23	1 MONKEY
Dec 6	1 LIZARD
Dec 19	1 INCENSE
1929	
Jan 1	1 DOG
Jan 14	1 NIGHT
Jan 27	1 VULTURE
Feb 9	1 WATER
Feb 22	1 WIND
Mar 7	1 EAGLE
Mayan Year	**8 WIND (Mar 14)**
Mar 20	1 RABBIT
Apr 2	1 CROCODILE
Apr 15	1 JAGUAR
Apr 28	1 DEER

*** indicates a leap year**

Gregorian Date	Mayan Date
May 11	1 ANCESTORS
May 24	1 CORN
Jun 6	1 DEATH
Jun 19	1 STORM
Jul 2	1 ROAD
Jul 15	1 SERPENT
Jul 28	1 FLINT
Aug 10	1 MONKEY
Aug 23	1 LIZARD
Sep 5	1 INCENSE
Sep 18	1 DOG
Oct 1	1 NIGHT
Oct 14	1 VULTURE
Oct 27	1 WATER
Nov 9	1 WIND
Nov 22	1 EAGLE
Dec 5	1 RABBIT
Dec 18	1 CROCODILE
Dec 31	1 JAGUAR
1930	
Jan 13	1 DEER
Jan 26	1 ANCESTORS
Feb 8	1 CORN
Feb 21	1 DEATH
Mar 6	1 STORM
Mayan Year 9 DEER (Mar 14)	
Mar 19	1 ROAD
Apr 1	1 SERPENT
Apr 14	1 FLINT
Apr 27	1 MONKEY
May 10	1 LIZARD
May 23	1 INCENSE
Jun 5	1 DOG
Jun 18	1 NIGHT
Jul 1	1 VULTURE
Jul 14	1 WATER
Jul 27	1 WIND

Gregorian Date	Mayan Date
Aug 9	1 EAGLE
Aug 22	1 RABBIT
Sep 4	1 CROCODILE
Sep 17	1 JAGUAR
Sep 30	1 DEER
Oct 13	1 ANCESTORS
Oct 26	1 CORN
Nov 8	1 DEATH
Nov 21	1 STORM
Dec 4	1 ROAD
Dec 17	1 SERPENT
Dec 30	1 FLINT
1931	
Jan 12	1 MONKEY
Jan 25	1 LIZARD
Feb 7	1 INCENSE
Feb 20	1 DOG
Mar 5	1 NIGHT
Mayan Year 10 ROAD (Mar 14)	
Mar 18	1 VULTURE
Mar 31	1 WATER
Apr 13	1 WIND
Apr 26	1 EAGLE
May 9	1 RABBIT
May 22	1 CROCODILE
Jun 4	1 JAGUAR
Jun 17	1 DEER
Jun 30	1 ANCESTORS
Jul 13	1 CORN
Jul 26	1 DEATH
Aug 8	1 STORM
Aug 21	1 ROAD
Sep 3	1 SERPENT
Sep 16	1 FLINT
Sep 29	1 MONKEY
Oct 12	1 LIZARD
Oct 25	1 INCENSE

*** indicates a leap year**

Gregorian Date	Mayan Date
Nov 7	1 DOG
Nov 20	1 NIGHT
Dec 3	1 VULTURE
Dec 16	1 WATER
Dec 29	1 WIND
***1932**	
Jan 11	1 EAGLE
Jan 24	1 RABBIT
Feb 6	1 CROCODILE
Feb 19	1 JAGUAR
Mar 3	1 DEER
Mayan Year	**11 INCENSE (Mar 13)**
Mar 16	1 ANCESTORS
Mar 29	1 CORN
Apr 11	1 DEATH
Apr 24	1 STORM
May 7	1 ROAD
May 20	1 SERPENT
Jun 2	1 FLINT
Jun 15	1 MONKEY
Jun 28	1 LIZARD
Jul 11	1 INCENSE
Jul 24	1 DOG
Aug 6	1 NIGHT
Aug 19	1 VULTURE
Sep 1	1 WATER
Sep 14	1 WIND
Sep 27	1 EAGLE
Oct 10	1 RABBIT
Oct 23	1 CROCODILE
Nov 5	1 JAGUAR
Nov 18	1 DEER
Dec 1	1 ANCESTORS
Dec 14	1 CORN
Dec 27	1 DEATH

Gregorian Date	Mayan Date
1933	
Jan 9	1 STORM
Jan 22	1 ROAD
Feb 4	1 SERPENT
Feb 17	1 FLINT
Mar 2	1 MONKEY
Mayan Year	**12 WIND (Mar 13)**
Mar 15	1 LIZARD
Mar 28	1 INCENSE
Apr 10	1 DOG
Apr 23	1 NIGHT
May 6	1 VULTURE
May 19	1 WATER
Jun 1	1 WIND
Jun 14	1 EAGLE
Jun 27	1 RABBIT
Jul 10	1 CROCODILE
Jul 23	1 JAGUAR
Aug 5	1 DEER
Aug 18	1 ANCESTORS
Aug 31	1 CORN
Sep 13	1 DEATH
Sep 26	1 STORM
Oct 9	1 ROAD
Oct 22	1 SERPENT
Nov 4	1 FLINT
Nov 17	1 MONKEY
Nov 30	1 LIZARD
Dec 13	1 INCENSE
Dec 26	1 DOG
1934	
Jan 8	1 NIGHT
Jan 21	1 VULTURE
Feb 3	1 WATER

END KATUN 12 AHAU (Feb 14)
BEGIN KATUN 10 AHAU

*** indicates a leap year**

Gregorian Date	Mayan Date
Feb 16	1 WIND
Mar 1	1 EAGLE
Mayan Year	**13 DEER (Mar 13)**
Mar 14	1 RABBIT
Mar 27	1 CROCODILE
Apr 9	1 JAGUAR
Apr 22	1 DEER
May 5	1 ANCESTORS
May 18	1 CORN
May 31	1 DEATH
Jun 13	1 STORM
Jun 26	1 ROAD
Jul 9	1 SERPENT
Jul 22	1 FLINT
Aug 4	1 MONKEY
Aug 17	1 LIZARD
Aug 30	1 INCENSE
Sep 12	1 DOG
Sep 25	1 NIGHT
Oct 8	1 VULTURE
Oct 21	1 WATER
Nov 3	1 WIND
Nov 16	1 EAGLE
Nov 29	1 RABBIT
Dec 12	1 CROCODILE
Dec 25	1 JAGUAR
1935	
Jan 7	1 DEER
Jan 20	1 ANCESTORS
Feb 2	1 CORN
Feb 15	1 DEATH
Feb 28	1 STORM
Mar 13	1 ROAD
Mayan Year	**1 ROAD (Mar 13)**
Mar 26	1 SERPENT
Apr 8	1 FLINT
Apr 21	1 MONKEY

Gregorian Date	Mayan Date
May 4	1 LIZARD
May 17	1 INCENSE
May 30	1 DOG
Jun 12	1 NIGHT
Jun 25	1 VULTURE
Jul 8	1 WATER
Jul 21	1 WIND
Aug 3	1 EAGLE
Aug 16	1 RABBIT
Aug 29	1 CROCODILE
Sep 11	1 JAGUAR
Sep 24	1 DEER
Oct 7	1 ANCESTORS
Oct 20	1 CORN
Nov 2	1 DEATH
Nov 15	1 STORM
Nov 28	1 ROAD
Dec 11	1 SERPENT
Dec 24	1 FLINT
***1936**	
Jan 6	1 MONKEY
Jan 19	1 LIZARD
Feb 1	1 INCENSE
Feb 14	1 DOG
Feb 27	1 NIGHT
Mar 11	1 VULTURE
Mayan Year	**2 INCENSE (Mar 12)**
Mar 24	1 WATER
Apr 6	1 WIND
Apr 19	1 EAGLE
May 2	1 RABBIT
May 15	1 CROCODILE
May 28	1 JAGUAR
Jun 10	1 DEER
Jun 23	1 ANCESTORS
Jul 6	1 CORN
Jul 19	1 DEATH

*** indicates a leap year**

Gregorian Date	Mayan Date
Aug 1	1 STORM
Aug 14	1 ROAD
Aug 27	1 SERPENT
Sep 9	1 FLINT
Sep 22	1 MONKEY
Oct 5	1 LIZARD
Oct 18	1 INCENSE
Oct 31	1 DOG
Nov 13	1 NIGHT
Nov 26	1 VULTURE
Dec 9	1 WATER
Dec 22	1 WIND
1937	
Jan 4	1 EAGLE
Jan 17	1 RABBIT
Jan 30	1 CROCODILE
Feb 12	1 JAGUAR
Feb 25	1 DEER
Mar 10	1 ANCESTORS
Mayan Year 3 WIND (Mar 12)	
Mar 23	1 CORN
Apr 5	1 DEATH
Apr 18	1 STORM
May 1	1 ROAD
May 14	1 SERPENT
May 27	1 FLINT
Jun 9	1 MONKEY
Jun 22	1 LIZARD
Jul 5	1 INCENSE
Jul 18	1 DOG
Jul 31	1 NIGHT
Aug 13	1 VULTURE
Aug 26	1 WATER
Sep 8	1 WIND
Sep 21	1 EAGLE
Oct 4	1 RABBIT
Oct 17	1 CROCODILE

Gregorian Date	Mayan Date
Oct 30	1 JAGUAR
Nov 12	1 DEER
Nov 25	1 ANCESTORS
Dec 8	1 CORN
Dec 21	1 DEATH
1938	
Jan 3	1 STORM
Jan 16	1 ROAD
Jan 29	1 SERPENT
Feb 11	1 FLINT
Feb 24	1 MONKEY
Mar 9	1 LIZARD
Mayan Year 4 DEER (Mar 12)	
Mar 22	1 INCENSE
Apr 4	1 DOG
Apr 17	1 NIGHT
Apr 30	1 VULTURE
May 13	1 WATER
May 26	1 WIND
Jun 8	1 EAGLE
Jun 21	1 RABBIT
Jul 4	1 CROCODILE
Jul 17	1 JAGUAR
Jul 30	1 DEER
Aug 12	1 ANCESTORS
Aug 25	1 CORN
Sep 7	1 DEATH
Sep 20	1 STORM
Oct 3	1 ROAD
Oct 16	1 SERPENT
Oct 29	1 FLINT
Nov 11	1 MONKEY
Nov 24	1 LIZARD
Dec 7	1 INCENSE
Dec 20	1 DOG
1939	
Jan 2	1 NIGHT

*** indicates a leap year**

Gregorian Date	Mayan Date
Jan 15	1 VULTURE
Jan 28	1 WATER
Feb 10	1 WIND
Feb 23	1 EAGLE
Mar 8	1 RABBIT
Mayan Year	**5 ROAD (Mar 12)**
Mar 21	1 CROCODILE
Apr 3	1 JAGUAR
Apr 16	1 DEER
Apr 29	1 ANCESTORS
May 12	1 CORN
May 25	1 DEATH
Jun 7	1 STORM
Jun 20	1 ROAD
Jul 3	1 SERPENT
Jul 16	1 FLINT
Jul 29	1 MONKEY
Aug 11	1 LIZARD
Aug 24	1 INCENSE
Sep 6	1 DOG
Sep 19	1 NIGHT
Oct 2	1 VULTURE
Oct 15	1 WATER
Oct 28	1 WIND
Nov 10	1 EAGLE
Nov 23	1 RABBIT
Dec 6	1 CROCODILE
Dec 19	1 JAGUAR
***1940**	
Jan 1	1 DEER
Jan 14	1 ANCESTORS
Jan 27	1 CORN
Feb 9	1 DEATH
Feb 22	1 STORM
Mar 6	1 ROAD
Mayan Year	**6 INCENSE (Mar 11)**
Mar 19	1 SERPENT

Gregorian Date	Mayan Date
Apr 1	1 FLINT
Apr 14	1 MONKEY
Apr 27	1 LIZARD
May 10	1 INCENSE
May 23	1 DOG
Jun 5	1 NIGHT
Jun 18	1 VULTURE
Jul 1	1 WATER
Jul 14	1 WIND
Jul 27	1 EAGLE
Aug 9	1 RABBIT
Aug 22	1 CROCODILE
Sep 4	1 JAGUAR
Sep 17	1 DEER
Sep 30	1 ANCESTORS
Oct 13	1 CORN
Oct 26	1 DEATH
Nov 8	1 STORM
Nov 21	1 ROAD
Dec 4	1 SERPENT
Dec 17	1 FLINT
Dec 30	1 MONKEY
1941	
Jan 12	1 LIZARD
Jan 25	1 INCENSE
Feb 7	1 DOG
Feb 20	1 NIGHT
Mar 5	1 VULTURE
Mayan Year	**7 WIND (Mar 11)**
Mar 18	1 WATER
Mar 31	1 WIND
Apr 13	1 EAGLE
Apr 26	1 RABBIT
May 9	1 CROCODILE
May 22	1 JAGUAR
Jun 4	1 DEER
Jun 17	1 ANCESTORS

*** indicates a leap year**

Gregorian Date	Mayan Date
Jun 30	1 CORN
Jul 13	1 DEATH
Jul 26	1 STORM
Aug 8	1 ROAD
Aug 21	1 SERPENT
Sep 3	1 FLINT
Sep 16	1 MONKEY
Sep 29	1 LIZARD
Oct 12	1 INCENSE
Oct 25	1 DOG
Nov 7	1 NIGHT
Nov 20	1 VULTURE
Dec 3	1 WATER
Dec 16	1 WIND
Dec 29	1 EAGLE
1942	
Jan 11	1 RABBIT
Jan 24	1 CROCODILE
Feb 6	1 JAGUAR
Feb 19	1 DEER
Mar 4	1 ANCESTORS
Mayan Year	**8 DEER (Mar 11)**
Mar 17	1 CORN
Mar 30	1 DEATH
Apr 12	1 STORM
Apr 25	1 ROAD
May 8	1 SERPENT
May 21	1 FLINT
Jun 3	1 MONKEY
Jun 16	1 LIZARD
Jun 29	1 INCENSE
Jul 12	1 DOG
Jul 25	1 NIGHT
Aug 7	1 VULTURE
Aug 20	1 WATER
Sep 2	1 WIND
Sep 15	1 EAGLE
Sep 28	1 RABBIT
Oct 11	1 CROCODILE
Oct 24	1 JAGUAR
Nov 6	1 DEER
Nov 19	1 ANCESTORS
Dec 2	1 CORN
Dec 15	1 DEATH
Dec 28	1 STORM
1943	
Jan 10	1 ROAD
Jan 23	1 SERPENT
Feb 5	1 FLINT
Feb 18	1 MONKEY
Mar 3	1 LIZARD
Mayan Year	**9 ROAD (Mar 11)**
Mar 16	1 INCENSE
Mar 29	1 DOG
Apr 11	1 NIGHT
Apr 24	1 VULTURE
May 7	1 WATER
May 20	1 WIND
Jun 2	1 EAGLE
Jun 15	1 RABBIT
Jun 28	1 CROCODILE
Jul 11	1 JAGUAR
Jul 24	1 DEER
Aug 6	1 ANCESTORS
Aug 19	1 CORN
Sep 1	1 DEATH
Sep 14	1 STORM
Sep 27	1 ROAD
Oct 10	1 SERPENT
Oct 23	1 FLINT
Nov 5	1 MONKEY
Nov 18	1 LIZARD
Dec 1	1 INCENSE
Dec 14	1 DOG

*** indicates a leap year**

Gregorian Date	Mayan Date
Dec 27	1 NIGHT
***1944**	
Jan 9	1 VULTURE
Jan 22	1 WATER
Feb 4	1 WIND
Feb 17	1 EAGLE
Mar 1	1 RABBIT
Mayan Year	**10 INCENSE (Mar 10)**
Mar 14	1 CROCODILE
Mar 27	1 JAGUAR
Apr 9	1 DEER
Apr 22	1 ANCESTORS
May 5	1 CORN
May 18	1 DEATH
May 31	1 STORM
Jun 13	1 ROAD
Jun 26	1 SERPENT
Jul 9	1 FLINT
Jul 22	1 MONKEY
Aug 4	1 LIZARD
Aug 17	1 INCENSE
Aug 30	1 DOG
Sep 12	1 NIGHT
Sep 25	1 VULTURE
Oct 8	1 WATER
Oct 21	1 WIND
Nov 3	1 EAGLE
Nov 16	1 RABBIT
Nov 29	1 CROCODILE
Dec 12	1 JAGUAR
Dec 25	1 DEER
1945	
Jan 7	1 ANCESTORS
Jan 20	1 CORN
Feb 2	1 DEATH
Feb 15	1 STORM
Feb 28	1 ROAD

Gregorian Date	Mayan Date
Mayan Year	**11 WIND (Mar 10)**
Mar 13	1 SERPENT
Mar 26	1 FLINT
Apr 8	1 MONKEY
Apr 21	1 LIZARD
May 4	1 INCENSE
May 17	1 DOG
May 30	1 NIGHT
Jun 12	1 VULTURE
Jun 25	1 WATER
Jul 8	1 WIND
Jul 21	1 EAGLE
Aug 3	1 RABBIT
Aug 16	1 CROCODILE
Aug 29	1 JAGUAR
Sep 11	1 DEER
Sep 24	1 ANCESTORS
Oct 7	1 CORN
Oct 20	1 DEATH
Nov 2	1 STORM
Nov 15	1 ROAD
Nov 28	1 SERPENT
Dec 11	1 FLINT
Dec 24	1 MONKEY
1946	
Jan 6	1 LIZARD
Jan 19	1 INCENSE
Feb 1	1 DOG
Feb 14	1 NIGHT
Feb 27	1 VULTURE
Mayan Year	**12 DEER (Mar 10)**
Mar 12	1 WATER
Mar 25	1 WIND
Apr 7	1 EAGLE
Apr 20	1 RABBIT
May 3	1 CROCODILE
May 16	1 JAGUAR

*** indicates a leap year**

Gregorian Date	Mayan Date
May 29	1 DEER
Jun 11	1 ANCESTORS
Jun 24	1 CORN
Jul 7	1 DEATH
Jul 20	1 STORM
Aug 2	1 ROAD
Aug 15	1 SERPENT
Aug 28	1 FLINT
Sep 10	1 MONKEY
Sep 23	1 LIZARD
Oct 6	1 INCENSE
Oct 19	1 DOG
Nov 1	1 NIGHT
Nov 14	1 VULTURE
Nov 27	1 WATER
Dec 10	1 WIND
Dec 23	1 EAGLE
1947	
Jan 5	1 RABBIT
Jan 18	1 CROCODILE
Jan 31	1 JAGUAR
Feb 13	1 DEER
Feb 26	1 ANCESTORS
Mayan Year	**13 ROAD (Mar 10)**
Mar 11	1 CORN
Mar 24	1 DEATH
Apr 6	1 STORM
Apr 19	1 ROAD
May 2	1 SERPENT
May 15	1 FLINT
May 28	1 MONKEY
Jun 10	1 LIZARD
Jun 23	1 INCENSE
Jul 6	1 DOG
Jul 19	1 NIGHT
Aug 1	1 VULTURE
Aug 14	1 WATER

Gregorian Date	Mayan Date
Aug 27	1 WIND
Sep 9	1 EAGLE
Sep 22	1 RABBIT
Oct 5	1 CROCODILE
Oct 18	1 JAGUAR
Oct 31	1 DEER
Nov 13	1 ANCESTORS
Nov 26	1 CORN
Dec 9	1 DEATH
Dec 22	1 STORM
***1948**	
Jan 4	1 ROAD
Jan 17	1 SERPENT
Jan 30	1 FLINT
Feb 12	1 MONKEY
Feb 25	1 LIZARD
Mar 9	1 INCENSE
Mayan Year	**1 INCENSE (Mar 9)**
Mar 22	1 DOG
Apr 4	1 NIGHT
Apr 17	1 VULTURE
Apr 30	1 WATER
May 13	1 WIND
May 26	1 EAGLE
Jun 8	1 RABBIT
Jun 21	1 CROCODILE
Jul 4	1 JAGUAR
Jul 17	1 DEER
Jul 30	1 ANCESTORS
Aug 12	1 CORN
Aug 25	1 DEATH
Sep 7	1 STORM
Sep 20	1 ROAD
Oct 3	1 SERPENT
Oct 16	1 FLINT
Oct 29	1 MONKEY
Nov 11	1 LIZARD

*** indicates a leap year**

Gregorian Date	Mayan Date
Nov 24	1 INCENSE
Dec 7	1 DOG
Dec 20	1 NIGHT

1949

Gregorian Date	Mayan Date
Jan 2	1 VULTURE
Jan 15	1 WATER
Jan 28	1 WIND
Feb 10	1 EAGLE
Feb 23	1 RABBIT
Mar 8	1 CROCODILE

Mayan Year 2 WIND (Mar 9)

Gregorian Date	Mayan Date
Mar 21	1 JAGUAR
Apr 3	1 DEER
Apr 16	1 ANCESTORS
Apr 29	1 CORN
May 12	1 DEATH
May 25	1 STORM
Jun 7	1 ROAD
Jun 20	1 SERPENT
Jul 3	1 FLINT
Jul 16	1 MONKEY
Jul 29	1 LIZARD
Aug 11	1 INCENSE
Aug 24	1 DOG
Sep 6	1 NIGHT
Sep 19	1 VULTURE
Oct 2	1 WATER
Oct 15	1 WIND
Oct 28	1 EAGLE
Nov 10	1 RABBIT
Nov 23	1 CROCODILE
Dec 6	1 JAGUAR
Dec 19	1 DEER

1950

Gregorian Date	Mayan Date
Jan 1	1 ANCESTORS
Jan 14	1 CORN
Jan 27	1 DEATH
Feb 9	1 STORM
Feb 22	1 ROAD
Mar 7	1 SERPENT

Mayan Year 3 DEER (Mar 9)

Gregorian Date	Mayan Date
Mar 20	1 FLINT
Apr 2	1 MONKEY
Apr 15	1 LIZARD
Apr 28	1 INCENSE
May 11	1 DOG
May 24	1 NIGHT
Jun 6	1 VULTURE
Jun 19	1 WATER
Jul 2	1 WIND
Jul 15	1 EAGLE
Jul 28	1 RABBIT
Aug 10	1 CROCODILE
Aug 23	1 JAGUAR
Sep 5	1 DEER
Sep 18	1 ANCESTORS
Oct 1	1 CORN
Oct 14	1 DEATH
Oct 27	1 STORM
Nov 9	1 ROAD
Nov 22	1 SERPENT
Dec 5	1 FLINT
Dec 18	1 MONKEY
Dec 31	1 LIZARD

1951

Gregorian Date	Mayan Date
Jan 13	1 INCENSE
Jan 26	1 DOG
Feb 8	1 NIGHT
Feb 21	1 VULTURE
Mar 6	1 WATER

Mayan Year 4 ROAD (Mar 9)

Gregorian Date	Mayan Date
Mar 19	1 WIND
Apr 1	1 EAGLE
Apr 14	1 RABBIT

*** indicates a leap year**

Gregorian Date	Mayan Date
Apr 27	1 CROCODILE
May 10	1 JAGUAR
May 23	1 DEER
Jun 5	1 ANCESTORS
Jun 18	1 CORN
Jul 1	1 DEATH
Jul 14	1 STORM
Jul 27	1 ROAD
Aug 9	1 SERPENT
Aug 22	1 FLINT
Sep 4	1 MONKEY
Sep 17	1 LIZARD
Sep 30	1 INCENSE
Oct 13	1 DOG
Oct 26	1 NIGHT
Nov 8	1 VULTURE
Nov 21	1 WATER
Dec 4	1 WIND
Dec 17	1 EAGLE
Dec 30	1 RABBIT

***1952**

Gregorian Date	Mayan Date
Jan 12	1 CROCODILE
Jan 25	1 JAGUAR
Feb 7	1 DEER
Feb 20	1 ANCESTORS
Mar 4	1 CORN

Mayan Year 5 INCENSE (Mar 8)

Gregorian Date	Mayan Date
Mar 17	1 DEATH
Mar 30	1 STORM
Apr 12	1 ROAD
Apr 25	1 SERPENT
May 8	1 FLINT
May 21	1 MONKEY
Jun 3	1 LIZARD
Jun 16	1 INCENSE
Jun 29	1 DOG
Jul 12	1 NIGHT
Jul 25	1 VULTURE
Aug 7	1 WATER
Aug 20	1 WIND
Sep 2	1 EAGLE
Sep 15	1 RABBIT
Sep 28	1 CROCODILE
Oct 11	1 JAGUAR
Oct 24	1 DEER
Nov 6	1 ANCESTORS
Nov 19	1 CORN
Dec 2	1 DEATH
Dec 15	1 STORM
Dec 28	1 ROAD

1953

Gregorian Date	Mayan Date
Jan 10	1 SERPENT
Jan 23	1 FLINT
Feb 5	1 MONKEY
Feb 18	1 LIZARD
Mar 3	1 INCENSE

Mayan Year 6 WIND (Mar 8)

Gregorian Date	Mayan Date
Mar 16	1 DOG
Mar 29	1 NIGHT
Apr 11	1 VULTURE
Apr 24	1 WATER
May 7	1 WIND
May 20	1 EAGLE
Jun 2	1 RABBIT
Jun 15	1 CROCODILE
Jun 28	1 JAGUAR
Jul 11	1 DEER
Jul 24	1 ANCESTORS
Aug 6	1 CORN
Aug 19	1 DEATH
Sep 1	1 STORM
Sep 14	1 ROAD
Sep 27	1 SERPENT
Oct 10	1 FLINT

*** indicates a leap year**

Gregorian Date	Mayan Date
Oct 23	1 MONKEY
END KATUN 10 AHAU (Nov 1)	
BEGIN KATUN 8 AHAU	
Nov 5	1 LIZARD
Nov 18	1 INCENSE
Dec 1	1 DOG
Dec 14	1 NIGHT
Dec 27	1 VULTURE
1954	
Jan 9	1 WATER
Jan 22	1 WIND
Feb 4	1 EAGLE
Feb 17	1 RABBIT
Mar 2	1 CROCODILE
Mayan Year 7 DEER (Mar 8)	
Mar 15	1 JAGUAR
Mar 28	1 DEER
Apr 10	1 ANCESTORS
Apr 23	1 CORN
May 6	1 DEATH
May 19	1 STORM
Jun 1	1 ROAD
Jun 14	1 SERPENT
Jun 27	1 FLINT
Jul 10	1 MONKEY
Jul 23	1 LIZARD
Aug 5	1 INCENSE
Aug 18	1 DOG
Aug 31	1 NIGHT
Sep 13	1 VULTURE
Sep 26	1 WATER
Oct 22	1 EAGLE
Nov 4	1 RABBIT
Nov 17	1 CROCODILE
Nov 30	1 JAGUAR
Dec 13	1 DEER
Dec 26	1 ANCESTORS

Gregorian Date	Mayan Date
1955	
Jan 8	1 CORN
Jan 21	1 DEATH
Feb 3	1 STORM
Feb 16	1 ROAD
Mar 1	1 SERPENT
Mayan Year 8 ROAD (Mar 8)	
Mar 14	1 FLINT
Mar 27	1 MONKEY
Apr 9	1 LIZARD
Apr 22	1 INCENSE
May 5	1 DOG
May 18	1 NIGHT
May 31	1 VULTURE
Jun 13	1 WATER
Jun 26	1 WIND
Jul 9	1 EAGLE
Jul 22	1 RABBIT
Aug 4	1 CROCODILE
Aug 17	1 JAGUAR
Aug 30	1 DEER
Sep 12	1 ANCESTORS
Sep 25	1 CORN
Oct 8	1 DEATH
Oct 21	1 STORM
Nov 3	1 ROAD
Nov 16	1 SERPENT
Nov 29	1 FLINT
Dec 12	1 MONKEY
Dec 25	1 LIZARD
***1956**	
Jan 7	1 INCENSE
Jan 20	1 DOG
Feb 2	1 NIGHT
Feb 15	1 VULTURE
Feb 28	1 WATER
Mayan Year 9 INCENSE (Mar 7)	

*** indicates a leap year**

Gregorian Date	Mayan Date
Mar 12	1 WIND
Mar 25	1 EAGLE
Apr 7	1 RABBIT
Apr 20	1 CROCODILE
May 3	1 JAGUAR
May 16	1 DEER
May 29	1 ANCESTORS
Jun 11	1 CORN
Jun 24	1 DEATH
Jul 7	1 STORM
Jul 20	1 ROAD
Aug 2	1 SERPENT
Aug 15	1 FLINT
Aug 28	1 MONKEY
Sep 10	1 LIZARD
Sep 23	1 INCENSE
Oct 6	1 DOG
Oct 19	1 NIGHT
Nov 1	1 VULTURE
Nov 14	1 WATER
Nov 27	1 WIND
Dec 10	1 EAGLE
Dec 23	1 RABBIT
1957	
Jan 5	1 CROCODILE
Jan 18	1 JAGUAR
Jan 31	1 DEER
Feb 13	1 ANCESTORS
Feb 26	1 CORN
Mayan Year	**10 WIND (Mar 7)**
Mar 11	1 DEATH
Mar 24	1 STORM
Apr 6	1 ROAD
Apr 19	1 SERPENT
May 2	1 FLINT
May 15	1 MONKEY
May 28	1 LIZARD

Gregorian Date	Mayan Date
Jun 10	1 INCENSE
Jun 23	1 DOG
Jul 6	1 NIGHT
Jul 19	1 VULTURE
Aug 1	1 WATER
Aug 14	1 WIND
Aug 27	1 EAGLE
Sep 9	1 RABBIT
Sep 22	1 CROCODILE
Oct 5	1 JAGUAR
Oct 18	1 DEER
Oct 31	1 ANCESTORS
Nov 13	1 CORN
Nov 26	1 DEATH
Dec 9	1 STORM
Dec 22	1 ROAD
1958	
Jan 4	1 SERPENT
Jan 17	1 FLINT
Jan 30	1 MONKEY
Feb 12	1 LIZARD
Feb 25	1 INCENSE
Mayan Year	**11 DEER (Mar 7)**
Mar 10	1 DOG
Mar 23	1 NIGHT
Apr 5	1 VULTURE
Apr 18	1 WATER
May 1	1 WIND
May 14	1 EAGLE
May 27	1 RABBIT
Jun 9	1 CROCODILE
Jun 22	1 JAGUAR
Jul 5	1 DEER
Jul 18	1 ANCESTORS
Jul 31	1 CORN
Aug 13	1 DEATH
Aug 26	1 STORM

*** indicates a leap year**

Gregorian Date	Mayan Date
Sep 8	1 ROAD
Sep 21	1 SERPENT
Oct 4	1 FLINT
Oct 17	1 MONKEY
Oct 30	1 LIZARD
Nov 12	1 INCENSE
Nov 25	1 DOG
Dec 8	1 NIGHT
Dec 21	1 VULTURE
1959	
Jan 3	1 WATER
Jan 16	1 WIND
Jan 29	1 EAGLE
Feb 11	1 RABBIT
Feb 24	1 CROCODILE
Mayan Year	**12 ROAD (Mar 7)**
Mar 9	1 JAGUAR
Mar 22	1 DEER
Apr 4	1 ANCESTORS
Apr 17	1 CORN
Apr 30	1 DEATH
May 13	1 STORM
May 26	1 ROAD
Jun 8	1 SERPENT
Jun 21	1 FLINT
Jul 4	1 MONKEY
Jul 17	1 LIZARD
Jul 30	1 INCENSE
Aug 12	1 DOG
Aug 25	1 NIGHT
Sep 7	1 VULTURE
Sep 20	1 WATER
Oct 3	1 WIND
Oct 16	1 EAGLE
Oct 29	1 RABBIT
Nov 11	1 CROCODILE
Nov 24	1 JAGUAR

Gregorian Date	Mayan Date
Dec 7	1 DEER
Dec 20	1 ANCESTORS
***1960**	
Jan 2	1 CORN
Jan 15	1 DEATH
Jan 28	1 STORM
Feb 10	1 ROAD
Feb 23	1 SERPENT
Mayan Year	**13 INCENSE (Mar 6)**
Mar 7	1 FLINT
Mar 20	1 MONKEY
Apr 2	1 LIZARD
Apr 15	1 INCENSE
Apr 28	1 DOG
May 11	1 NIGHT
May 24	1 VULTURE
Jun 6	1 WATER
Jun 19	1 WIND
Jul 2	1 EAGLE
Jul 15	1 RABBIT
Jul 28	1 CROCODILE
Aug 10	1 JAGUAR
Aug 23	1 DEER
Sep 5	1 ANCESTORS
Sep 18	1 CORN
Oct 1	1 DEATH
Oct 14	1 STORM
Oct 27	1 ROAD
Nov 9	1 SERPENT
Nov 22	1 FLINT
Dec 5	1 MONKEY
Dec 18	1 LIZARD
Dec 31	1 INCENSE
1961	
Jan 13	1 DOG
Jan 26	1 NIGHT
Feb 8	1 VULTURE

*** indicates a leap year**

Gregorian Date	Mayan Date
Feb 21	1 WATER
Mar 6	1 WIND
Mayan Year	**1 WIND (Mar 6)**
Mar 19	1 EAGLE
Apr 1	1 RABBIT
Apr 14	1 CROCODILE
Apr 27	1 JAGUAR
May 10	1 DEER
May 23	1 ANCESTORS
Jun 5	1 CORN
Jun 18	1 DEATH
Jul 1	1 STORM
Jul 14	1 ROAD
Jul 27	1 SERPENT
Aug 9	1 FLINT
Aug 22	1 MONKEY
Sep 4	1 LIZARD
Sep 17	1 INCENSE
Sep 30	1 DOG
Oct 13	1 NIGHT
Oct 26	1 VULTURE
Nov 8	1 WATER
Nov 21	1 WIND
Dec 4	1 EAGLE
Dec 17	1 RABBIT
Dec 30	1 CROCODILE
1962	
Jan 12	1 JAGUAR
Jan 25	1 DEER
Feb 7	1 ANCESTORS
Feb 20	1 CORN
Mar 5	1 DEATH
Mayan Year	**2 DEER (Mar 6)**
Mar 18	1 STORM
Mar 31	1 ROAD
Apr 13	1 SERPENT
Apr 26	1 FLINT

Gregorian Date	Mayan Date
May 9	1 MONKEY
May 22	1 LIZARD
Jun 4	1 INCENSE
Jun 17	1 DOG
Jun 30	1 NIGHT
Jul 13	1 VULTURE
Jul 26	1 WATER
Aug 8	1 WIND
Aug 21	1 EAGLE
Sep 3	1 RABBIT
Sep 16	1 CROCODILE
Sep 29	1 JAGUAR
Oct 12	1 DEER
Oct 25	1 ANCESTORS
Nov 7	1 CORN
Nov 20	1 DEATH
Dec 3	1 STORM
Dec 16	1 ROAD
Dec 29	1 SERPENT
1963	
Jan 11	1 FLINT
Jan 24	1 MONKEY
Feb 6	1 LIZARD
Feb 19	1 INCENSE
Mar 4	1 DOG
Mayan Year	**3 ROAD (Mar 6)**
Mar 17	1 NIGHT
Mar 30	1 VULTURE
Apr 12	1 WATER
Apr 25	1 WIND
May 8	1 EAGLE
May 21	1 RABBIT
Jun 3	1 CROCODILE
Jun 16	1 JAGUAR
Jun 29	1 DEER
Jul 12	1 ANCESTORS
Jul 25	1 CORN

*** indicates a leap year**

Gregorian Date	Mayan Date
Aug 7	1 DEATH
Aug 20	1 STORM
Sep 2	1 ROAD
Sep 15	1 SERPENT
Sep 28	1 FLINT
Oct 11	1 MONKEY
Oct 24	1 LIZARD
Nov 6	1 INCENSE
Nov 19	1 DOG
Dec 2	1 NIGHT
Dec 15	1 VULTURE
Dec 28	1 WATER
***1964**	
Jan 10	1 WIND
Jan 23	1 EAGLE
Feb 5	1 RABBIT
Feb 18	1 CROCODILE
Mar 2	1 JAGUAR
Mayan Year 4 INCENSE (Mar 5)	
Mar 15	1 DEER
Mar 28	1 ANCESTORS
Apr 10	1 CORN
Apr 23	1 DEATH
May 6	1 STORM
May 19	1 ROAD
Jun 1	1 SERPENT
Jun 14	1 FLINT
Jun 27	1 MONKEY
Jul 10	1 LIZARD
Jul 23	1 INCENSE
Aug 5	1 DOG
Aug 18	1 NIGHT
Aug 31	1 VULTURE
Sep 13	1 WATER
Sep 26	1 WIND
Oct 9	1 EAGLE
Oct 22	1 RABBIT

Gregorian Date	Mayan Date
Nov 4	1 CROCODILE
Nov 17	1 JAGUAR
Nov 30	1 DEER
Dec 13	1 ANCESTORS
Dec 26	1 CORN
1965	
Jan 8	1 DEATH
Jan 21	1 STORM
Feb 3	1 ROAD
Feb 16	1 SERPENT
Mar 1	1 FLINT
Mayan Year 5 WIND (Mar 5)	
Mar 14	1 MONKEY
Mar 27	1 LIZARD
Apr 9	1 INCENSE
Apr 22	1 DOG
May 5	1 NIGHT
May 18	1 VULTURE
May 31	1 WATER
Jun 13	1 WIND
Jun 26	1 EAGLE
Jul 9	1 RABBIT
Jul 22	1 CROCODILE
Aug 4	1 JAGUAR
Aug 17	1 DEER
Aug 30	1 ANCESTORS
Sep 12	1 CORN
Sep 25	1 DEATH
Oct 8	1 STORM
Oct 21	1 ROAD
Nov 3	1 SERPENT
Nov 16	1 FLINT
Nov 29	1 MONKEY
Dec 12	1 LIZARD
Dec 25	1 INCENSE
1966	
Jan 7	1 DOG

*** indicates a leap year**

Gregorian Date	Mayan Date
Jan 20	1 NIGHT
Feb 2	1 VULTURE
Feb 15	1 WATER
Feb 28	1 WIND
Mayan Year	**6 DEER (Mar 5)**
Mar 13	1 EAGLE
Mar 26	1 RABBIT
Apr 8	1 CROCODILE
Apr 21	1 JAGUAR
May 4	1 DEER
May 17	1 ANCESTORS
May 30	1 CORN
Jun 12	1 DEATH
Jun 25	1 STORM
Jul 8	1 ROAD
Jul 21	1 SERPENT
Aug 3	1 FLINT
Aug 16	1 MONKEY
Aug 29	1 LIZARD
Sep 11	1 INCENSE
Sep 24	1 DOG
Oct 7	1 NIGHT
Oct 20	1 VULTURE
Nov 2	1 WATER
Nov 15	1 WIND
Nov 28	1 EAGLE
Dec 11	1 RABBIT
Dec 24	1 CROCODILE
1967	
Jan 6	1 JAGUAR
Jan 19	1 DEER
Feb 1	1 ANCESTORS
Feb 14	1 CORN
Feb 27	1 DEATH
Mayan Year	**7 ROAD (Mar 5)**
Mar 12	1 STORM
Mar 25	1 ROAD

Gregorian Date	Mayan Date
Apr 7	1 SERPENT
Apr 20	1 FLINT
May 3	1 MONKEY
May 16	1 LIZARD
May 29	1 INCENSE
Jun 11	1 DOG
Jun 24	1 NIGHT
Jul 7	1 VULTURE
Jul 20	1 WATER
Aug 2	1 WIND
Aug 15	1 EAGLE
Aug 28	1 RABBIT
Sep 10	1 CROCODILE
Sep 23	1 JAGUAR
Oct 6	1 DEER
Oct 19	1 ANCESTORS
Nov 1	1 CORN
Nov 14	1 DEATH
Nov 27	1 STORM
Dec 10	1 ROAD
Dec 23	1 SERPENT
***1968**	
Jan 5	1 FLINT
Jan 18	1 MONKEY
Jan 31	1 LIZARD
Feb 13	1 INCENSE
Feb 26	1 DOG
Mayan Year	**8 INCENSE (Mar 4)**
Mar 10	1 NIGHT
Mar 23	1 VULTURE
Apr 5	1 WATER
Apr 18	1 WIND
May 1	1 EAGLE
May 14	1 RABBIT
May 27	1 CROCODILE
Jun 9	1 JAGUAR
Jun 22	1 DEER

*** indicates a leap year**

Gregorian Date	Mayan Date
Jul 5	1 ANCESTORS
Jul 18	1 CORN
Jul 31	1 DEATH
Aug 13	1 STORM
Aug 26	1 ROAD
Sep 8	1 SERPENT
Sep 21	1 FLINT
Oct 4	1 MONKEY
Oct 17	1 LIZARD
Oct 30	1 INCENSE
Nov 12	1 DOG
Nov 25	1 NIGHT
Dec 8	1 VULTURE
Dec 21	1 WATER

1969

Gregorian Date	Mayan Date
Jan 3	1 WIND
Jan 16	1 EAGLE
Jan 29	1 RABBIT
Feb 11	1 CROCODILE
Feb 24	1 JAGUAR

Mayan Year 9 WIND (Mar 4)

Gregorian Date	Mayan Date
Mar 9	1 DEER
Mar 22	1 ANCESTORS
Apr 4	1 CORN
Apr 17	1 DEATH
Apr 30	1 STORM
May 13	1 ROAD
May 26	1 SERPENT
Jun 8	1 FLINT
Jun 21	1 MONKEY
Jul 4	1 LIZARD
Jul 17	1 INCENSE
Jul 30	1 DOG
Aug 12	1 NIGHT
Aug 25	1 VULTURE
Sep 7	1 WATER
Sep 20	1 WIND

Gregorian Date	Mayan Date
Oct 3	1 EAGLE
Oct 16	1 RABBIT
Oct 29	1 CROCODILE
Nov 11	1 JAGUAR
Nov 24	1 DEER
Dec 7	1 ANCESTORS
Dec 20	1 CORN

1970

Gregorian Date	Mayan Date
Jan 2	1 DEATH
Jan 15	1 STORM
Jan 28	1 ROAD
Feb 10	1 SERPENT
Feb 23	1 FLINT

Mayan Year 10 DEER (Mar 4)

Gregorian Date	Mayan Date
Mar 8	1 MONKEY
Mar 21	1 LIZARD
Apr 3	1 INCENSE
Apr 16	1 DOG
Apr 29	1 NIGHT
May 12	1 VULTURE
May 25	1 WATER
Jun 7	1 WIND
Jun 20	1 EAGLE
Jul 3	1 RABBIT
Jul 16	1 CROCODILE
Jul 29	1 JAGUAR
Aug 11	1 DEER
Aug 24	1 ANCESTORS
Sep 6	1 CORN
Sep 19	1 DEATH
Oct 2	1 STORM
Oct 15	1 ROAD
Oct 28	1 SERPENT
Nov 10	1 FLINT
Nov 23	1 MONKEY
Dec 6	1 LIZARD
Dec 19	1 INCENSE

*** indicates a leap year**

Gregorian Date	Mayan Date
1971	
Jan 1	1 DOG
Jan 14	1 NIGHT
Jan 27	1 VULTURE
Feb 9	1 WATER
Feb 22	1 WIND
Mayan Year	**11 ROAD (Mar 4)**
Mar 7	1 EAGLE
Mar 20	1 RABBIT
Apr 2	1 CROCODILE
Apr 15	1 JAGUAR
Apr 28	1 DEER
May 11	1 ANCESTORS
May 24	1 CORN
Jun 6	1 DEATH
Jun 19	1 STORM
Jul 2	1 ROAD
Jul 15	1 SERPENT
Jul 28	1 FLINT
Aug 10	1 MONKEY
Aug 23	1 LIZARD
Sep 5	1 INCENSE
Sep 18	1 DOG
Oct 1	1 NIGHT
Oct 14	1 VULTURE
Oct 27	1 WATER
Nov 9	1 WIND
Nov 22	1 EAGLE
Dec 5	1 RABBIT
Dec 18	1 CROCODILE
Dec 31	1 JAGUAR
***1972**	
Jan 13	1 DEER
Jan 26	1 ANCESTORS
Feb 8	1 CORN
Feb 21	1 DEATH
Mayan Year	**12 INCENSE (Mar 3)**

Gregorian Date	Mayan Date
Mar 5	1 STORM
Mar 18	1 ROAD
Mar 31	1 SERPENT
Apr 13	1 FLINT
Apr 26	1 MONKEY
May 9	1 LIZARD
May 22	1 INCENSE
Jun 4	1 DOG
Jun 17	1 NIGHT
Jun 30	1 VULTURE
Jul 13	1 WATER
Jul 26	1 WIND
Aug 8	1 EAGLE
Aug 21	1 RABBIT
Sep 3	1 CROCODILE
Sep 16	1 JAGUAR
Sep 29	1 DEER
Oct 12	1 ANCESTORS
Oct 25	1 CORN
Nov 7	1 DEATH
Nov 20	1 STORM
Dec 3	1 ROAD
Dec 16	1 SERPENT
Dec 29	1 FLINT
1973	
Jan 11	1 MONKEY
Jan 24	1 LIZARD
Feb 6	1 INCENSE
Feb 19	1 DOG
Mayan Year	**13 WIND (Mar 3)**
Mar 4	1 NIGHT
Mar 17	1 VULTURE
Mar 30	1 WATER
Apr 12	1 WIND
Apr 25	1 EAGLE
May 8	1 RABBIT
May 21	1 CROCODILE

*** indicates a leap year**

Gregorian Date	Mayan Date
Jun 3	1 JAGUAR
Jun 16	1 DEER
Jun 29	1 ANCESTORS
Jul 12	1 CORN
END KATUN 8 AHAU (July 19)	
BEGIN KATUN 6 AHAU	
Jul 25	1 DEATH
Aug 7	1 STORM
Aug 20	1 ROAD
Sep 2	1 SERPENT
Sep 15	1 FLINT
Sep 28	1 MONKEY
Oct 11	1 LIZARD
Oct 24	1 INCENSE
Nov 6	1 DOG
Nov 19	1 NIGHT
Dec 2	1 VULTURE
Dec 15	1 WATER
Dec 28	1 WIND
1974	
Jan 10	1 EAGLE
Jan 23	1 RABBIT
Feb 5	1 CROCODILE
Feb 18	1 JAGUAR
Mar 3	1 DEER
Mayan Year 1 DEER (Mar 3)	
Mar 16	1 ANCESTORS
Mar 29	1 CORN
Apr 11	1 DEATH
Apr 24	1 STORM
May 7	1 ROAD
May 20	1 SERPENT
Jun 2	1 FLINT
Jun 15	1 MONKEY
Jun 28	1 LIZARD
Jul 11	1 INCENSE
Jul 24	1 DOG

Gregorian Date	Mayan Date
Aug 6	1 NIGHT
Aug 19	1 VULTURE
Sep 1	1 WATER
Sep 14	1 WIND
Sep 27	1 EAGLE
Oct 10	1 RABBIT
Oct 23	1 CROCODILE
Nov 5	1 JAGUAR
Nov 18	1 DEER
Dec 1	1 ANCESTORS
Dec 14	1 CORN
Dec 27	1 DEATH
1975	
Jan 9	1 STORM
Jan 22	1 ROAD
Feb 4	1 SERPENT
Feb 17	1 FLINT
Mar 2	1 MONKEY
Mayan Year 2 ROAD (Mar 3)	
Mar 15	1 LIZARD
Mar 28	1 INCENSE
Apr 10	1 DOG
Apr 23	1 NIGHT
May 6	1 VULTURE
May 19	1 WATER
Jun 1	1 WIND
Jun 14	1 EAGLE
Jun 27	1 RABBIT
Jul 10	1 CROCODILE
Jul 23	1 JAGUAR
Aug 5	1 DEER
Aug 18	1 ANCESTORS
Aug 31	1 CORN
Sep 13	1 DEATH
Sep 26	1 STORM
Oct 9	1 ROAD
Oct 22	1 SERPENT

*** indicates a leap year**

Gregorian Date	Mayan Date
Nov 4	1 FLINT
Nov 17	1 MONKEY
Nov 30	1 LIZARD
Dec 13	1 INCENSE
Dec 26	1 DOG
***1976**	
Jan 8	1 NIGHT
Jan 21	1 VULTURE
Feb 3	1 WATER
Feb 16	1 WIND
Feb 29	1 EAGLE
Mayan Year	**3 INCENSE (Mar 2)**
Mar 13	1 RABBIT
Mar 26	1 CROCODILE
Apr 8	1 JAGUAR
Apr 21	1 DEER
May 4	1 ANCESTORS
May 17	1 CORN
May 30	1 DEATH
Jun 12	1 STORM
Jun 25	1 ROAD
Jul 8	1 SERPENT
Jul 21	1 FLINT
Aug 3	1 MONKEY
Aug 16	1 LIZARD
Aug 29	1 INCENSE
Sep 11	1 DOG
Sep 24	1 NIGHT
Oct 7	1 VULTURE
Oct 20	1 WATER
Nov 2	1 WIND
Nov 15	1 EAGLE
Nov 28	1 RABBIT
Dec 11	1 CROCODILE
Dec 24	1 JAGUAR
1977	
Jan 6	1 DEER

Gregorian Date	Mayan Date
Jan 19	1 ANCESTORS
Feb 1	1 CORN
Feb 14	1 DEATH
Feb 27	1 STORM
Mayan Year	**4 WIND (Mar 2)**
Mar 12	1 ROAD
Mar 25	1 SERPENT
Apr 7	1 FLINT
Apr 20	1 MONKEY
May 3	1 LIZARD
May 16	1 INCENSE
May 29	1 DOG
Jun 11	1 NIGHT
Jun 24	1 VULTURE
Jul 7	1 WATER
Jul 20	1 WIND
Aug 2	1 EAGLE
Aug 15	1 RABBIT
Aug 28	1 CROCODILE
Sep 10	1 JAGUAR
Sep 23	1 DEER
Oct 6	1 ANCESTORS
Oct 19	1 CORN
Nov 1	1 DEATH
Nov 14	1 STORM
Nov 27	1 ROAD
Dec 10	1 SERPENT
Dec 23	1 FLINT
1978	
Jan 5	1 MONKEY
Jan 18	1 LIZARD
Jan 31	1 INCENSE
Feb 13	1 DOG
Feb 26	1 NIGHT
Mayan Year	**5 DEER (Mar 2)**
Mar 11	1 VULTURE
Mar 24	1 WATER

*** indicates a leap year**

Gregorian Date	Mayan Date
Apr 6	1 WIND
Apr 19	1 EAGLE
May 2	1 RABBIT
May 15	1 CROCODILE
May 28	1 JAGUAR
Jun 10	1 DEER
Jun 23	1 ANCESTORS
Jul 6	1 CORN
Jul 19	1 DEATH
Aug 1	1 STORM
Aug 14	1 ROAD
Aug 27	1 SERPENT
Sep 9	1 FLINT
Sep 22	1 MONKEY
Oct 5	1 LIZARD
Oct 18	1 INCENSE
Oct 31	1 DOG
Nov 13	1 NIGHT
Nov 26	1 VULTURE
Dec 9	1 WATER
Dec 22	1 WIND

1979

Gregorian Date	Mayan Date
Jan 4	1 EAGLE
Jan 17	1 RABBIT
Jan 30	1 CROCODILE
Feb 12	1 JAGUAR
Feb 25	1 DEER

Mayan Year 6 ROAD (Mar 2)

Gregorian Date	Mayan Date
Mar 10	1 ANCESTORS
Mar 23	1 CORN
Apr 5	1 DEATH
Apr 18	1 STORM
May 1	1 ROAD
May 14	1 SERPENT
May 27	1 FLINT
Jun 9	1 MONKEY
Jun 22	1 LIZARD
Jul 5	1 INCENSE
Jul 18	1 DOG
Jul 31	1 NIGHT
Aug 13	1 VULTURE
Aug 26	1 WATER
Sep 8	1 WIND
Sep 21	1 EAGLE
Oct 4	1 RABBIT
Oct 17	1 CROCODILE
Oct 30	1 JAGUAR
Nov 12	1 DEER
Nov 25	1 ANCESTORS
Dec 8	1 CORN
Dec 21	1 DEATH

*1980

Gregorian Date	Mayan Date
Jan 3	1 STORM
Jan 16	1 ROAD
Jan 29	1 SERPENT
Feb 11	1 FLINT
Feb 24	1 MONKEY

Mayan Year 7 INCENSE (Mar 1)

Gregorian Date	Mayan Date
Mar 8	1 LIZARD
Mar 21	1 INCENSE
Apr 3	1 DOG
Apr 16	1 NIGHT
Apr 29	1 VULTURE
May 12	1 WATER
May 25	1 WIND
Jun 7	1 EAGLE
Jun 20	1 RABBIT
Jul 3	1 CROCODILE
Jul 16	1 JAGUAR
Jul 29	1 DEER
Aug 11	1 ANCESTORS
Aug 24	1 CORN
Sep 6	1 DEATH
Sep 19	1 STORM

*** indicates a leap year**

Gregorian Date	Mayan Date
Oct 2	1 ROAD
Oct 15	1 SERPENT
Oct 28	1 FLINT
Nov 10	1 MONKEY
Nov 23	1 LIZARD
Dec 6	1 INCENSE
Dec 19	1 DOG
1981	
Jan 1	1 NIGHT
Jan 14	1 VULTURE
Jan 27	1 WATER
Feb 9	1 WIND
Feb 22	1 EAGLE
Mayan Year	**8 WIND (Mar 1)**
Mar 7	1 RABBIT
Mar 20	1 CROCODILE
Apr 2	1 JAGUAR
Apr 15	1 DEER
Apr 28	1 ANCESTORS
May 11	1 CORN
May 24	1 DEATH
Jun 6	1 STORM
Jun 19	1 ROAD
Jul 2	1 SERPENT
Jul 15	1 FLINT
Jul 28	1 MONKEY
Aug 10	1 LIZARD
Aug 23	1 INCENSE
Sep 5	1 DOG
Sep 18	1 NIGHT
Oct 1	1 VULTURE
Oct 14	1 WATER
Oct 27	1 WIND
Nov 9	1 EAGLE
Nov 22	1 RABBIT
Dec 5	1 CROCODILE
Dec 18	1 JAGUAR

Gregorian Date	Mayan Date
Dec 31	1 DEER
1982	
Jan 13	1 ANCESTORS
Jan 26	1 CORN
Feb 8	1 DEATH
Feb 21	1 STORM
Mayan Year	**9 DEER (Mar 1)**
Mar 6	1 ROAD
Mar 19	1 SERPENT
Apr 1	1 FLINT
Apr 14	1 MONKEY
Apr 27	1 LIZARD
May 10	1 INCENSE
May 23	1 DOG
Jun 5	1 NIGHT
Jun 18	1 VULTURE
Jul 1	1 WATER
Jul 14	1 WIND
Jul 27	1 EAGLE
Aug 9	1 RABBIT
Aug 22	1 CROCODILE
Sep 4	1 JAGUAR
Sep 17	1 DEER
Sep 30	1 ANCESTORS
Oct 13	1 CORN
Oct 26	1 DEATH
Nov 8	1 STORM
Nov 21	1 ROAD
Dec 4	1 SERPENT
Dec 17	1 FLINT
Dec 30	1 MONKEY
1983	
Jan 12	1 LIZARD
Jan 25	1 INCENSE
Feb 7	1 DOG
Feb 20	1 NIGHT
Mayan Year	**10 ROAD (Mar 1)**

*** indicates a leap year**

Gregorian Date	Mayan Date
Mar 5	1 VULTURE
Mar 18	1 WATER
Mar 31	1 WIND
Apr 13	1 EAGLE
Apr 26	1 RABBIT
May 9	1 CROCODILE
May 22	1 JAGUAR
Jun 4	1 DEER
Jun 17	1 ANCESTORS
Jun 30	1 CORN
Jul 13	1 DEATH
Jul 26	1 STORM
Aug 8	1 ROAD
Aug 21	1 SERPENT
Sep 3	1 FLINT
Sep 16	1 MONKEY
Sep 29	1 LIZARD
Oct 12	1 INCENSE
Oct 25	1 DOG
Nov 7	1 NIGHT
Nov 20	1 VULTURE
Dec 3	1 WATER
Dec 16	1 WIND
Dec 29	1 EAGLE
***1984**	
Jan 11	1 RABBIT
Jan 24	1 CROCODILE
Feb 6	1 JAGUAR
Feb 19	1 DEER
Mayan Year	**11 INCENSE (Feb 29)**
Mar 3	1 ANCESTORS
Mar 16	1 CORN
Mar 29	1 DEATH
Apr 11	1 STORM
Apr 24	1 ROAD
May 7	1 SERPENT
May 20	1 FLINT
Jun 2	1 MONKEY
Jun 15	1 LIZARD
Jun 28	1 INCENSE
Jul 11	1 DOG
Jul 24	1 NIGHT
Aug 6	1 VULTURE
Aug 19	1 WATER
Sep 1	1 WIND
Sep 14	1 EAGLE
Sep 27	1 RABBIT
Oct 10	1 CROCODILE
Oct 23	1 JAGUAR
Nov 5	1 DEER
Nov 18	1 ANCESTORS
Dec 1	1 CORN
Dec 14	1 DEATH
Dec 27	1 STORM
1985	
Jan 9	1 ROAD
Jan 22	1 SERPENT
Feb 4	1 FLINT
Feb 17	1 MONKEY
Mayan Year	**12 WIND (Feb 28)**
Mar 2	1 LIZARD
Mar 15	1 INCENSE
Mar 28	1 DOG
Apr 10	1 NIGHT
Apr 23	1 VULTURE
May 6	1 WATER
May 19	1 WIND
Jun 1	1 EAGLE
Jun 14	1 RABBIT
Jun 27	1 CROCODILE
Jul 10	1 JAGUAR
Jul 23	1 DEER
Aug 5	1 ANCESTORS
Aug 18	1 CORN

*** indicates a leap year**

Gregorian Date	Mayan Date
Aug 31	1 DEATH
Sep 13	1 STORM
Sep 26	1 ROAD
Oct 9	1 SERPENT
Oct 22	1 FLINT
Nov 4	1 MONKEY
Nov 17	1 LIZARD
Nov 30	1 INCENSE
Dec 13	1 DOG
Dec 26	1 NIGHT

1986

Gregorian Date	Mayan Date
Jan 8	1 VULTURE
Jan 21	1 WATER
Feb 3	1 WIND
Feb 16	1 EAGLE

Mayan Year 13 DEER (Feb 28)

Gregorian Date	Mayan Date
Mar 1	1 RABBIT
Mar 14	1 CROCODILE
Mar 27	1 JAGUAR
Apr 9	1 DEER
Apr 22	1 ANCESTORS
May 5	1 CORN
May 18	1 DEATH
May 31	1 STORM
Jun 13	1 ROAD
Jun 26	1 SERPENT
Jul 9	1 FLINT
Jul 22	1 MONKEY
Aug 4	1 LIZARD
Aug 17	1 INCENSE
Aug 30	1 DOG
Sep 12	1 NIGHT
Sep 25	1 VULTURE
Oct 8	1 WATER
Oct 21	1 WIND
Nov 3	1 EAGLE
Nov 16	1 RABBIT
Nov 29	1 CROCODILE
Dec 12	1 JAGUAR
Dec 25	1 DEER

1987

Gregorian Date	Mayan Date
Jan 7	1 ANCESTORS
Jan 20	1 CORN
Feb 2	1 DEATH
Feb 15	1 STORM
Feb 28	1 ROAD

Mayan Year 1 ROAD (Feb 28)

Gregorian Date	Mayan Date
Mar 13	1 SERPENT
Mar 26	1 FLINT
Apr 8	1 MONKEY
Apr 21	1 LIZARD
May 4	1 INCENSE
May 17	1 DOG
May 30	1 NIGHT
Jun 12	1 VULTURE
Jun 25	1 WATER
Jul 8	1 WIND
Jul 21	1 EAGLE
Aug 3	1 RABBIT
Aug 16	1 CROCODILE
Aug 29	1 JAGUAR
Sep 11	1 DEER
Sep 24	1 ANCESTORS
Oct 7	1 CORN
Oct 20	1 DEATH
Nov 2	1 STORM
Nov 15	1 ROAD
Nov 28	1 SERPENT
Dec 11	1 FLINT
Dec 24	1 MONKEY

*1988

Gregorian Date	Mayan Date
Jan 6	1 LIZARD
Jan 19	1 INCENSE
Feb 1	1 DOG

*** indicates a leap year**

Gregorian Date	Mayan Date
Feb 14	1 NIGHT
Feb 27	1 VULTURE
Mayan Year	**2 INCENSE (Feb 28)**
Mar 11	1 WATER
Mar 24	1 WIND
Apr 6	1 EAGLE
Apr 19	1 RABBIT
May 2	1 CROCODILE
May 15	1 JAGUAR
May 28	1 DEER
Jun 10	1 ANCESTORS
Jun 23	1 CORN
Jul 6	1 DEATH
Jul 19	1 STORM
Aug 1	1 ROAD
Aug 14	1 SERPENT
Aug 27	1 FLINT
Sep 9	1 MONKEY
Sep 22	1 LIZARD
Oct 5	1 INCENSE
Oct 18	1 DOG
Oct 31	1 NIGHT
Nov 13	1 VULTURE
Nov 26	1 WATER
Dec 9	1 WIND
Dec 22	1 EAGLE
1989	
Jan 4	1 RABBIT
Jan 17	1 CROCODILE
Jan 30	1 JAGUAR
Feb 12	1 DEER
Feb 25	1 ANCESTORS
Mayan Year	**3 WIND (Feb 27)**
Mar 10	1 CORN
Mar 23	1 DEATH
Apr 5	1 STORM
Apr 18	1 ROAD

Gregorian Date	Mayan Date
May 1	1 SERPENT
May 14	1 FLINT
May 27	1 MONKEY
Jun 9	1 LIZARD
Jun 22	1 INCENSE
Jul 5	1 DOG
Jul 18	1 NIGHT
Jul 31	1 VULTURE
Aug 13	1 WATER
Aug 26	1 WIND
Sep 8	1 EAGLE
Sep 21	1 RABBIT
Oct 4	1 CROCODILE
Oct 17	1 JAGUAR
Oct 30	1 DEER
Nov 12	1 ANCESTORS
Nov 25	1 CORN
Dec 8	1 DEATH
Dec 21	1 STORM
1990	
Jan 3	1 ROAD
Jan 16	1 SERPENT
Jan 29	1 FLINT
Feb 11	1 MONKEY
Feb 24	1 LIZARD
Mayan Year	**4 DEER (Feb 27)**
Mar 9	1 INCENSE
Mar 22	1 DOG
Apr 4	1 NIGHT
Apr 17	1 VULTURE
Apr 30	1 WATER
May 13	1 WIND
May 26	1 EAGLE
Jun 8	1 RABBIT
Jun 21	1 CROCODILE
Jul 4	1 JAGUAR
Jul 17	1 DEER

*** indicates a leap year**

Gregorian Date	Mayan Date
Jul 30	1 ANCESTORS
Aug 12	1 CORN
Aug 25	1 DEATH
Sep 7	1 STORM
Sep 20	1 ROAD
Oct 3	1 SERPENT
Oct 16	1 FLINT
Oct 29	1 MONKEY
Nov 11	1 LIZARD
Nov 24	1 INCENSE
Dec 7	1 DOG
Dec 20	1 NIGHT

1991

Gregorian Date	Mayan Date
Jan 2	1 VULTURE
Jan 15	1 WATER
Jan 28	1 WIND
Feb 10	1 EAGLE
Feb 23	1 RABBIT

Mayan Year 5 ROAD (Feb 27)

Gregorian Date	Mayan Date
Mar 8	1 CROCODILE
Mar 21	1 JAGUAR
Apr 3	1 DEER
Apr 16	1 ANCESTORS
Apr 29	1 CORN
May 12	1 DEATH
May 25	1 STORM
Jun 7	1 ROAD
Jun 20	1 SERPENT
Jul 3	1 FLINT
Jul 16	1 MONKEY
Jul 29	1 LIZARD
Aug 11	1 INCENSE
Aug 24	1 DOG
Sep 6	1 NIGHT
Sep 19	1 VULTURE
Oct 2	1 WATER

Gregorian Date	Mayan Date
Oct 15	1 WIND
Oct 28	1 EAGLE
Nov 10	1 RABBIT
Nov 23	1 CROCODILE
Dec 6	1 JAGUAR
Dec 19	1 DEER

***1992**

Gregorian Date	Mayan Date
Jan 1	1 ANCESTORS
Jan 14	1 CORN
Jan 27	1 DEATH
Feb 9	1 STORM
Feb 22	1 ROAD

Mayan Year 6 INCENSE (Feb 27)

Gregorian Date	Mayan Date
Mar 6	1 SERPENT
Mar 19	1 FLINT
Apr 1	1 MONKEY
Apr 14	1 LIZARD
Apr 27	1 INCENSE
May 10	1 DOG
May 23	1 NIGHT
Jun 5	1 VULTURE
Jun 18	1 WATER
Jul 1	1 WIND
Jul 14	1 EAGLE
Jul 27	1 RABBIT
Aug 9	1 CROCODILE
Aug 22	1 JAGUAR
Sep 4	1 DEER
Sep 17	1 ANCESTORS
Sep 30	1 CORN
Oct 13	1 DEATH
Oct 26	1 STORM
Nov 8	1 ROAD
Nov 21	1 SERPENT
Dec 4	1 FLINT
Dec 17	1 MONKEY
Dec 30	1 LIZARD

*** indicates a leap year**

Gregorian Date	Mayan Date
1993	
Jan 12	1 INCENSE
Jan 25	1 DOG
Feb 7	1 NIGHT
Feb 20	1 VULTURE
Mayan Year 7 WIND (Feb 26)	
Mar 5	1 WATER
Mar 18	1 WIND
Mar 31	1 EAGLE
END KATUN 6 AHAU (April 5)	
BEGIN KATUN 4 AHAU	
Apr 13	1 RABBIT
Apr 26	1 CROCODILE
May 9	1 JAGUAR
May 22	1 DEER
Jun 4	1 ANCESTORS
Jun 17	1 CORN
Jun 30	1 DEATH
Jul 13	1 STORM
Jul 26	1 ROAD
Aug 8	1 SERPENT
Aug 21	1 FLINT
Sep 3	1 MONKEY
Sep 16	1 LIZARD
Sep 29	1 INCENSE
Oct 12	1 DOG
Oct 25	1 NIGHT
Nov 7	1 VULTURE
Nov 20	1 WATER
Dec 3	1 WIND
Dec 16	1 EAGLE
Dec 29	1 RABBIT
1994	
Jan 11	1 CROCODILE
Jan 24	1 JAGUAR
Feb 6	1 DEER
Feb 19	1 ANCESTORS

Gregorian Date	Mayan Date
Mayan Year 8 DEER (Feb 26)	
Mar 4	1 CORN
Mar 17	1 DEATH
Mar 30	1 STORM
Apr 12	1 ROAD
Apr 25	1 SERPENT
May 8	1 FLINT
May 21	1 MONKEY
Jun 3	1 LIZARD
Jun 16	1 INCENSE
Jun 29	1 DOG
Jul 12	1 NIGHT
Jul 25	1 VULTURE
Aug 7	1 WATER
Aug 20	1 WIND
Sep 2	1 EAGLE
Sep 15	1 RABBIT
Sep 28	1 CROCODILE
Oct 11	1 JAGUAR
Oct 24	1 DEER
Nov 6	1 ANCESTORS
Nov 19	1 CORN
Dec 2	1 DEATH
Dec 15	1 STORM
Dec 28	1 ROAD
1995	
Jan 10	1 SERPENT
Jan 23	1 FLINT
Feb 5	1 MONKEY
Feb 18	1 LIZARD
Mayan Year 9 ROAD (Feb 26)	
Mar 3	1 INCENSE
Mar 16	1 DOG
Mar 29	1 NIGHT
Apr 11	1 VULTURE
Apr 24	1 WATER
May 7	1 WIND

*** indicates a leap year**

Gregorian Date	Mayan Date
May 20	1 EAGLE
Jun 2	1 RABBIT
Jun 15	1 CROCODILE
Jun 28	1 JAGUAR
Jul 11	1 DEER
Jul 24	1 ANCESTORS
Aug 6	1 CORN
Aug 19	1 DEATH
Sep 1	1 STORM
Sep 14	1 ROAD
Sep 27	1 SERPENT
Oct 10	1 FLINT
Oct 23	1 MONKEY
Nov 5	1 LIZARD
Nov 18	1 INCENSE
Dec 1	1 DOG
Dec 14	1 NIGHT
Dec 27	1 VULTURE
***1996**	
Jan 9	1 WATER
Jan 22	1 WIND
Feb 4	1 EAGLE
Feb 17	1 RABBIT
Mayan Year	**10 INCENSE (Feb 26)**
Mar 1	1 CROCODILE
Mar 14	1 JAGUAR
Mar 27	1 DEER
Apr 9	1 ANCESTORS
Apr 22	1 CORN
May 5	1 DEATH
May 18	1 STORM
May 31	1 ROAD
Jun 13	1 SERPENT
Jun 26	1 FLINT
Jul 9	1 MONKEY
Jul 22	1 LIZARD
Aug 4	1 INCENSE

Gregorian Date	Mayan Date
Aug 17	1 DOG
Aug 30	1 NIGHT
Sep 12	1 VULTURE
Sep 25	1 WATER
Oct 8	1 WIND
Oct 21	1 EAGLE
Nov 3	1 RABBIT
Nov 16	1 CROCODILE
Nov 29	1 JAGUAR
Dec 12	1 DEER
Dec 25	1 ANCESTORS
1997	
Jan 7	1 CORN
Jan 20	1 DEATH
Feb 2	1 STORM
Feb 15	1 ROAD
Mayan Year	**11 WIND (Feb 25)**
Feb 28	1 SERPENT
Mar 13	1 FLINT
Mar 26	1 MONKEY
Apr 8	1 LIZARD
Apr 21	1 INCENSE
May 4	1 DOG
May 17	1 NIGHT
May 30	1 VULTURE
Jun 12	1 WATER
Jun 25	1 WIND
Jul 8	1 EAGLE
Jul 21	1 RABBIT
Aug 3	1 CROCODILE
Aug 16	1 JAGUAR
Aug 29	1 DEER
Sep 11	1 ANCESTORS
Sep 24	1 CORN
Oct 7	1 DEATH
Oct 20	1 STORM
Nov 2	1 ROAD

*** indicates a leap year**

Gregorian Date	Mayan Date
Nov 15	1 SERPENT
Nov 28	1 FLINT
Dec 11	1 MONKEY
Dec 24	1 LIZARD
1998	
Jan 6	1 INCENSE
Jan 19	1 DOG
Feb 1	1 NIGHT
Feb 14	1 VULTURE
Mayan Year	**12 DEER (Feb 25)**
Feb 27	1 WATER
Mar 12	1 WIND
Mar 25	1 EAGLE
Apr 7	1 RABBIT
Apr 20	1 CROCODILE
May 3	1 JAGUAR
May 16	1 DEER
May 29	1 ANCESTORS
Jun 11	1 CORN
Jun 24	1 DEATH
Jul 7	1 STORM
Jul 20	1 ROAD
Aug 2	1 SERPENT
Aug 15	1 FLINT
Aug 28	1 MONKEY
Sep 10	1 LIZARD
Sep 23	1 INCENSE
Oct 6	1 DOG
Oct 19	1 NIGHT
Nov 1	1 VULTURE
Nov 14	1 WATER
Nov 27	1 WIND
Dec 10	1 EAGLE
Dec 23	1 RABBIT
1999	
Jan 5	1 CROCODILE
Jan 18	1 JAGUAR

Gregorian Date	Mayan Date
Jan 31	1 DEER
Feb 13	1 ANCESTORS
Mayan Year	**13 ROAD (Feb 25)**
Feb 26	1 CORN
Mar 11	1 DEATH
Mar 24	1 STORM
Apr 6	1 ROAD
Apr 19	1 SERPENT
May 2	1 FLINT
May 15	1 MONKEY
May 28	1 LIZARD
Jun 10	1 INCENSE
Jun 23	1 DOG
Jul 6	1 NIGHT
Jul 19	1 VULTURE
Aug 1	1 WATER
Aug 14	1 WIND
Aug 27	1 EAGLE
Sep 9	1 RABBIT
Sep 22	1 CROCODILE
Oct 5	1 JAGUAR
Oct 18	1 DEER
Oct 31	1 ANCESTORS
Nov 13	1 CORN
Nov 26	1 DEATH
Dec 9	1 STORM
Dec 22	1 ROAD
***2000**	
Jan 4	1 SERPENT
Jan 17	1 FLINT
Jan 30	1 MONKEY
Feb 12	1 LIZARD
Feb 25	1 INCENSE
Mayan Year	**1 INCENSE (Feb 25)**
Mar 9	1 DOG
Mar 22	1 NIGHT
Apr 4	1 VULTURE

*** indicates a leap year**

Gregorian Date	Mayan Date
Apr 17	1 WATER
Apr 30	1 WIND
May 13	1 EAGLE
May 26	1 RABBIT
Jun 8	1 CROCODILE
Jun 21	1 JAGUAR
Jul 4	1 DEER
Jul 17	1 ANCESTORS
Jul 30	1 CORN
Aug 12	1 DEATH
Aug 25	1 STORM
Sep 7	1 ROAD
Sep 20	1 SERPENT
Oct 3	1 FLINT
Oct 16	1 MONKEY
Oct 29	1 LIZARD
Nov 11	1 INCENSE
Nov 24	1 DOG
Dec 7	1 NIGHT
Dec 20	1 VULTURE
2001	
Jan 2	1 WATER
Jan 15	1 WIND
Jan 28	1 EAGLE
Feb 10	1 RABBIT
Feb 23	1 CROCODILE
Mayan Year 2 WIND (Feb 24)	
Mar 8	1 JAGUAR
Mar 21	1 DEER
Apr 3	1 ANCESTORS
Apr 16	1 CORN
Apr 29	1 DEATH
May 12	1 STORM
May 25	1 ROAD
Jun 7	1 SERPENT
Jun 20	1 FLINT
Jul 3	1 MONKEY
Jul 16	1 LIZARD
Jul 29	1 INCENSE
Aug 11	1 DOG
Aug 25	1 NIGHT
Sep 6	1 VULTURE
Sep 19	1 WATER
Oct 2	1 WIND
Oct 15	1 EAGLE
Oct 28	1 RABBIT
Nov 10	1 CROCODILE
Nov 23	1 JAGUAR
Dec 6	1 DEER
Dec 19	1 ANCESTORS
2002	
Jan 1	1 CORN
Jan 14	1 DEATH
Jan 27	1 STORM
Feb 9	1 ROAD
Feb 22	1 SERPENT
Mayan Year 3 DEER (Feb 24)	
Mar 7	1 FLINT
Mar 20	1 MONKEY
Apr 2	1 LIZARD
Apr 15	1 INCENSE
Apr 28	1 DOG
May 11	1 NIGHT
May 24	1 VULTURE
Jun 6	1 WATER
Jun 19	1 WIND
Jul 2	1 EAGLE
Jul 15	1 RABBIT
Jul 28	1 CROCODILE
Aug 10	1 JAGUAR
Aug 23	1 DEER
Sep 5	1 ANCESTORS
Sep 18	1 CORN
Oct 1	1 DEATH

*** indicates a leap year**

Gregorian Date	Mayan Date
Oct 14	1 STORM
Oct 27	1 ROAD
Nov 9	1 SERPENT
Nov 22	1 FLINT
Dec 5	1 MONKEY
Dec 18	1 LIZARD
Dec 31	1 INCENSE
2003	
Jan 13	1 DOG
Jan 26	1 NIGHT
Feb 8	1 VULTURE
Feb 21	1 WATER
Mayan Year 4 ROAD (Feb 24)	
Mar 6	1 WIND
Mar 19	1 EAGLE
Apr 1	1 RABBIT
Apr 14	1 CROCODILE
Apr 27	1 JAGUAR
May 10	1 DEER
May 23	1 ANCESTORS
Jun 5	1 CORN
Jun 18	1 DEATH
Jul 1	1 STORM
Jul 14	1 ROAD
Jul 27	1 SERPENT
Aug 9	1 FLINT
Aug 22	1 MONKEY
Sep 4	1 LIZARD
Sep 17	1 INCENSE
Sep 30	1 DOG
Oct 13	1 NIGHT
Oct 26	1 VULTURE
Nov 8	1 WATER
Nov 21	1 WIND
Dec 4	1 EAGLE
Dec 17	1 RABBIT
Dec 30	1 CROCODILE

Gregorian Date	Mayan Date
***2004**	
Jan 12	1 JAGUAR
Jan 25	1 DEER
Feb 7	1 ANCESTORS
Feb 20	1 CORN
Mayan Year 5 INCENSE (Feb 24)	
Mar 4	1 DEATH
Mar 17	1 STORM
Mar 30	1 ROAD
Apr 12	1 SERPENT
Apr 25	1 FLINT
May 8	1 MONKEY
May 21	1 LIZARD
Jun 3	1 INCENSE
Jun 16	1 DOG
Jun 29	1 NIGHT
Jul 12	1 VULTURE
Jul 25	1 WATER
Aug 7	1 WIND
Aug 20	1 EAGLE
Sep 2	1 RABBIT
Sep 15	1 CROCODILE
Sep 28	1 JAGUAR
Oct 11	1 DEER
Oct 24	1 ANCESTORS
Nov 6	1 CORN
Nov 19	1 DEATH
Dec 2	1 STORM
Dec 15	1 ROAD
Dec 28	1 SERPENT
2005	
Jan 10	1 FLINT
Jan 23	1 MONKEY
Feb 5	1 LIZARD
Feb 18	1 INCENSE
Mayan Year 6 WIND (Feb 23)	
Mar 3	1 DOG

*** indicates a leap year**

Gregorian Date	Mayan Date
Mar 16	1 NIGHT
Mar 29	1 VULTURE
Apr 11	1 WATER
Apr 24	1 WIND
May 7	1 EAGLE
May 20	1 RABBIT
Jun 2	1 CROCODILE
Jun 15	1 JAGUAR
Jun 28	1 DEER
Jul 11	1 ANCESTORS
Jul 24	1 CORN
Aug 6	1 DEATH
Aug 19	1 STORM
Sep 1	1 ROAD
Sep 14	1 SERPENT
Sep 27	1 FLINT
Oct 10	1 MONKEY
Oct 23	1 LIZARD
Nov 5	1 INCENSE
Nov 18	1 DOG
Dec 1	1 NIGHT
Dec 14	1 VULTURE
Dec 27	1 WATER

2006

Gregorian Date	Mayan Date
Jan 9	1 WIND
Jan 22	1 EAGLE
Feb 4	1 RABBIT
Feb 17	1 CROCODILE

Mayan Year 7 DEER (Feb 23)

Gregorian Date	Mayan Date
Mar 2	1 JAGUAR
Mar 15	1 DEER
Mar 28	1 ANCESTORS
Apr 10	1 CORN
Apr 23	1 DEATH
May 6	1 STORM
May 19	1 ROAD
Jun 1	1 SERPENT
Jun 14	1 FLINT
Jun 27	1 MONKEY
Jul 10	1 LIZARD
Jul 23	1 INCENSE
Aug 5	1 DOG
Aug 18	1 NIGHT
Aug 31	1 VULTURE
Sep 13	1 WATER
Sep 26	1 WIND
Oct 9	1 EAGLE
Oct 22	1 RABBIT
Nov 4	1 CROCODILE
Nov 17	1 JAGUAR
Nov 30	1 DEER
Dec 13	1 ANCESTORS
Dec 26	1 CORN

2007

Gregorian Date	Mayan Date
Jan 8	1 DEATH
Jan 21	1 STORM
Feb 3	1 ROAD
Feb 16	1 SERPENT

Mayan Year 8 ROAD (Feb 23)

Gregorian Date	Mayan Date
Mar 1	1 FLINT
Mar 14	1 MONKEY
Mar 27	1 LIZARD
Apr 9	1 INCENSE
Apr 22	1 DOG
May 5	1 NIGHT
May 18	1 VULTURE
May 31	1 WATER
Jun 13	1 WIND
Jun 26	1 EAGLE
Jul 9	1 RABBIT
Jul 22	1 CROCODILE
Aug 4	1 JAGUAR
Aug 17	1 DEER
Aug 30	1 ANCESTORS

*** indicates a leap year**

Gregorian Date	Mayan Date
Sep 12	1 CORN
Sep 25	1 DEATH
Oct 8	1 STORM
Oct 21	1 ROAD
Nov 3	1 SERPENT
Nov 16	1 FLINT
Nov 29	1 MONKEY
Dec 12	1 LIZARD
Dec 25	1 INCENSE

*2008

Gregorian Date	Mayan Date
Jan 7	1 DOG
Jan 20	1 NIGHT
Feb 2	1 VULTURE
Feb 15	1 WATER
Mayan Year	**9 INCENSE (Feb 23)**
Feb 28	1 WIND
Mar 12	1 EAGLE
Mar 25	1 RABBIT
Apr 7	1 CROCODILE
Apr 20	1 JAGUAR
May 3	1 DEER
May 16	1 ANCESTORS
May 29	1 CORN
Jun 11	1 DEATH
Jun 24	1 STORM
Jul 7	1 ROAD
Jul 20	1 SERPENT
Aug 2	1 FLINT
Aug 15	1 MONKEY
Aug 28	1 LIZARD
Sep 10	1 INCENSE
Sep 23	1 DOG
Oct 6	1 NIGHT
Oct 19	1 VULTURE
Nov 1	1 WATER
Nov 27	1 WIND
Nov 27	1 EAGLE
Dec 10	1 RABBIT
Dec 23	1 CROCODILE

2009

Gregorian Date	Mayan Date
Jan 5	1 JAGUAR
Jan 18	1 DEER
Jan 31	1 ANCESTORS
Feb 13	1 CORN
Mayan Year	**10 WIND (Feb 22)**
Feb 26	1 DEATH
Mar 11	1 STORM
Mar 24	1 ROAD
Apr 6	1 SERPENT
Apr 19	1 FLINT
May 2	1 MONKEY
May 15	1 LIZARD
May 28	1 INCENSE
Jun 10	1 DOG
Jun 23	1 NIGHT
Jul 6	1 VULTURE
Jul 19	1 WATER
Aug 1	1 WIND
Aug 14	1 EAGLE
Aug 27	1 RABBIT
Sep 9	1 CROCODILE
Sep 22	1 JAGUAR
Oct 5	1 DEER
Oct 18	1 ANCESTORS
Oct 31	1 CORN
Nov 13	1 DEATH
Nov 26	1 STORM
Dec 9	1 ROAD
Dec 22	1 SERPENT

2010

Gregorian Date	Mayan Date
Jan 4	1 FLINT
Jan 17	1 MONKEY
Jan 30	1 LIZARD
Feb 12	1 INCENSE

*** indicates a leap year**

Gregorian Date	Mayan Date
Mayan Year	**11 DEER (Feb 22)**
Feb 25	1 DOG
Mar 10	1 NIGHT
Mar 23	1 VULTURE
Apr 5	1 WATER
Apr 18	1 WIND
May 1	1 EAGLE
May 14	1 RABBIT
May 27	1 CROCODILE
Jun 9	1 JAGUAR
Jun 22	1 DEER
Jul 5	1 ANCESTORS
Jul 18	1 CORN
Jul 31	1 DEATH
Aug 13	1 STORM
Aug 26	1 ROAD
Sep 8	1 SERPENT
Sep 21	1 FLINT
Oct 4	1 MONKEY
Oct 17	1 LIZARD
Oct 30	1 INCENSE
Nov 12	1 DOG
Nov 25	1 NIGHT
Dec 8	1 VULTURE
Dec 21	1 WATER
2011	
Jan 3	1 WIND
Jan 16	1 EAGLE
Jan 29	1 RABBIT
Feb 11	1 CROCODILE
Mayan Year	**12 ROAD (Feb 22)**
Feb 24	1 JAGUAR
Mar 9	1 DEER
Mar 22	1 ANCESTORS
Apr 4	1 CORN
Apr 17	1 DEATH
Apr 30	1 STORM

Gregorian Date	Mayan Date
May 13	1 ROAD
May 26	1 SERPENT
Jun 8	1 FLINT
Jun 21	1 MONKEY
Jul 4	1 LIZARD
Jul 17	1 INCENSE
Jul 30	1 DOG
Aug 12	1 NIGHT
Aug 25	1 VULTURE
Sep 7	1 WATER
Sep 20	1 WIND
Oct 3	1 EAGLE
Oct 16	1 RABBIT
Oct 29	1 CROCODILE
Nov 11	1 JAGUAR
Nov 24	1 DEER
Dec 7	1 ANCESTORS
Dec 20	1 CORN
***2012**	
Jan 2	1 DEATH
Jan 15	1 STORM
Jan 28	1 ROAD
Feb 10	1 SERPENT
Mayan Year	**13 INCENSE (Feb 22)**
Feb 23	1 FLINT
Mar 7	1 MONKEY
Mar 20	1 LIZARD
Apr 2	1 INCENSE
Apr 15	1 DOG
Apr 28	1 NIGHT
May 11	1 VULTURE
May 24	1 WATER
Jun 6	1 WIND
Jun 19	1 EAGLE
Jul 2	1 RABBIT
Jul 15	1 CROCODILE
Jul 28	1 JAGUAR

*** indicates a leap year**

Gregorian Date	Mayan Date
Aug 10	1 DEER
Aug 23	1 ANCESTORS
Sep 5	1 CORN
Sep 18	1 DEATH
Oct 1	1 STORM
Oct 14	1 ROAD
Oct 27	1 SERPENT
Nov 9	1 FLINT
Nov 22	1 MONKEY
Dec 5	1 LIZARD
Dec 18	1 INCENSE
END OF THE GREAT CYCLE	
Dec 21	**4 Ancestors**

Glossary

Mayan Terminology

ahau, ahauob (Yucatec Mayan)—The word literally means "lord." The sacred kings of the Classic Mayan city-states were ahauob or lords—but so were the spirits of departed ancestors whom the sacred kings invoked during their rituals. The ahauob represent the continuity of the ancestral stream—our sacredness or lordliness in the present as well as in extension towards an infinite past and future.

ceiba (Yucatec)—This tree, called tz'ite in Quiché Mayan, was the sacred World Tree of the Classic Maya. Souls blossom like flowers on the World Tree in order to be born into this world. Even today, Quiché Calendar diviners often gather their divining seeds from this tree.

copal—Resin of the ceiba tree. Copal is used as incense among the Maya and among Mexican Indians in general. In contrast to frankincense or "church" incense, copal is more often used in traditional or indigenous ceremonies.

costumbre (Spanish)—The customs and traditions of the contemporary Maya, especially those that have ancient roots in pre-Columbian times.

coyopa (Quiché Mayan)—The "body lightning." Often compared to a bolt of lightning striking the quiet waters of a lake, coyopa is an inner psychic energy upon which Mayan shamans draw on for their power. In comparative terms, it is equivalent to the Hindu kundalini.

dzib (Yucatec)—Literally "scribe," this word can also be used to denote an artist or artisan. It also implies speaking in a sacred manner: prophecy is sometimes called *akab dzib*, or "night speaking."

Ek Ue (Yucatec)—Literally, "Black Dreamplace" or "Black Transformer Place." The hole in the Milky Way wherein the souls of the dead vanished into the Otherworld after traveling the "white road" of the Milky Way.

h-men (Yucatec)—Literally "one who knows" or "knower." An h-men is a shaman in modern-day Yucatán.

itz (Yucatec)—Literally "the dew of heaven." Divine energy flowing down from Heaven, which has its correspondence in the human body. See *coyopa*.

Nantat (Quiché)—The Ancestors. The Nantat constitute the "third person" of the Quiché Maya trinity: God, Sacred Earth, and the Ancestors.

Sac Be (Yucatec)—Literally "White Road." Straight-line roads, built by the Classic or Post-Classic Maya, were called sac be. The Milky Way, another "white road" and the pathway of departed souls, was also known as Sac Be.

Santo Mundo (Spanish)—This term, used by the Quiché Maya, means "Holy Earth" or "Holy World." It signifies the earth personified as deity, an Earth Father whose antecedents lie in the old pre-Columbian Lord of the Underworld. The Gregorian Calendar is the calendar of the Christian world; the Mayan Calendar is the calendar of Santo Mundo.

sastun (Yucatec)—"Stone of Light." This may be any kind of stone, but its purpose is always magical—used for healing, divining, and other occult arts.

Tiox (Quiché)—A Quiché word derived from the Spanish "Dios." Although it literally means "the Christian God," the term Tiox also includes Jesus, Mary, and all the Christian saints.

tz'ite (Quiché)—See *ceiba*.

x-men (Yucatec)—A female shaman or healer. See *h-men*.

Xibalba (Yucatec)—Literally "The Awesome Place," this was the name of the Mayan Underworld, land of the dead.

yaxche (Yucatec)—Literally "green tree," the yaxche is the World Tree at the center of all things.

Nahuatl Terminology

ihiyotl—The energy associated with the inner center of power that dwells in the liver and governs our fear and courage, sensual emotions, etc.

malinalli—The primal energy that gives life and spirit to human beings, equivalent to the Mayan *itz* or *coyopa*. This is the energy or power known in India as kundalini.

nagual—In many different Native cultures of Mesoamerica, our double or "free soul," embodied in a totem animal, is called the nagual.

ollin—Literally "movement" or "motion." The Nahuatl words for "life" and "heart" are both derived from this important root word.

teyolia—The energy associated with the inner center of power that dwells in the heart and governs our soul and vital force.

tonalli—The energy associated with the inner center of power that dwells in the head and represents our gift of enlightenment from the Creator.

Calendar Terminology

baktun (Yucatec)—A Mayan calendrical cycle of 144,000 days or twenty katuns. Approximately 395 Gregorian years.

Calendar Round—A cycle of approximately 52 years, defined by the correspondence of the day 0 Pop (the Mayan New Year) with a particular day of the Sacred Calendar.

Great Cycle—A complete cycle of thirteen *baktuns*, 5,125 years. The present Great Cycle began Agust 13, 3114 B.C. and ends on December 21, A.D. 2012.

haab (Yucatec)—The 365-day solar year, comprised of eighteen months of twenty days each, followed by the five "dead days" (see *uayeb*) at the end of the year.

katun (Yucatec)—A cycle of twenty *tuns*. The katun cycle was the one most commonly used for historical and political prophecy.

kin (Yucatec)—A single day, counted from sunrise to sunrise. The kin was the smallest unit of the *Great Cycle*; in addition to its meaning of "day," the word kin also means "sun" and "priest."

Long Count—A Mayan system of time computation, which encompassed various cycles of time (see *baktun*, *katun*, *kin*, *tun*) and gave rise to Mayan historical prophecy.

tun (Yucatec)—A 360-day "year," comprised of eighteen uinal cycles.

tzolkin (Yucatec)—Literally "count of days." The tzolkin is the 260-day Sacred Calendar or divinatory almanac, sometimes (but not always) measured from Imix to Ahau.

uayeb (Yucatec)—The five "dead days" at the end of every haab or solar year. They were considered unlucky; no work was done during the uayeb period.

uinal (Yucatec)—A cycle of twenty days, sometimes (but not always) measured from Imix to Ahau.

Year Bearers—The four days of the Sacred Calendar which, on consecutive years, correspond to 0 Pop, the New Year's day of the solar calendar. Different Mesoamerican civilizations recognized different Year Bearers.

Bibliography

Arguelles, Jose. *The Mayan Factor: Path Beyond Technology*. Santa Fe: Bear and Co., 1987.

Arvigo, Rosita, with Nadine Epstein and Marilyn Yaquinto. *Sastun: My Apprenticeship with a Maya Healer*. San Francisco: Harper and Row, 1994.

Aveni, Anthony F. "Astronomy in Ancient Mesoamerica." In *In Serach of Ancient Astronomies*. Edited by Dr. E. C. Krupp, 185-190. New York: McGraw–Hill, 1979.

———. "Concepts of Positional Astronomy in Ancient Mesoamerican Architecture." In *Native American Astronomy*. Edited by Anthony F. Aveni, 9–14. Austin: University of Texas Press, 1977.

———. *Skywatchers of Ancient Mexico*. Austin: University of Texas Press, 1980.

Barrera Vasquez, Alfredo. *Horoscopos Mayas*. Merida: Area Maya, 1986.

Bowditch, Charles P. *The Numeration, Calendar Systems and Astronomical Knowledge of the Mayas*. Cambridge: Harvard University Press, 1910.

Bunzel, Ruth. *Chichicastenango*. Seattle: University of Washington Press, 1959.

Carrasco, David. *Quetzalcoatl and the Irony of Empire: Myths and Prophecies in the Aztec Tradition*. Chicago and London: University of Chicago Press, 1982.

———. *Religions of Mesoamerica: Cosmovision and Ceremonial Centers.* San Francisco: Harper and Row, 1990.

Coe, Michael. *Breaking the Maya Code.* New York: Thames and Hudson, 1992.

Craine, Eugene, and Reginald Reindorp. *The Codex Perez and the Book of Chilam Balam of Mani.* Norman: University of Oklahoma, 1979.

Edmonson, Munro. *The Ancient Future of the Itzá: The Book of Chilam Balam of Tizimin.* Austin: University of Texas, 1982.

———. *Heaven Born Merida and Its Destiny: The Book of Chilam Balam of Chumayel.* Austin: University of Texas, 1986.

———. *The Book of the Year: Middle American Calendrical Systems.* Salt Lake City: University of Utah, 1988.

Freidel, David, Linda Schele and Joy Parker. *Maya Cosmos: Three Thousand Years on the Shaman's Path.* New York: William Morrow and Co., 1993.

Heyden, Doris. "An Interpretation of the Cave Underneath the Pyramid of the Sun in Teotihuacán, Mexico." *American Antiquity* 40, no. 2 (1975): 131–47.

Ivanoff, Pierre. *Monuments of Civilization: The Maya.* New York: Grosset and Dunlap, 1973.

Jenkins, John Major, "The How and Why of the Mayan End Date in 2012 A.D." *The Mountain Astrologer* 8, no. 1 (Dec/Jan 1994–95): 52–7.

Landa, Fray Diego de. Yucatán *Before and After the Conquest.* Translated by William Gates. New York: Dover, 1978.

Leon–Portilla, Miguel. *Aztec Thought and Culture: A Study of the Ancient Nahuatl Mind.* Norman: University of Oklahoma, 1982.

Lopez Austin, Alfredo. *Human Body and Ideology.* Translated by Bernardo Ortiz de Montellano. Salt Lake City: University of Utah Press, 1988.

Love, Bruce, trans. *The Paris Codex: Handbook for a Maya Priest.* Austin: University of Texas, 1994.

Men, Hunbatz. *Secrets of Mayan Science/Religion.* Translated by Diana Gubiseh Ayala and James Jennings Dunlap II. Santa Fe: Bear and Co., 1990.

Mendelson, E. Michael. "Maximon: An Iconographical Introduction." *Man* 59 (1959): 56–60.

Nicholson, Irene. *Mexican and Central American Mythology*. London: Paul Hamlyn, 1967.

Nuttall, Zelia. "Nouvelles lumiéres sur les civilisations americaines et le système du calendrier." *Proceedings of the 22nd International Congress of Americanists*. Vol. 1 (1928) Rome: 1926, 119–48.

Oakes, Maud. *The Two Crosses of Todos Santos: Survivals of Mayan Religious Ritual*. New York: Pantheon, Bollingen Series, 1951.

Proskouriakoff, Tatiana. "Historical Implications of a Pattern of Dates at Piedras Negras, Guatemala," *American Antiquity* 25: 454–475.

Roys, Ralph L. *The Book of Chilam Balam of Chumayel*. Norman: University of Oklahoma, 1967.

Sahagún, Bernardino de. *General History of the Things of New Spain*. Translated by Charles Dibble and Arthur Anderson. 13 vols. School of American Research (Santa Fe) and University of Utah (Salt Lake City).

Schele, Linda and David Freidel. *A Forest of Kings: The Untold Story of the Ancient Maya*. New York: William Morrow and Co., 1990.

Schele, Linda and Mary Ellen Miller. *The Blood of Kings: Dynasty and Ritual in Maya Art*. New York: George Braziller and Kimbell Art Museum, 1986.

Sejourne, Laurette. *Burning Water: Thought and Religion in Ancient Mexico*. Boulder: Shambhala Publications, 1977.

Shearer, Tony. *Beneath the Moon and Under the Sun*. Santa Fe: Sun Books, 1987.

Stephens, John Lloyd. *Incidents of Travel in Central America, Chiapas and Yucatán*. New York: Dover Publications, 1969.

———. *Incidents of Travel in Yucatán*. New York: Dover Publications, 1963.

Sullivan, Paul. *Unfinished Conversations: Mayas and Foreigners Between Two Wars*. Berkeley and Los Angeles: University of California Press, 1991.

Tedlock, Barbara. *Time and the Highland Maya*. Albuquerque: University of New Mexico Press, 1992.

———. *The Beautiful and the Dangerous: Encounters with the Zuni Indians*. New York: Viking Penguin, 1992.

Tedlock, Dennis, trans. *Popol Vuh: The Mayan Book of the Dawn of Life*. New York: Touchstone, 1985.

Thompson, J. E. S. *A Commentary on the Dresden Codex*. Philadelphia: American Philosophical Society, 1972.

———. *Maya Hieroglyphic Writing: An Introduction*. Norman: University of Oklahoma Press, 1950.

Tompkins, Peter. *Mysteries of the Mexican Pyramids*. New York: Harper and Row, 1976.

Tozzer, Alfred. *A Maya Grammar*. New York: Dover, 1977.

Waters, Frank. *Book of the Hopi*. Harmondsworth: Penguin Books, 1977.

———. *Mexico Mystique*. Chicago: Sage Books, 1975.

Wilhelm, Richard, trans. *The I Ching or Book of Changes*. English translation by Cary F. Baynes. Princeton: Princeton–Bollingen, 1970.

Index

B

C

D

G

H

I

M

N

O

P

T

Z

Stay in Touch...

Llewellyn publishes hundreds of books on your favorite subjects

On the following pages you will find listed some books now available on related subjects. Your local bookstore stocks most of these and will stock new Llewellyn titles as they become available. We urge your patronage.

Order by Phone

Call toll-free within the U.S. and Canada, **1–800–THE MOON.**
In Minnesota call **(612) 291–1970.**
We accept Visa, MasterCard, and American Express.

Order by Mail

Send the full price of your order (MN residents add 7% sales tax) in U.S. funds to:

Llewellyn Worldwide
P.O. Box 64383, Dept. K372-7
St. Paul, MN 55164–0383, U.S.A.

Postage and Handling

- $4.00 for orders $15.00 and under
- $5.00 for orders over $15.00
- No charge for orders over $100.00 (US, Mexico, and Canada only)

We ship UPS in the continental United States. Orders shipped to P.O. boxes sent via standard mail. Orders shipped to Alaska, Hawaii, Virgin Islands, and Puerto Rico will be sent first-class mail.Orders to Mexico and Canada are shipped via surface mail.
International orders: Airmail—add freight equal to price of each book to the total price of order, plus $5.00 for each non-book item (audiotapes, etc.). Surface mail—add $1.00 per item.
Allow 4–6 weeks delivery on all orders. Postage and handling rates subject to change.

Group Discounts

We offer a 20% quantity discount to group leaders or agents. You must order a minimum of 5 copies of the same book to get our special quantity price.

Free Catalog

Get a free copy of our color catalog, *New Worlds of Mind and Spirit.* Subscribe for just $10.00 in the United States and Canada ($30.00 overseas, airmail). Many bookstores carry *New Worlds*—ask for it!

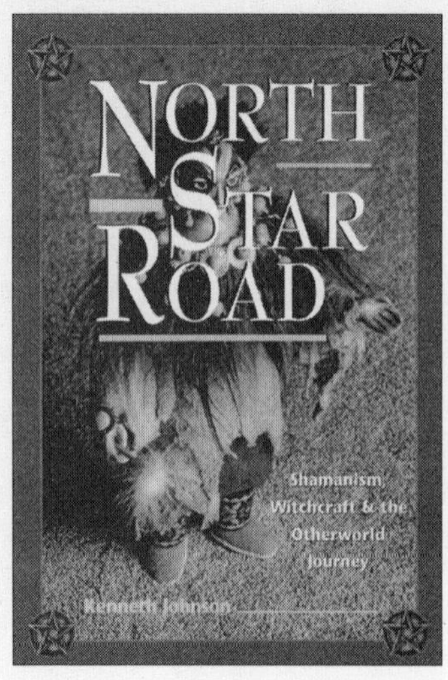
NORTH
STAR
ROAD
Shamanism
Witchcraft & the
Otherworld
Journey
Kenneth Johnson

The Silver Wheel

Women's Myths and Mysteries in the Celtic Tradition

Marguerite Elsbeth & Kenneth Johnson

Myth is one of the foundations of the spiritual path. For those who are disillusioned with their own religious history, myth has become the cornerstone of Western wisdom.

For today's women, the old Celtic stories have genuine relevance. Celtic heroines come to us full of fire and spirit, fresh from the Otherworld and part of wild Nature. Their stories speak the eternal truths about power, self-identity, relationships, love, creativity, passion, and death.

The Silver Wheel is a direct exploration of women's mythic past, and it offers exercises aimed at awakening and integrating the archetypes within the female personality. Revel in your own transformation as you resonate with the goddess Rhiannon and her ever-spiraling life-path to the heart of the Silver Wheel, wherein lies the Lady of the Otherworld, the primal Wild Woman within us all.

1-56718-371-9, 224 pp., 6 x 9, illus., softcover **$14.95**

To order, call 1–800–THE MOON
Prices subject to change without notice

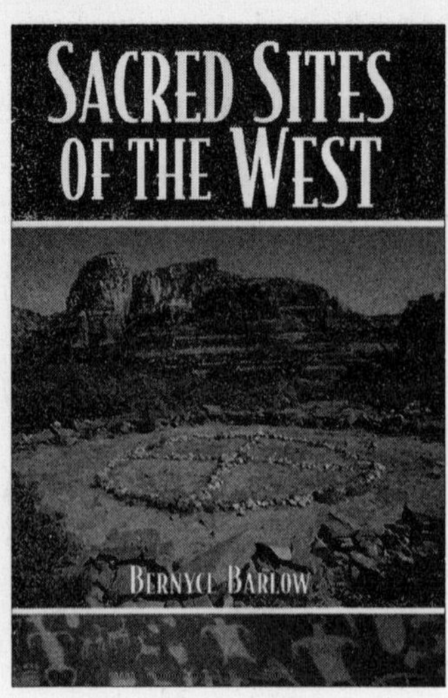

Sacred Sites of the West

Bernyce Barlow

Stroll through a forest of the world's oldest living trees, explore secret healing caves, or take a midnight dip in the hallowed waters of Big Sur! *Sacred Sites of the West* takes you on an exciting journey of enchantment and explains how the earth's energies can heal you, rejuvenate your inner energies, and affect your dreams. Investigate ley lines and grid networks, vortexes, and energy wellsprings—all here in the United States! Visit the "Lourdes of America" in New Mexico, tour the inner temple of a Hawaiian heiau, then raft the most treacherous rapids on the North American continent. See the never-before-documented Albino Redwood of California and the Child Nest Rock of Nevada. Dream spots, healing centers, goddess and warrior sites, temples, and vision caves are just a few of the places you'll encounter. Plus, color photographs, holy history, earth physics and legends become an integral part of each site narration, leaving you with a clear understanding of just what makes these sites so captivating.

0-87542-056-6, 240 pp., 6 x 9, 8-pg. color insert **$19.95**

To order, call 1–800–THE MOON

Prices subject to change without notice